PENGUIN BOOKS

THE UNITED STATES OF EUROPE

Tom Reid was head of *The Washington Post*'s London bureau, where he chronicled the rise of the European Union, pondered the Eurovision Song Contest and marvelled at the provision of free health care. He has covered four presidential campaigns for the paper in the US, and headed their bureau in Tokyo. He is the author of three books in Japanese, and five in English.

THE UNITED STATES OF EUROPE

THE UNITED STATES OF EUROPE

THE UNITED STATES OF EUROPE

THE UNITED STATES OF EUROPE

THE UNITED STATES OF EUROPE

The Superpower nobody talks about —

from the euro to eurovision

THE UNITED STATES OF EUROPE

THE UNITED STATES OF EUROPE

T. R. REID

PENGUIN BOOKS

PENGUIN BOOKS

Published by the Penguin Group
Penguin Books Ltd, 80 Strand, London WC2R 0RL, England
Penguin Group (USA) Inc., 375 Hudson Street, New York, New York 10014, USA
Penguin Group (Canada), 90 Eglinton Avenue East, Suite 700, Toronto, Ontario, Canada M4P 3YZ
(a division of Pearson Penguin Canada Inc.)
Penguin Ireland, 25 St Stephen's Green, Dublin 2, Ireland (a division of Penguin Books Ltd)
Penguin Group (Australia), 250 Camberwell Road,
Camberwell, Victoria 3124, Australia (a division of Pearson Australia Group Pty Ltd)
Penguin Books India Pvt Ltd, 11 Community Centre,
Panchsheel Park, New Delhi – 110 017, India
Penguin Group (NZ), cnr Airborne and Rosedale Roads, Albany,
Auckland 1310, New Zealand (a division of Pearson New Zealand Ltd)
Penguin Books (South Africa) (Pty) Ltd, 24 Sturdee Avenue,
Rosebank 2196, South Africa

Penguin Books Ltd, Registered Offices: 80 Strand, London WC2R 0RL, England

www.penguin.com

First published in the United States of America by The Penguin Press 2004
First published in Great Britain by Penguin Books 2005
1

Printed in England by Clays Ltd, St Ives plc

To Margaret M. McMahon
With love that has spanned the continents

Contents

THE UNITED STATES OF EUROPE

Sleeping Through the Revolution

At the dawn of the twenty-first century, a geopolitical revolution of historic dimensions is under way across the Atlantic: the unification of Europe. Twenty-five nations have joined together—with another dozen or so on the waiting list—to build a common economy, government, and culture. Europe is a more integrated place today than at any time since the Roman Empire. Americans have largely ignored this European revolution. Like one of those heavy, powerful SUVs that Detroit turns out, the United States has been cruising along at a comfortable speed, completely unaware of the well-engineered European sedan coming up fast in the passing lane. It's time to take a look over our shoulder. The new United States of Europe—to use Winston Churchill's phrase—has more people, more wealth, and more trade than the United States of America. The New Europe cannot match American military strength (and doesn't want to, for that matter). But it has more votes in every international organization than the United States, and it gives away far more money in development aid. The result is global economic and political clout that makes the European Union exactly what its leaders want it to be: a second superpower that can stand on equal footing with the United States.

Since it was born, in the rubble of World War II, the vision of a united Europe has grown dramatically from a coal-and-steel trading arrangement to a "common market" to a "community" to today's European Union, a new kind of state in which the member nations have handed over much of their sovereignty to a transcontinental government in a community that is becoming legally, commercially, and culturally borderless. The EU, with a population of nearly half a billion people stretching from Ireland to Estonia, has a president, a parliament, a constitution, a cabinet, a central bank, a bill of rights, a unified patent office, and a court system with the power to overrule the highest courts of every member nation. It has a 60,000-member army (or "European Rapid Reaction Force," to be precise) that is independent of NATO or any other outside control. It has its own space agency with 200 satellites in orbit and a project under way to send a European to Mars before Americans get there. It has a 22,000-person bureaucracy and an 80,000-page legal code governing everything from criminal trials and corporate taxation to peanut butter labels and lawn mower safety.

In pursuit of economic union, Europeans have thrown their marks, francs, lira, escudos, drachma, and so on into history's trash can and replaced them all with the new common currency, the euro, a form of money that has more daily users than the U.S. dollar. At the end of the twentieth century, the strong U.S. dollar reigned supreme. Five years into the new century, the young upstart, the euro, ranks as the world's strongest currency. In the first three years after it hit the streets of Europe, the common currency rose more than 50 percent in value against a struggling dollar. Europeans want to see the euro replace the dollar as the world's reserve currency—a development that would cost the United States a pretty penny, as we'll see in chapter 9. But Europe's new money is more than money. It is also a political statement—a daily message in every pocket that cooperation has replaced conflict across the continent.

To forge a physical linkage that enhances their political and economic union, Europeans have invested hundreds of billions of those euros in an ambitious network of bridges, tunnels, ports, and rail lines. Most of the continent has done away with customs and immigrations controls. When I drove recently from the Arctic Circle to the Mediterranean, I passed through eight countries, never saw a border guard, and never had to bother with foreign exchange. The New Europe has all the symbolic apparatus of a unified political entity. The citizens of the EU use a standard license plate, birth certificate, and passport (although each country still gets to pick its preferred passport color: a red cover for Britain, dark blue for Poland, and of course green for Ireland). The whole continent plays a common lottery. Europeans tune in by the tens of millions each May to watch the Eurovision song contest, the pancontinental TV extravaganza we'll meet in chapter 8. The EU has its own flag, its own anthem, and its own national day (which is May 9, for reasons we'll see in chapter 2). Europe's new constitution even establishes an official EU motto: "Unity in diversity," or "Unité dans la diversité," or "In varietate concordia," and so on in three dozen languages.

At first glance, the disagreements in 2003 surrounding the Iraq war seemed to expose more *diversité* than *unité* in Europe. In fact, the dispute over Iraq turned out to be another powerful unifying force for Europeans, particularly for the largely borderless young people known as Generation E—people who consider themselves not Spaniards or Czechs but rather Europeans who happen to be living in Toledo or Prague. No matter what their prime ministers said about the war, large majorities of the population in every European state opposed the American-led effort. The war enhanced the growing feeling across the continent (which we'll look at more closely in chapter 1) that Europe and America are fundamentally different places—and that Europeans need to stick together to confront the behemoth across the Atlantic. Among diplomats and scholars who study the transatlantic relationship, the concept of a united Europe standing as a superpower to match the United States is taken so seriously that the idea has a name of its own: the "counterweight thesis," or the "countervailing power thesis." Naturally, this theory is more popular in Europe than in the United States. And it is not just Europe's professional America-bashers—a fairly large category on the continent these days—who see the EU as a counterweight to U.S. dominance. At one of the union's endless summit meetings—the one where the Finnish and

Italian prime ministers argued bitterly for two days whether the European Food Agency should be headquartered in Helsinki or in Parma—I went up to Britain's prime minister, Tony Blair, the closest U.S. ally in Europe. I asked him whether these long, wordy sessions around the conference table were worthwhile.

"They do go on a bit," Blair said. He sounded bored and weary. But then, as he got talking about the prospects for the EU's future, he came to life. "You know, these summits makes sense if you try to have a sense of history. I mean, when the thing is getting tiresome, you have to remember what we are doing here. We are building a new world superpower. The European Union is about the projection of collective power, wealth, and influence. That collective strength makes individual nations more powerful—and it will make the EU as a whole a global power.

"Look—the United States is plainly the superpower of the world today," Blair continued, now rising to his rhetorical finish. "But the argument is that a single-power world is inherently unstable. I mean, that's the rationale for Europe to unite. When we work together, the European Union can stand on par as a superpower and a partner with the U.S. The world needs that right now."

While this historic transformation has been taking place, Americans have been asleep. For decades the American foreign policy establishment, both Democratic and Republican, didn't seem to notice—or, perhaps, didn't want to notice—the emergence of a new kind of political entity on the European continent. It was easier for the United States to continue dealing with familiar national governments in Paris, Rome, Madrid, and Dublin than to face up to the rapidly growing power and authority of the EU government in Brussels.

Official Washington particularly scoffed at the idea that the proud nations of Europe would jettison their traditional currencies. In 1999, Henry Kissinger opined that the euro was one of those good ideas that would not come to fruition, because the people of Europe would never accept it.

In fact, euro coins and notes did replace the national currencies of twelve European countries on New Year's Day of 2002—the largest currency conversion in history. The changeover was carried off smoothly and successfully, with universal acceptance (in chapter 3, we'll see how the Europeans did it.) A little more than three months after the conversion was completed, at a time when 350 million people were contentedly using the euro every day, I attended a lavish breakfast—the meal must have cost 40 euros per person—where Kissinger spoke to a group of continental leaders. After his remarks, he agreed to take a few questions from the audience. The first questioner, predictably enough, asked "how the eminent Dr. Kissinger could explain his totally misguided prediction about the new common currency." The eminent doctor ate crow, more or less. "I am often right," he replied, "but I have never claimed to be infallible."

As we'll see in chapter 5, the American business community has also suffered—grievously, in some cases—from its failure to understand the processes, the ambition, and the sheer market power of the European Union. The legendary CEO Jack Welch learned the hard way (see chapter 4) that American companies have to follow European rules these days. Because the united Europe is the world's largest trade market, it is the "Eurocrats" in Brussels, more and more, who make the business regulations that govern global industry. There's a reason why the quintessential American whiskey, Kentucky bourbon, is sold today in 75 cl bottles. It's not because American consumers suddenly demanded to sip their sour mash by the centiliter.

Sometimes Americans seem to be in a state of denial about what Europe has achieved. American presidents from both parties, for example, have repeatedly declared that the United States has "the greatest health-care system in the world." That claim is hard to support. The unified Europe has higher life expectancy, lower infant mortality, lower rates of heart disease and cancer, and health insurance that covers every person—all for about half as much per capita as the United States spends. (We'll see how they do it in chapter 6.) Since the United States pays much more and gets much less in return, it might behoove American policymakers to stop bragging about their own health-care system long enough to take a look at what the EU nations have done.

This book will take a careful look at what the Europeans have done: how and why they launched their revolution, what they've done right and wrong as they built their new borderless continent and its supranational government, and how the planet's new superpower will change the world. That's the key point: the leaders and the people of the EU are determined to change a world that had been dominated by Americans. Indeed, that goal has become a powerful motivator for the New Europe—to create a United States of Europe that is not the United States of America. One clear result of the unification of Europe is that the gap between the two sides of the Atlantic Ocean is growing wider every day.

ONE

The Atlantic Widens

The Lardburgers were going at it again. "Ah got no gas in mah SUV," Stacey Lardburger screamed at her husband. "And you spent all our money buyin' ammo for your stoooo-pid rifles. So how'm ah goin' to git to the welfare office? Will you tell me that?" Jeff Lardburger was in no mood to take that kind of grief from a mere woman, even the woman who happened to be his fourth wife. "Button it, you slut," he roared, hurling his beer can in the general direction of Stacey's huge head of bleached hair. "You shet that big mouth of your'n, or ah'll sendya to Texas and puttya in the chair." Stacey had heard warnings like that dozens of times before, but this time she had a comeback. "You gonna be one sorry asshole when ah get finished witya," she shouted back. "Got me a lawyer now. He says, next time you threaten me like 'at, we's gonna sue your ass bigtime."

And thus passed another interlude of domestic bliss in the typical American home depicted on "The Lardburgers," a regular segment on the satirical British TV show *Big Breakfast*. Jeff and Stacey, both so obese they resemble the Michelin Man, are presented for the enjoyment of the British public as the kind of couple Britons like to conjure up when they think about Americans. The Lardburgers are fat, loud, and ignorant.

They argue all the time, except when they're talking about chili cheese dogs or the death penalty, the only things they both appreciate. They constantly throw beer cans, vases, and lamps at each other, knocking over piles of the tacky knickknacks that fill their mobile home. Jeff and Stacey don't have jobs, so they spend their time looking for the lawsuit that will make them rich. Their big hero, other than George W. Bush, is the woman who sued McDonald's, and won, because her coffee was too hot.

The Lardburgers, who have never known a moment of quiet, hardly make great comedy, particularly after you've caught their one-joke act a couple of times. Still, this caricature of an American couple, offered on a morning entertainment program aimed primarily at young professionals on the way to the office, does fit into a great European theatrical and literary tradition. Making fun of Americans—those crude, overweight folks in Bermuda shorts and cowboy boots who think Birmingham is in Michigan, Rome is in Georgia, and Notre Dame rhymes with "motor frame"—is one of Europe's favorite pastimes. It is a pleasure that knows no borders. The Italians make fun of American pizza. The Norwegians make fun of American sports. The English make fun of American accents. The French make fun of Americans' French. A standing joke in French TV comedies is the American couple who swagger into a restaurant, hurriedly consult their French-English dictionary, and place their order: "Doox vine blank." When the waitress looks back with a mystified expression, the Americans panic and switch to English: "Honey, we'll have two wot wahns." When that draws another blank look, the American says the same thing again, only louder: "Ah said, TWO WOT WAHNS!"

Determined to prove that I had the strength of character to laugh at myself, I used to go out of my way to take in this European species of comedy. As a result, I sat through a lot of dreck, like "The Lardburgers" or the German comedian who always portrayed the U.S. president as a simpleton with a teddy bear in one hand and a pistol in the other. I went to a mindless student satire called *The Madness of George Dubya*, in which a bloodthirsty U.S. president leads his cabinet in a rousing musical number called "Might Makes Right." As theater, *Madness* was basically junk, with all the subtlety of a cement truck. But it struck a chord with British audiences and sold out for weeks in the West End, London's equivalent of Broadway.

Occasionally, though, this rather masochistic habit of mine led me to some real theater—such as the hottest play on the London stage of 2003–4, the National Theatre's production of a musical entitled *Jerry Springer—The Opera*. For most theatergoers, the title alone made the thing irresistible. The posters advertising this work added to the allure, promising "the classic elements of grand opera: Triumph. Tragedy. Trailer Park trash."

Jerry Springer—The Opera has two jokes. First, it has all the paraphernalia of grand opera—choruses, septets, lyric arias—but the singing is mainly about Jerry Springer kinds of things: sex, violence, infidelity, weird sex. The opening chorus of the work is "My Brother's Girlfriend Used to Be My Dad." Early in the first act, a soprano playing an American housewife named Peaches steps demurely to the front of the stage for her big aria, which begins, "The strangest thing happened last night when I went to take a leak." The action of the "opera" is punctuated by a heroic chorus that continually bursts out in its chief refrain, "You're a loser! You're a slut!" For a while, this mockery of the operatic tradition is entertaining, but gradually the joke gets old.

The second joke in *Jerry Springer* is the same one that animates the Lardburgers and so much other European satire: a portrayal of rude, crude, boorish Americans, with all the classic stereotypes. Except for Springer himself (a native of England, as the Brits all know), every character in this "opera" is fat, stupid, prejudiced, cheating on his spouse, and carrying a gun. When the Springer character turns to his TV audience on stage and asks, "What do you want to see today?" the chorus fires right back: "Lesbians fighting! Open crotch sightings!" The story of the opera, to the extent there is one, is interrupted now and then for "commercials," and the products being touted are right out of American trash TV: plastic surgery, Viagra, and guaranteed weight-loss programs. Just to rub it in, at the end of the first act the Ku Klux Klan dances onto the stage, complete with white hoods and pointed caps, and burns a cross. Despite my long experience watching Europeans make fun of my country, I found *Jerry Springer—The Opera* to be debilitating. "Really, we're not like that," I said defensively during the intermission to the kind British woman sitting next to me. She noticed that I was disturbed, and did her best to cheer me up. "Don't worry, dahling," she said. "We have daft chat shows over here as well. And look on the bright side: at least this play is providing employment for a lot of really fat opera singers."

And the play—so popular it was the toughest ticket to land in London for more than a year—provided Europeans with a basic entertainment staple they have been enjoying for two centuries. Almost as long as there has been a United States of America, the people of Europe have found a certain delicious pleasure in deploring American ways and making fun of them. Much has been made of the sharp decline in mutual respect and admiration between the United States and Europe in the first few years of the twenty-first century. All over Europe, west and east, opinion surveys show a steep plunge in positive feelings toward the United States, a trend that became even more obvious following the war in Iraq. (And Americans have returned the favor, from "liberty fries" in the congressional cafeteria to learned seminars where thinkers like Robert Kagan, whom we'll see more of in chapter 7, argue that Europe is a pitiful weakling that can safely be ignored.)

This pancontinental America-bashing can be funny (for a while), and it can be exasperating. But it is an important mindset for Americans to understand, because the sheer pleasure that Europeans take in denigrating America has become another bond unifying the continent. Widespread anti-Americanism has strengthened Europeans' belief that an integrated European Union should stand up as a counterweight to the American brute. Until the early years of the twenty-first century, a majority of Europeans reacted warily to the suggestion that the European Union should become a "superpower." Today, Europeans have broadly embraced the notion that their united continent should be the superpower that stands up to super America. Surveys taken in the summer of 2003, after the intensely unpopular military action in Iraq, showed that more than 70 percent of Europeans want the EU to become a superpower—and more than 70 percent expect that this will happen.

To a large extent, the zeal for America-bashing stems from opposition to U.S. foreign policy—and particularly the foreign policy of George W. Bush, the most unpopular American president in a century among Europeans. But the sour feeling toward America among the people of Europe goes well beyond foreign policy issues. Across the continent today, there are all sorts of things about the United States that people can't stand, or can't understand, or both.

As with the rest of the world, Europe's attitude toward the behemoth across the Atlantic is not purely negative; it's a love-hate kind of thing. American products, and American pop culture, are pervasive in Europe and immensely popular. U.S. exports like *Beverly Hills 90210, Dawson's Creek, The West Wing, Sex and the City,* and, yes, *Jerry Springer,* fill the airwaves, often on the prestigious public networks. (*Seinfeld* has not been as successful, apparently because the jokes don't translate to a continental setting.) Belgium is one of the countries where U.S. global policies are most bitterly condemned by the general public, but Belgium's home-grown version of McDonald's, the burger-and-*frites* chain called Quick, uses the characters from *Friends* as its drawing card, with Phoebe serving Ross a Quickburger in the ads. On European MTV, more than half of the videos feature American bands; no translation is provided, on the theory that Generation E can understand the lyrics as well as an American audience. The only time MTV Europe changes this pattern is each May 9, when the network celebrates Europe Day by playing only European bands. (Actually, the producers tend to cheat by claiming Madonna and Gwen Stefani as Europeans, because both pop divas now live in London with their European husbands. Thus May 9 is the day to see videos of "Papa Don't Preach" or "Just a Girl" on European TV.) All over the continent, fashionable people gather at predawn parties each spring to watch the Oscar broadcast from Los Angeles. Most years, this is followed the next day with a series of angry newspaper columns complaining that, once again, the Oscar voters showed a disgraceful bias against all European movies. The one time when the voters proved they were not biased—that was 1999, when Roberto Benigni won the Best Actor award for his performance in *La Vita e Bella* (*Life Is Beautiful*)—all of Italy celebrated for a week.

To the consternation of the great continental fashion houses, American labels—Levi's, Gap, Tommy Hilfiger, Abercrombie—are de rigueur for Generation E. For Europe's youth movement, any article of clothing genuinely "from the States" has innate value. Walking past a trendy boot store in London's Camden Town neighborhood one day, I was offered 200 pounds on the spot for the cowboy boots I was wearing. That was $370, more than twice what I had paid for the boots, new, back home in Colorado. When I hesitated, the shopkeeper threw in a cheap pair of trainers (that's British for "gym shoes") to get me home. I laughed all the way to the bank to cash my cheque.

American fast food is ubiquitous on the continent; that explains why the standard for price transparency is the "Big Mac Index," as we will see in chapter 3 of this book. The sheep farmer José Bové became a national hero, of sorts, in France by wrecking a McDonald's outlet and defending himself on the grounds that "it's American, from the country that promotes globalization and industrial food production and unfairly penalizes the small French farmer." (Bové was sentenced to twenty days in jail for vandalism, which only increased the size of his following.) Still, France has more than 1,000 McDonald's outlets that do quite nicely, thank you, even when situated right next to a traditional *boulangerie*. No matter what the Bové-istes might say, it is hard to call this an American "invasion," since every one of the French outlets belongs to a French franchisee. Nobody is forcing the Belgians, the Spaniards, or the Danes to drink Coca-Cola or wear Nikes; the fact is, Europeans like American stuff. The novelist Arthur Koestler, a prominent America-basher in his day, had the intellectual honesty to admit this point in a 1951 essay: "Who coerced us into buying all this? The United States do not rule

Europe as the British rule India; they waged no Opium War to force the revolting 'Coke' down our throats. Europe bought the whole package because Europe wanted it."

Almost despite themselves, Europeans visiting "the States" often find themselves charmed by American ways. Even a lefty columnist like John Sutherland, of London's *Guardian* newspaper, was so taken by the little things of life in the United States that he made a list of "fifty-two things they do better in America." Among the items that caught his eye—none of them common in Europe—were:

- Free refills of coffee (without asking)
- Newspaper vendomats on street corners
- "Paper or plastic?" (what the bagger says in your friendly 24-hour supermarket)
- Drive-through banking
- High school graduation ceremonies, and regular class reunions
- Free or cut-price parking at cinemas and restaurants
- Ubiquitous 24-hour convenience stores
- Fridges big enough for a 30-pound turkey

There is a whole genre of contemporary European literature involving people who have moved to, or spent some time in, the United States and are surprised to find themselves adopting American habits. The English novelist Zoe Heller, in an essay titled "Help! I'm Turning into an American Parent," described how she was at first appalled at the way American parents constantly praise their children: "To an English sensibility, these anthologies of praise seem mawkish. Unseemly. Deleterious to an appropriate sense of modesty." But gradually, Heller wrote, she began to see her own daughter responding positively to the endless encouragement she got at preschool in Santa Monica. "One of the things most admired about Americans is their can-do spirit, their optimism and self-belief and so on," Heller concluded. "It occurs to me that their child-rearing techniques might have something to do with that sunny outlook. . . . What, indeed, if the Americans' cosseting methods are the real reason they are a superpower?"

Europeans also appreciate some of the larger virtues of American life: the nation's youthful vigor, its open-armed acceptance of new ideas, its great universities, and the classlessness that means the American dream really works. Even the staunchest European leftists admire America's willingness to take in refugees by the millions, accept them as American, and then hold a fancy ceremony, with a judge or a senator presiding, to make their citizenship official. (In Europe, in contrast, becoming a new citizen generally involves nothing more than a bureaucrat stamping a form in a cluttered office, and payment of the required fee.) Almost every European—particularly east of the former iron curtain—has a neighbor or cousin or grandchild who has emigrated to Milwaukee or Portland or Tallahassee. These relatives recognize the symbolic power of the Statue of Liberty and the generosity of a rich, powerful nation that embraces poor, powerless newcomers from anywhere on earth. In the beautiful old city of Riga, Latvia, I got to talking with Marie Rabinovich, whose daughter had emigrated to Denver a decade earlier. Marie told me proudly that her daughter had become an American citizen, and was about to cast her first vote in the 2000 election between George W. Bush and Al Gore. "It is amazing thing," Marie told me, in decent English, "that my daughter, a peasant, is allowed to choosing the most powerful man in the world." No matter how fashionable America-bashing has become, people all over the continent still get letters every month from their cousins in Chicago urging them to emigrate to the U.S.A.

But the Europeans also know what they don't like about the United States. These views tend to be set forth in a series of best-selling books, one after another, with titles like *Dangereuse Amerique* or *The Eagle's Shadow* or *Pourquoi le monde deteste-t-il l'Amerique?* The depiction of the United States in these popular volumes has been summarized neatly by the American scholar Anthony Judt: "The U.S. is a selfish, individualistic society devoted to commerce, profit, and the despoliation of the planet. It is uncaring of the poor and sick and it is indifferent to the rest of humankind. The U.S. rides roughshod over international laws and treaties and threatens the moral, environmental, and physical future of humanity. It is inconsistent and hypocritical in its foreign dealings, and it wields unparalleled military clout. It is, in short, a bull in the global china shop."

As we will discuss in chapter 6 of this book, most Europeans are appalled by the death penalty. And because each American execution tends to get big play in the French, German, Spanish, and British media, Europeans think American electric chairs are used much more frequently than is actually the case. The constitutional "right to keep and bear arms," and the gun lobby that defends it, also tend to mystify the people of Europe, even those who are strongly pro-American on most issues. In September of 1999, I was watching the TV news in Norway, reporting on Hurricane Floyd, which swept up the east coast of the United States and wreaked considerable destruction. The Norwegian correspondent on the scene was deeply impressed by the fact that some 2.6 million people— equivalent to half the population of Norway!—had been successfully evacuated from coastal areas to escape danger. On the same day, though, one of those tragic gun massacres had left seven Americans dead and a dozen badly wounded in a church (!) in Texas. "What kind of society is it," the reporter asked plaintively, "that can move millions of people overnight in the name of safety, but then expose them to crazy men wielding guns on every street?"

I was surprised to find that the open display of patriotism—something I had taken to be a universal human impulse—is widely sneered at in Europe. After all, it was a European who turned that impulse into death-less verse:

> *Breathes there the man with soul so dead*
> *Who never to himself hath said,*
> *"This is my own, my native land!"*

But when the great Scot Sir Walter Scott wrote that in 1805, it was still an acceptable, even admirable, point of view for Europeans. Today, the way of thinking that says, "This is my native land, and I love it," is considered an American peculiarity. The Europeans, of course, are working hard to move away from their nationalistic tendencies and toward a supranational union that eviscerates borders and traditional national rivalries, and this perhaps explains the exasperation with old-style love of country in the United States. Ian Buruma, a Dutchman living in Britain, caught this mood perfectly after seeing the American flag everywhere during a visit to New York:

> To most Europeans born after the second world war, it is a somewhat bewildering sight, this massive outpouring of patriotism. . . . Those of us who pride ourselves on a certain degree of sophistication view flag-waving with lofty disdain. It is embarrassing, mawkish, potentially bellicose. I must confess that I find the sight of grown men touching their hearts at the sound of the national anthem a little ridiculous, too. And the ubiquitous incantations of "God Bless America" seem absurdly over the top. Mawkishness and a beady eye on commercial opportunity go together in the land of the free in a way that can be quite disconcerting.

The place where American patriotism seems to annoy Europeans the most is at international sporting events. Chants of "USA! USA!" and "We're number one!" may seem like normal fan behavior to Americans, but they drive Europe crazy. When Russian competitors lost gold medals due to disputed calls by referees in hockey, figure skating, and Nordic skiing in the 2002 Winter Olympics, President Vladimir Putin condemned the International Olympic Committee for "biased decisions and pro-American judgements at the Winter Games." Most Americans put this down as sour grapes; almost all Europeans, however, agreed with Putin that the noisy home fans in Salt Lake City—where 93 percent of all tickets were sold to Americans—had put impossible pressure on the officials. "What the Russians are upset about," wrote Simon Barnes, the sports columnist for the *Times* of London, when the Salt Lake games ended, "is the transformation of the Olympic Games into yet another American

Festival of Victory. The world has been treated to 17 days of whooping crowds and American athletes hysterical with their adrenalin-stoned patriotism. I've had many wonderful times in the States and have many good American friends. But whooping, en masse, up-yours patriotism is not endearing. . . . And so the world watched the Winter Games . . . hoping that the American in the race would fall over."

I don't think Barnes is overstating the case here. The Europeans really do want to see American competitors fall over and lose—and thus give the "whooping, up-yours patriots" in the American cheering section their due comeuppance. Even the ever-so-proper world of golf erupts in rage again and again at the conduct of U.S. players and fans. There was the infamous (in Europe, at least) "Battle of Brookline" during the 1999 Ryder Cup, the biennial competition where a team of European pro golfers takes on an American all-star team. With the match all even on the last hole in Brookline, Massachusetts, an American sank a long birdie putt that put the U.S. team ahead by one stroke. The fans erupted— "USA! USA!"—and swarmed onto the green in glee to applaud their heroes. The problem was, the match wasn't over. A European player still had a putt to make that could have tied the score; after all the hoopla, and the crowd's footprints covering the green, he missed. "Evidently, they care more about an American victory than they do about sportsmanship," declared an angry European player, José Maria Olazabal of Spain. A year later, when the Solheim Cup competition—the female version of the Ryder Cup—was played in Scotland, the American team caused a pan-European furor. The Swedish star Annika Sorenstam sunk a long chip shot from off the green that seemed to sew up a European victory. But then the American captain, Pat Bradley, approached the referee and said Sorenstam's great birdie should be disallowed, because the Swede had shot out of turn. It was a technicality—indeed, a tiny technicality—but the judges decided, once the issue had been raised, that they had to enforce the rule. In a scene played over and over on European TV news, Sorenstam broke into tears and denounced American competitiveness. "I was shocked that they took my shot away," she said. "The entire European team is disgusted with America. We all ask ourselves, 'Is this how badly they need to win?'"

Another common grievance among Europeans is the sense—it is, indeed, conventional wisdom almost everywhere—that Americans are insular people, ignorant of and indifferent to the rest of the planet. This has been a standard European complaint for more than a century. In her 1852 best-seller *Domestic Manners of the Americans,* the British traveler Frances Trollope—aunt of the great Victorian novelist—established the theme with her conclusion about the American worldview. "If the citizens of the United States were indeed the devoted patriots they call themselves, they would surely not thus encrust themselves in the hard, dry, stubborn persuasion that they are the first and best of the human race, that nothing is to be learnt, but what they are able to teach, and that nothing is worth having, which they do not possess." In the contemporary version of this stereotype, the paradigm American is that Texan tourist on the French comedy shows who walks into a Paris café and orders "two wot wahns." Brian Reade, a columnist for the London tabloid the *Mirror,* summarizes this widespread European belief:

They are wonderfully courteous to strangers, yet indiscriminately shoot kids in schools. They believe they are masters of the world, yet know nothing about what goes on outside their shores. Yanks . . . the people whose IQ is smaller than their waist size. People who believe the world stretches from California to Boston and everything outside is the bit they have to bomb to keep the price of oil down. When I first visited America in 1976, teenagers asked if we had cars, and, if so, how we could drive them on our cobbled streets. Two months ago, a man from Chicago asked me how often we vote for a new Queen. Only one in five Americans hold a passport and the only foreign stories that make their news are floods, famine, and wars, because it makes them feel good to be an American. Feeling good to be American is what they live for. It's why they call their baseball league The World Series, why they can't take our football because they didn't invent it.

As I often argued in Europe, the charge that Americans are insular is absurdly off-base. No country on earth has a broader distribution of races, creeds, and nationalities than the United States, and each of the ethnic groups in America maintains a close interest in developments back in the old country. One day on the BBC's excellent *Dateline* program, Gavin Esler, the presenter—that's the British word for "anchorman"—was haranguing me about Americans' ignorance of the outside world, and their inability to master foreign languages. "You know, the way Americans speak French is just to say the word in English, only louder," he said, laughing. I know Gavin loves a good debate, so I took him on. I said that the citizenry of the United States is the world's largest repository of language skills. "We have a couple of million Polish speakers," I said. "We have more Estonian speakers than there are in Tallinn. We have 100,000 people in America who read a Cambodian newspaper every week. I'll bet there aren't 100 people in all of Britain who can read Cambodian." Esler was undeterred by this line of argument. He responded, in essence, that America shouldn't get credit for its formidable body of Cambodian linguistic talent because we imported it rather than teaching the language in our schools.

What really annoys the Europeans is that this nation perceived to be ignorant of the rest of the world has the wealth and power to dominate much of it. The French parliamentarian Noel Mamere racked up strong sales with a book—title: *No Thanks, Uncle Sam*—arguing that "it is appropriate to be downright anti-American" because of this combination of strength and stupidity. "Ominipotence and ignorace," he wrote, "is a questionable cocktail. It would be great if they saw what they looked like from over here. But they are not interested. They think they are the best in the world, that they are way ahead of everyone, and everyone needs to learn from them."

This mix of experience, attitudes, and urban myths, some dating back many decades, meant that ordinary Europeans' view of the United States was fairly critical even before the earth-shaking developments at the start of the twenty-first century. The French polling firm Groupe CSA regularly surveys opinon across France about contemporary issues, and periodically takes a poll titled "L'Image des Etats-Unis." Almost every French citizen feels knowledgeable enough to answer the questions— only a tiny minority say they aren't familiar with the details of American life—and the results are generally unflattering. The image of the United States tends to vary slightly in these polls depending on recent events— predictably, esteem for America dropped during and after the Iraq war of 2003—but the general pattern is fairly constant over the years. A survey taken in the fall of 2000 gives a baseline reading on French attitudes toward life in the United States. Asked the question, "As far as you're concerned, what kind of country is the United States?" the French public gave the following answers:

1. A nation of violence   50%
2. A nation that uses the death penalty   48%
3. A nation of great social inequality   45%
4. A nation of innovation   37%
5. A racist nation   33%
6. A nation where anything goes   27%
7. A nation where anyone can get rich   24%
8. A nation that welcomes immigrants   15%
9. A society where religion is pervasive   15%
(No opinion about America)   3%

Given those broad impressions, it's not surprising that only 12 percent of French people surveyed said they felt "admiration" for the United States. Another 14 percent reported a generally "positive" view. In contrast to the 26 percent who held a favorable view of America, 12 percent said the United States makes them worried, and 34 percent of those polled said their view of the United States was "critical."

Other European populations were perhaps not so critical as the French, but the general pattern across the continent in the year 2000 would have been roughly similar to what that CSA survey found. And then came the Bush presidency, the horrific events of 9/11, and Iraq. In November of 2004, when Americans awarded George W. Bush a second term in the White House, the gap in understanding, respect, and friendship seemed wider than it had ever been before.

At first, September 11, 2001, seemed to shrink the Atlantic. Just hours after the buildings toppled in New York and Washington, British prime minister Tony Blair assured Americans that Europe "stands shoulder to shoulder with you." In a unanimous vote on September 12, NATO invoked—for the first time in its fifty-year history—Article 5 of its founding treaty, the clause that says an attack on one member is considered an attack on all NATO nations. Even that venerable organ of Euro-left anti-Americanism, France's *Le Monde,* declared "Nous sommes tous Américains"—"We are all Americans." On September 13, Queen Elizabeth II broke all precedent by ordering the Royal Marine Band to play "The Star-Spangled Banner" during the changing of the guard at Buckingham Palace. A survey two weeks after the attack by the Swiss polling company Isopublic found that the peace-minded Europeans were ready to go to war against the perpetrators of the attack, or their host nation. Asked if their own countries should support a U.S. military assault, 80 percent of Danish respondents backed the idea, as did 79 percent in Britain, 73 percent in France, 58 percent in Spain and Norway, and about 53 percent in Germany. The only European nation that resisted the idea of fighting alongside the Americans was Greece, where only 29 percent supported military action.

To be an American in Europe in those troubled, frightening days after 9/11 was to be surrounded by support, sympathy, and unsolicited words of encouragement. When people realized an American was present—usually from hearing an American accent—they would go out of their way to express consolation and friendship. On a nondescript traffic island near Grosvenor Square in London, somebody tied an American flag around an old oak tree early on September 12. Over the next few days, a mountain grew beside the tree—a mountain of flowers, flags, cards, candles, tear-stained notes, pictures, paintings, and a New York Yankees cap. This was the British people's spontaneous tribute to the Americans who were murdered on 9/11. There were no instructions about this, no coordination. These were simply ordinary people who felt a need to send America a message—people like Rob Anderson of London, who left a big spray of roses with a handwritten card: "Dear America, You supported us in two world wars. We stand with you now." Similar floral mountains went up outside the U.S. embassies in Moscow, Copenhagen, Lisbon, and Madrid. London's largest cathedral, St. Paul's, invited every Yank in town to a memorial service on September 14. The local paper in Ipswich devoted its entire front page on September 12 to a banner headline: "God Bless America." Across the continent, there was an overwhelming sense that the whole of the West was under attack. We were all Americans now. We were all in this thing together.

This initial rush of good feeling was accompanied by action. The first arrests of conspirators charged with planning the 9/11 attacks were made in Germany. European intelligence agencies basically opened their files on suspected Muslim militants to investigators from the CIA and the FBI. When the United States went to war in Afghanistan a month after the attacks, European public opinion strongly supported the move; more important, nearly every NATO member sent troops, weapons, and money to help topple the Taliban. The vaunted "Atlantic Alliance" was working together more closely than at any time since the depths of the cold war.

But over the next three years, that moment of transatlantic togetherness in the fall of 2001 came to look like a momentary blip, an aberration caused more by the sudden shock of those burning buildings than by common bonds of interest and policy. Within a year of 9/11, European government ministers, columnists, and academics were once again depicting the United States as a selfish, gun-happy "hyperpower" that had shifted into "unilateralist overdrive," to borrow a term from Chris Patten, the European Union's commissioner for external affairs, a man who was supposed to be diplomatic about such things. "The whole concept of the 'West' feels out of date now," said Dominique Moisi, of the Institut

Français des Relations Internationales in Paris, about eighteen months after the attacks. "September 11 brought us together, but only temporarily. We have to realize that major differences exist across the Atlantic, and will not go away. Europe and the U.S. will have to live with them." The transatlantic chill stemmed in part from one man; President George W. Bush has been highly unpopular among the people of Europe. "Almost everyone on the European side agrees that the relationship is far worse since George W. Bush was elected," Moisi said. The war in Iraq, opposed by large popular majorities in every EU country—even nations like Britain, Spain, and Poland, which the United States counted as allies in the war—exacerbated the split. Spain's José María Aznar, who supported Bush in Iraq, paid a high price for his prowar stance. In the spring of 2004, in the wake of a terrorist bombing, the voters of Spain dumped Aznar's Popular Party and handed the government in Madrid to the strongly antiwar Socialists.

The process of "continental drift" driving the United States and Europe apart was also propelled by venerable European complaints about America, feelings dating back at least to Mrs. Trollope. The Bush administration strengthened all the old prejudices, and tended to confirm the old stereotypes. The new president, a pro-death-penalty oil man swaggering into the White House despite winning half a million fewer votes than his opponent, was "a walking gift to every European anti-American caricaturist." It was repeatedly reported in the European press that America's new leader had never been to Europe. This claim was false—Bush had made half a dozen trips to across the Atlantic before he entered the White House—but it neatly fit the common perception of an American president who didn't know the first thing about Europe. Bush fueled this European view with some unfortunate policy blunders. As we'll see in chapter 4 of this book, the Bush administration's ham-handed effort to intervene in the General Electric dispute between Jack Welch and Mario Monti damaged the new president's stature among European leaders just months after he took office. Two years later, President Bush personally phoned European prime ministers to urge them to admit Turkey to the

European Union. This lobbying mission was doomed to fail, and it did. Worse than that, the president angered the leaders on the receiving end of his calls. "How could the White House possibly think that they could play in a role in determining who joins the EU?" Chris Patten commented later.

Opinion polls demonstrate how far the image of the U.S. has fallen since that brief moment of post-9/11 togetherness. A U.S. State Department poll in 1998 found that 78 percent of Germans had a favorable view of the United States. In 2002, a survey by the Pew Research Center in Washington, D.C., found that 61 percent of Germans were favorable. Two years later, in the wake of the war in Iraq, only 38 percent of Germans had a positive feeling toward the United States, the nation that had been Germany's strongest ally, and military defender, for fifty-nine years. In France, positive feelings toward America fell from 62 percent in 1999 to 37 percent in the spring of 2004. "If anything, fear and loathing of the U.S. has increased," wrote the Pew Center's pollster, Andrew Kohut, a few months after the fall of Baghdad. "Even in the United Kingdom, the United States' most trusted European ally, 55% see the U.S. as a threat to global peace. And in four EU countries—Greece, Spain, Finland, and Sweden—the United States is viewed as the greatest threat to world peace, more menacing than Iran or North Korea."

In a geopolitical application of Newton's third law, the actions tending to divide the old Atlantic Alliance have sparked an equal and opposite reaction in Europe: divisions with America have prompted the Europeans to draw closer together, to look even harder for unity among themselves. The growing sense that the United States is no longer the continent's protector, but rather a potential threat—or even, perhaps, the "greatest threat"—has strengthened the movement toward "ever closer union" among the members of the EU. Since the Europeans can no longer trust or align themselves with the world's only superpower, they have no choice but to build a superpower of their own. That, at least, is the reasoning of many EU leaders, including the most recent president of the European Commission, Romano Prodi. "There is a rhythm of global dominance," Prodi observed a couple of years after 9/11. "No country remains the first player forever. Maybe this American hour will not last. And who will be the next leading player? Maybe next will be China. But more probably, before China, it will be the united Europe. Europe's time is almost here. In fact, there are many areas of world affairs where the objective conclusion would have to be that Europe is already the super-power, and the United States must follow our lead."

While this deeply felt need to be the un-America, to be different from the much-mocked nation across the sea, has been a key force in building European unity, it was not the motivation that sparked the creation of a unified New Europe in the first place. The initial steps toward a United States of Europe were propelled by a different dream. Amid the misery and ruin left behind by the twentieth century's two lethal world wars, a group of Europeans set out to create a lasting peace on the continent and a shared economy. They did not aim low. Their dream was to produce, once and for all, an end to war on the continent, and an end to poverty.

TWO

The Invention of Peace

and the Pursuit of Prosperity

In Flanders fields the poppies still blow, between the crosses, row on row. Amid the flowering meadows around the small Flanders town of Ypres, there are more than 170 military cemeteries, an archipelago of perfectly manicured green lawns lined with row on row of crosses and memorial stones recording why soldiers from at least twenty different countries fought and died in the world wars there:

Morts pour la France
For King and Country
Gestorven voor het vaderland
Deutschland muss leben

For the merchants of Ypres, an ancient market center, the cemeteries are now the main source of income. The Belgian town has built a bustling economy around memories of war. This is fitting, because the broad valleys and long, steep hills of Flanders—stretching across northern France and southern Belgium from Dunkirk, on the Atlantic Coast, to Waterloo, some fifty miles inland—have served Europeans as battlefields for two thousand years. In all that time, the basic war plan has not changed:

one army sets up on a high ridge, the other takes the opposite ridge, and the valley between them becomes a blood-drenched no-man's-land.

Readers old enough to have gone to school when students still had to memorize the opening lines of Julius Caesar's *Gallic Wars* will remember that Caesar himself went to war in Flanders. "Gallia est omnis divisa in partes tres," Caesar began; "quarum unam incolunt Belgae" ("All Gaul is divided into three parts; one of those regions is inhabited by the Belgians"). The rest of Caesar's great war journal has little to say about the fighting in Flanders—not surprisingly, because it was one part of Gaul that he never managed to conquer. The "Belgae," arrayed on the northern ridge, rained so much damage upon the Roman legions in the wide valleys below that mighty Caesar was stopped in his tracks. Ever since, the fertile Flanders farmland has marked a dividing line between Roman and Germanic Europe. This is where the Latin-derived languages gradually give way to German and its low-country variants, Dutch and Flemish.

To this day, the maps and road signs of Flanders show two names for every town—one in French, the flower of the Romance languages, and the other in Flemish. If you go to Ypres to visit the cemeteries and the fine museum of warfare there, a sign at the edge of town welcomes you both to "Ypres" and to "Ieper." The British soldiers who trooped in by the hundreds of thousands at the start of World War I did their best to pronounce that French name, "Ypres," and ended up calling the town "Wipers." They even published a newspaper called the *Wipers Times*.

Flanders went on to become a battleground, and effectively a burial ground, for a long series of would-be conquerors of Europe. The frustrations of the Spanish Hapsburgs as they tried in vain to maintain control of the low countries spawned a common Spanish aphorism, *Poner una pica en Flandes* ("To station a spearman in Flanders"), meaning to attempt too much, to reach too far. Napoleon's final trip to the region in 1815 made the humdrum Belgian village of Waterloo a global synonym for crushing defeat.

The deadliest years in the long, bellicose history of Flanders came during World War I, when the region known as the "Ypres salient" hosted the mother of all trench warfare. From 1914 to 1918 the opposing sides lobbed shells and grenades and poison gas back and forth across the muddy lowlands. This long exercise in futility left millions of young men blind or maimed and a half-million dead, but produced almost no military result for any of the armies involved. The toll of death and injury in the trenches of Flanders did help, though, to produce an even bloodier European war just twenty-one years later. Among the German victims at Ypres was a twenty-nine-year-old private first class named Adolf Hitler, who was caught in a British gas attack on October 13, 1918, and temporarily blinded. "I stumbled back with burning eyes," Hitler recalled in his memoir, *Mein Kampf,* "taking with me my last regret of the war. A few hours later, my eyes had turned into burning coals." The memory burned even hotter. "We do not pardon, we do not forget," Hitler told the German people four years later. "We demand vengeance!"

The death and destruction of the Ypres salient also produced deathless literature, as doomed young men on both sides sat in the muddy trenches writing poetry that perfectly captured the horror and the grisly fascination of warfare. During its brief existence, the *Wipers Times* published such distinguished writers as Rupert Brooke, who fell in the first year of the war but left behind a classic lyric:

If I should die, think only this of me
That there's some corner of a foreign field
That is for ever England. There shall be
In that rich earth a richer dust concealed
A dust whom England bore, shaped, made aware . . .

as well as his comrade Julian Grenfell, another casualty of 1915 who saw what was coming beforehand:

The thundering line of battle stands,
And in the air Death moans and sings;

But Day shall clasp him with strong hands
And Night shall fold him in his wings.

These voices from the Ypres salient are generally presented today as spokesmen of an antiwar sentiment. A few of them fit that description, such as Wilfred Owen, killed in the trenches fourteen days before the war ended ("What passing bells for these who die as cattle?/Only the monstrous anger of the guns"). But most of the battlefield poetry was about the rectitude of the war, the manly importance of the call to battle, and the glory of fighting for one's country, native or adopted. Alan Seeger, an American poet living in Paris, signed up to fight for France within days of the outbreak of the war. He was killed by machine-gun fire at age twenty-eight, charging a German barricade. He probably died happy, for he had written that death in the Great War was his mission in life:

I have a rendezvous with Death
At some disputed barricade
When spring comes back with rustling shade
And apple blossoms fill the air.

. . . And I to my pledged word am true
I shall not fail that rendezvous.

The most famous battle poem to come out of the Flanders fields was an outright plea for more battle. Dr. John McCrae, a sometime poet assigned as a surgeon to the Canadian Army forces at Ypres, watched in agony as his troops were slaughtered and buried, day after day. On May 2, 1915, McCrae's closest friend, Alexis Helmer, killed by a German chlorine gas attack, was buried under a white cross in a field of wildflowers beside the Canadian encampment. That evening, Colonel McCrae imagined the message Helmer would wish to convey to his fellow soldiers: Keep on fighting. McCrae worked through the night putting the thought into poetry, creating a lyric that quickly became a global favorite and is still being anthologized around the world:

In Flanders Fields the poppies blow
Between the crosses, row on row
That mark our place; and in the sky
The larks, still bravely singing, fly
Scarce heard among the guns below.

We are the Dead. Short days ago
We lived, felt dawn, saw sunset glow,
Loved and were loved. And now we lie
In Flanders Fields.

Take up our quarrel with the foe!
To you from falling hands we throw
The torch: be yours to hold it high.
If ye break faith with us who die
We shall not sleep, though poppies grow
In Flanders Fields.

McCrae himself sleeps now in the same Flanders field, having succumbed to pneumonia in the last year of the war.

In twenty-first-century Europe, such nationalistic and belligerent attitudes are out of place; nobody today would see much glory in an admonition to "take up our quarrel with the foe," particularly if the foe were a fellow European nation. The new pancontinental mindset is apparent at the war museum—it's called the In Flanders Fields Museum—in downtown Ypres, where the suffering of soldiers from every country is recorded, with all nations treated equally and no suggestion that either side was right or wrong. The same universal antiwar sentiment comes through at the Menin Gate, a giant marble arch at the entrance to the town. Each evening at sunset, buglers from the Ypres fire brigade gather under the arch to play "The Last Post," the European version of "Taps," in memory of the fallen. The brief, sad ceremony draws thousands of people every night from all over Europe. Many of them cry as the bugles play. The mournful sobs and the ringing call of the horns rise up into the darkening Belgian sky, there to mingle with the spirits of tens of millions of innocents killed in the hot and cold wars of Europe's lethal twentieth century.

But barely an hour's drive across the Flanders fields rises a gleaming memorial to a new Europe in a new century. The relentlessly modern office towers of Brussels' Quartier Européen house most of the major institutions of the European Union, the ambitious effort to create a continent so integrated, so connected, that war will be impossible. With the sidewalks full of sharply dressed Eurocrats racing back and forth among the Euro-agencies with their bulging briefcases, the European Quarter looks and feels like the seat of a major government. It brings to mind Washington's Federal Triangle or London's Whitehall or Tokyo's Kasumigaseki, except that the buildings are newer and there are many more flags.

Just about any time you turn a corner in the EU section of Brussels, you come upon a forest of flags—twenty-five national flags, plus the EU's blue banner with its circle of twelve gold stars. The flags flap in the wind at the entrance to each of the EU's office buildings. For my money, the most attractive piece of architecture in Belgium's sprawling EU quarter is the European Parliament, an imposing block-long structure with the requisite flags lined up outside a broad covered portico where important people—or at least, people who clearly think they are important people—continually step into and out of limousines.

That huge parliament and the other massive buildings of the Quartier Européen represent the concrete manifestation of an idea that has been floating around Europe for several centuries, a dream that gained strength each time the various countries went to war with one another.

This dream was identified by many names in many languages: The Idea of Europe. *L'Europe. Pax Europa.* A Common European Home. In 1916, in *A Portrait of the Artist as a Young Man,* James Joyce gave the Idea of Europe an interesting name:

> I'm a democrat: and I'll work and act for the social liberty and equality among all classes and sexes in the United States of the Europe of the future.

This suggests either that Joyce had an amazing talent for seeing into the geopolitical future, or that—as most scholars believe—he was simply engaging in typical Joycean wordplay.

In the years after World War I, as European leaders looked back in horror on the four years that had virtually eliminated a whole generation of the continent's young men, the Idea of Europe had considerable appeal. The French foreign minister, Aristide Briand—a bold if somewhat unrealistic thinker whose other great idea was an international treaty in which all nations would renounce war forever—toured the continent with his proposal for "A Moral Union of Europe." This European Union was to be made up initially of the twenty-seven continental members of the League of Nations; it would have a legislative body with members elected from every country, and an executive branch with pan-European jurisdiction. In the late 1920s, committees were formed and multinational conferences were gathered to forward the Briand plan. But then the Great Depression came along. Ex-PFC Hitler, with his demand for vengeance, started winning elections in Germany. Briand died in 1932, and his Moral Union died with him. Europe was quickly engulfed in preparations for yet another war. World War II would kill five times as many Europeans as World War I.

Amid the smoke and splinters of the blasted, impoverished continent that emerged from World War II, a group of visionaries from several countries took up anew the dream of a united Europe. A loose aggregation emerged of government leaders, academics, business leaders, and writers, known collectively as the European Movement. In essence, they offered a completely new approach to an ancient concept. The Romans had forged a united Europe with a conquering army and a genius for government. The Holy Roman Emperors, the Hapsburgs (both Austrian and Spanish), Napoleon, and Hitler had all tried to unify Europe using force. The European Movement set out to do the same thing using the popular will. Their timing was perfect. The shock of a war that had killed some 55 million people, together with the ruin and hunger that came in its wake—even for the countries that won, rationing was stricter in the immediate postwar years that it had been during combat—made this old idea more palatable than ever before.

For Americans, who often think of the European Union as an economic entity, a free-trade zone and little more, it is easy to forget the moral passion and the enormous hunger for peace that motivated the union in the first place. The European Movement had massive support in Germany and Italy, among people who felt a painful guilt about the horrific war their nations had started. A group of German church leaders, led by the Reverend Martin Niemoller, drew up a formal "Declaration of Guilt" in late 1945; posted and read to the congregation at churches throughout the Axis nations, it promoted the notion that Germany and Italy must now seek reconciliation and common ground with the countries they had attacked in the war. Catholic priests and lay organizations across Europe and Protestant movements like Moral Rearmament also campaigned for a single Europe as a way to avoid the sin of mass killing in future wars.

The clarion voice advocating European unity as an essential antidote to further European wars was Winston Churchill. At the end of World War II, Churchill was revered all over Europe—all over the earth, for that matter—as the man who stood up to Adolph Hitler and rallied the free world to defeat the Nazi terror. Churchill, of course, was fully aware of his postwar stature. One day shortly after the war ended, his six-year-old grandson, Nicholas Soames, heard something astounding on the radio. He ran into Churchill's study to confirm it. "Grandpapa," the boy asked, "is it true that you are the greatest man in the world?" Churchill, deeply engaged in official papers, looked up briefly from his desk and answered, "Yes—and now bugger off."[1]

In 1946, however, the greatest man in the world had time on his hands. Just seven weeks after Churchill stood on the balcony at Buckingham Palace on May 8, 1945, to receive the adulation of millions celebrating VE-day, the prime minister and his Conservative Party were booted out of office by a British electorate already looking ahead to postwar arrangements. Churchill was crushed. When his wife, Clementine, told the exhausted seventy-year-old war leader that the election defeat might be a blessing in disguise, Churchill famously replied, "At the moment, my dear, it's certainly very well disguised."

Voted out of office, Churchill turned to work on his multivolume history of the war. With a cigar in his mouth and a team of stenographers on hand around the clock, he walked back and forth across the floor of his study, dictating each sentence of the book in rhythmic bursts that matched his paces.

In addition to his six-volume memoir of the war years, Churchill spent his postwar days looking ahead at Europe's future. He did not like what he saw. In one of those classic rhythmic sentences of his, he captured the brutal state of the continent after the war: "What is Europe? A rubble heap, a charnel house, a breeding ground for pestilence and hate." The Soviet Union's seizure of the eastern countries had divided the continent. The rubble, pestilence, and hate left over from the six years of all-out conflict seemed likely to spawn even more war. Something had to be done.

Churchill addressed these concerns in two famous speeches in 1946. For Americans, the better known of the two was the "iron curtain" speech in Fulton, Missouri, deploring the division between the Communist East of Europe and the (mainly) democratic West:

> From Stettin on the Baltic to Trieste on the Adriatic, an iron curtain
> has descended across the continent. Behind that line lie all the capitals

of the ancient states of central and Eastern Europe—Warsaw, Berlin, Prague, Vienna, Budapest, Belgrade, Bucharest, and Sofia. . . . This is certainly not the liberated Europe we fought to build up.

For Europeans, though—and for the purposes of this book—the most important Churchillian address of 1946 by far came on September 19, at Zurich. "I wish to speak to you today about the tragedy of Europe," the great orator began. He went on to lay out for a European audience, in that powerful rhythmic prose of his, the plight of the postwar continent. "Over wide areas a vast quivering mass of tormented, hungry, care-worn, and bewildered human beings gape at the ruins of their cities and homes, and scan the dark horizons for the approach of some new peril, tyranny, or terror. Among the victors there is a babel of jarring voices; among the vanquished the sullen silence of despair. That is all that Europeans, grouped in so many ancient states and nations, that is all that the Germanic powers have got by tearing each other to pieces and spreading havoc far and wide."

But Churchill had not traveled to Zurich simply to spread the word of doom. Rather, he promised a cure that would transform "as if by a miracle" the tragic state of postwar Europe. "What is this sovereign remedy?" Churchill went on. "It is to re-create the European Family, or as much of it as we can, and provide it with a structure under which it can dwell in peace, in safety, and in freedom."

The model for the structure Churchill had in mind was readily available for all to see: "The great Republic across the Atlantic Ocean." Europe had to become more like the United States of America, he argued. If Americans from places as distant and diverse as Texas and Massachusetts, Alabama and Oregon, could feel a shared sense of citizenship within their national framework, then surely Europeans could form their own "national grouping." "Why should there not be," Churchill went on, "a European group which could give a sense of shared patriotism and common citizenship to the distracted peoples of this turbulent and mighty continent? And why should it not take its rightful place with other great groupings in shaping the destinies of men?"

In short, Churchill told his fellow Europeans, the pathway to a future of peace and prominence on the world stage was clear: "We must build a kind of United States of Europe."

For some Europeans, there were problems with Churchill's prescription. He insisted that the French would have to set aside their burning hatred for the Germans who had attacked La Belle France twice in a single generation. "In this way only can France recover the moral leadership of Europe." He was right, of course, but it was still hard medicine for the embittered French, barely a year after the end of the war. Beyond that, Churchill didn't quite make it clear whether he expected Great Britain to play a role in his new United States of Europe, and that raised suspicions among the other countries. Was this just a British trick? (In Britain, the Europhiles and the Euroskeptics are arguing to this day about what Churchill had in mind about Britain's role in the new "United States.")

Overall, though, this forceful, ambitious, and optimistic vision of a united Europe, coming from the most respected leader on the continent, had an electrifying effect on a battered and war-weary people. It gave a huge burst of momentum to the nascent European Movement. Now a group of leaders in various countries began organizing and planning ways to create the new united states.

In addition to Churchill, the founding fathers of the European Union included political and religious figures from all of the countries that had suffered from Europe's assorted wars. Most were Roman Catholic, and they were largely motivated by a sense that Europe must regain its moral basis. The French statesman Robert Schuman had been a resistance leader against the Nazis; after the war, his countrymen thanked him repeatedly at the ballot box, twice choosing him as prime minister. The Belgian Paul-Henri Spaak held every senior post in his nation's government before and after the war; he was the first president of the United Nations General Assembly, in 1946, and decided that Europe needed the same kind of cooperative energy that had forged the UN.

Alcide de Gasperi was an anti-Fascist Italian who served as prime minister several times in Italy's constantly morphing postwar governments.

The German Konrad Adenauer had spent much of the war in a Nazi prison because he was suspected (accurately) of anti-Hitler sentiments. When he became the first chancellor of the new West Germany, he felt acutely Germany's need to express and demonstrate its remorse for what the nation had done to its European neighbors. The Spaniard Salvador de Madariaga, exiled because he dared to speak out publicly against his country's dictator, Francisco Franco, adopted the slogan "Fiat Europa!" or "Let there be one Europe!" The Spaniard was perhaps the most ambitious of all in his plan for a continent free of borders, both political and mental: "When Spaniards say 'our Chartres,' Englishmen say 'our Cracow,' Italians say 'our Copenhagen' and and Germans say 'our Bruges' . . . Then Europe will live."

If Winston Churchill was the voice of the United States of Europe, the pragmatic engineer who designed and built the foundations of this new political entity was a brandy salesman from the town of Cognac, France. Jean Monnet has often been called "the father of Europe." Not a man to hog the spotlight, Monnet himself spurned that title, but there's a good case to be made that he earned it. The young Monnet dropped out of high school at the age of sixteen to become a salesman for the family vineyard, J. G. Monnet Cognac. As the best English speaker in the company, he was dispatched to Britain, Canada, and the United States on sales missions at the start of the twentieth century. As he was packing for his first trip to London in 1904, his father offered some practical advice: "Don't take books. Your job is to talk to people."

In those foreign markets, the salesman from J. G. Monnet found his minuscule family firm competing against such titans of the cognac trade as Hennessy and Martell. And yet he found a pervasive atmosphere of cooperation among all the companies, large and small. By working together, Monnet noted in his memoirs, instead of constantly fighting, the cognac makers created a more prosperous, and a gentler, existence for everyone. Why couldn't nations learn the same lesson?

Charming, gregarious, a connoisseur of fine wine and cheese, Monnet was the kind of person who became friendly with everyone—including almost everyone who mattered in global affairs in the 1930s. Moving from the cognac business to international banking, he developed good working relationships with Franklin D. Roosevelt, Walter Lippmann, Philip and Katharine Graham, Churchill, Adenauer, Charles de Gaulle, and a host of other political and journalistic luminaries. During World War II, he did some ghostwriting for his friend the president of the United States; Monnet coined the description of the United States as the "Arsenal of Democracy," a ringing phrase that Roosevelt used to convince isolationist Americans that the States should help the anti-Nazi cause in Europe.

Even before the war ended, Monnet was giving speeches in Britain arguing that "a European entity, encompassing a common economic unit" was essential to create a cooperative atmosphere and avoid further mass slaughter on the continent. After VE-day, he went back to France and began working for a communal Europe.

For Monnet and the other visionaries, Churchill's great speech in Zurich served as the starting gun for a marathon run toward the goal of a united, communal Europe. For all the zeal and commitment, though, the first few years were unimpressive. A "Congress of Europe" was convened, with maximum hoopla, in The Hague in May 1948, featuring Winston Churchill as chairman and another inspiring Churchillian address to set the tone:

> We must proclaim the mission and the design of a United Europe, whose moral conception will win the respect and gratitude of mankind. I hope to see a Europe where men and women of every country will think of being European, and wherever they go in this wide domain will truly feel, "Here I am at home."

Out of the The Hague conference came a liaison committee, formally named "the European Movement," and two meetings of a new "Council of Europe Assembly" at Strasbourg—that handsome city on the German-

French border was picked because it had fallen to the opposing side, and thus changed its nationality, six times in the various wars between France and Germany from 1870 to 1945. These sessions were supposed to set the stage for a pan-European parliament. But the Strasbourg assembly turned out to be little more than a debating society. One of its key ideas, the creation of a European Defense Community—or "a unified European Army," as Churchill bluntly described it—never got off the ground and was forgotten by the mid-1950s.

These high-minded meetings, and the high-flown rhetoric they generated, served a purpose by committing political leaders across Europe to the ideal of a pancontinental union. But they didn't produce any practical result, in the 1940s at least. Rather, the major impetus for European unity in the half decade after the war came largely from the United States—a fact that many Europeans choose not to remember today.

Looking across the Atlantic at the "rubble heap" of postwar Europe, Harry Truman's secretary of state, George C. Marshall, created a "European Recovery Program"—more commonly known as the Marshall Plan—to finance European economic recovery. The fund paid out more than $12 billion between 1947 and 1951. The Marshall Plan also set up a coordinating committee, the Organization for Economic Cooperation and Development (OECD), which forced the World War II combatants to work together on postwar development.

The Marshall Plan was breathtaking in its sheer scope; the total fund was the equivalent of hundreds of billions of dollars in today's money. But the genuinely shocking facet of the American largesse was its evenhandedness. Marshall insisted that the money was to be shared among victors, vanquished, and neutrals. The Soviets refused to let their puppet nations east of the iron curtain accept the money, a key reason that Eastern Europe to this day has been unable to match the wealth and industrial might of the West. As the United States was sending those billions to Europe, Washington was also pouring hundreds of millions of dollars into the reconstruction of war-shattered Japan, a nation that had mounted a sneak attack on U.S. soil just five years earlier.

These huge grants of American aid to nations that had recently been bitter enemies were impelled somewhat by self-interest—the United States saw both Japan and Western Europe as bulwarks against the spread of communism—but also by a fundamentally generous spirit, a sense among the American people of a rich nation's responsibility to assist the poor. The notion of paying Germany to rebuild its industrial base particularly rankled the French; but Paris had to accept the American rules in order to get its share of Marshall aid. In Britain, the concept of Americans paying the nations that had attacked them prompted a small gem of the silver screen, *The Mouse That Roared*. In that film, Peter Sellers plays the prime minister of a small, impoverished European nation that declares war on the United States so that it, too, can cash in after the inevitable defeat and surrender. (Naturally, things go awry; Sellers and the Army of Grand Fenwick accidentally capture New York.)

In addition to this forced economic cooperation, the United States showed the Europeans how to work together on military and security concerns as well with the creation of NATO in 1949, linking West European nations with the United States and Canada in a common defense alliance. NATO successfully fulfilled its chief function, which was to deter the Soviet bloc from making war on Western Europe. Beyond that, it served another valuable purpose. Although France has never been comfortable about NATO—particularly since West Germany was admitted, in 1955—the organization demonstrated that bitter adversaries in the two world wars could cooperate on military matters.

While all this made-in-the-USA cooperation was proceeding in the late 1940s, Jean Monnet and his friends in the European Movement were looking for ideas, processes, mechanisms—basically anything that would forge voluntary alliances among European states. As Monnet wrote, the first step down the path of unity would be crucial; if it went smoothly, it could lead, over time, to a broad range of cooperative endeavors in Europe—economic, military, cultural, and governmental. Monnet, the visionary, had ideas for Europe so ambitious that even his fellow founding fathers thought them hopeless. As early as 1949, Monnet was openly talking about a European Parliament, a European court system to enforce a Europe-wide bill of rights, a tariff-free trade market, a common antitrust czar, borderless travel, and even a common currency. Anybody could see the man was daft.

But what should the first step be? Monnet knew that it had to involve some limitation on military power, because the immense public desire to avoid more wars was the strongest force driving the concept of a union. The program had to involve economic cooperation and a joint governmental apparatus, to show the Europeans that such common institutions could be made to work. The arrangement would have to involve both Germany and France, the chief antagonists in Europe's last three wars. If two or three other nations could be induced to sign up as well, all the better. And the plan needed the personal endorsement of a respected national leader.

In the spring of 1950, an opportunity came along, and Monnet jumped at it. The West German economy was reviving. Adenauer's government, with the backing of the United States and Britain, was eager to restart the great steel mills of the Ruhr and Saar valleys. This prospect both tempted and terrified Germany's neighbors. For the impoverished western regions of France and Belgium, the chance to sell coal in huge quantities to those German mills was tantalizing. For the struggling ports of Holland, German steel production promised a shipping boom. And yet the French, Belgians, and Dutch remembered all too well the shells and planes and Panzer tanks that had come out of the Ruhr and Saar the last time the Germans rebuilt their industrial base. Why let them do it again? Policymakers on both sides of the Atlantic looked at this dispute and saw a painful dilemma. The ever-inventive Jean Monnet looked at the same issue and saw the opening he had been waiting for.

A meeting among the French, British, and American governments was scheduled for May 10, 1950, to resolve the German steel question. Schuman, then the French foreign minister, went to his friend Monnet, desperate for a solution. Monnet sketched out a plan for a French-German industrial combine, with coal mining and steel production in both countries put under the control of a joint authority. In essence, France could sell its coal and Germany could build its steel, but the cross-border governing board would see to it that neither commodity could be used for any military purpose. It was a plan for profits and for peace at the same time.

Schuman quickly saw the genius in Monnet's idea. "Out of this," he said when he read the proposal, "will come forth Europe, a solid and united Europe." Monnet's plan not only solved the immediate problem of German steel production; it could also serve as the genesis of economic and governmental cooperation that could eventually lead to the dream of "L'Europe." With the media clamoring to know where France would stand at the May 10 meeting, Schuman called a press conference.

With Monnet at his side, the foreign minister set forth his ideas. This "Schuman Declaration" was so expansive, so ambitious—and, as it turned out, so accurate—that the text has become a sort of Declaration of Independence for the European Union. Just as Americans celebrate the declaration of 1776 with parties, picnics, and fireworks every July 4, the people of Europe today celebrate the declaration of 1950 with parties, picnics, and fireworks every May 9. The anniversary of the Schuman Declaration is feted in much of the continent as Europe Day—*Europatag, Festa dell' Europa, Le Jour d'Europe,* and so on in two dozen languages. (The British, still skittish about their connection with the union, make a careful practice of ignoring the celebrations altogether.)

Schuman met the assembled reporters on May 9, beneath the ornate chandeliers of an elegant chamber at the quai d'Orsay. He set forth Monnet's novel solution to the steel production issue: "Le Gouvernement Français propose de placer l'ensemble de la production franco-allemande de charbon et d'acier sous une Haute Autorité commune." ("The government of France proposes that French and German production of coal and steel should be placed under the control of a common authority.") Other European countries would be invited to join the combined operation. This would teach France and Germany how to work with, rather than against, each other, Schuman said. Beyond that, it would eliminate the risk of unilateral military production on either side: "The solidarity in production thus established will make it plain that any war between France and Germany becomes not merely unthinkable, but materially impossible."

But before the press could begin asking questions, Schuman offered an even more ambitious idea—a vastly broader vision of a united continent, with wartime adversaries joined together in a "European Federation" with a common economic system and unified political institutions. It was not a goal that would be achieved overnight, he added, but rather piece by piece, treaty by treaty, over a period of years or decades. In a statement that proved amazingly prescient about the next half century of unification, Schuman added: "The single Europe will not be made all at once, or according to a single comprehensive plan. Rather, it will be built through a series of concrete achievements, each of which will create a de facto solidarity."

Within days of this pronouncement, other European coal- and steel-producing nations asked to be included in the new communal undertaking. By the time the formal treaty creating the organization was signed the following spring, the new European Coal and Steel Community had six members: France, Germany, Italy, Belgium, Luxembourg, and the Netherlands. (In a response that would typify London's attitude toward European unity for the next fifty years, the British had an anguished debate over whether or not to join, finally decided to stay out, and eventually petitioned for membership ten years later, when the Coal and Steel Community had grown into a full-fledged Common Market.) The "Haute Autorité," or High Commission, that managed the business was headed by Jean Monnet. The board of directors was an assembly of members appointed by the governments of each of the six countries.

As was predictable at a time when war-torn countries were furiously rebuilding, the coal and steel operation at the heart of Western Europe was a rip-roaring economic success. That prompted the member nations to expand the cooperative concept until it applied to all commercial and economic activity. In the Treaty of Rome in 1957, the six countries formed the European Economic Community, popularly known as the Common Market, characterized by the elimination of all import tariffs, a common set of trade rules, and harmonized planning for transportation, agriculture, and taxes. That 1957 treaty was the source of three little words that have proven an accurate description of the sometimes sporadic European movement for the past half century: "ever closer union." There has been a clear momentum driving the nations and people of Europe closer, ever closer; and this momentum has so far proven strong enough to overcome almost every obstacle and argument against a closer union.

In the half century following the Schuman Declaration, "L'Europe" developed a bewildering network of councils, courts, commissions, and conferences (as we shall see in appendix 2). But the basic outlines of pan-European organization held fairly closely to the pattern Jean Monnet had designed for the European Coal and Steel Community in 1950. Just as Monnet's operation paid its own way, the European institutions today have their own dedicated revenue source—a value-added tax, or sales tax, assessed in each member nation—so that the union doesn't have to rely on voluntary contributions from governments. The underlying economic theory is that a sales tax, which is a tax on consumption, can be tolerated even in high-tax European countries because it does not penalize investment or production, the way income taxes might. Today that tax funds an annual EU budget well over $150 billion. Monnet's "Haute Autorité" has morphed over the years into the European Commission, the EU's cabinet, with members owing their allegiance not to their home countries but to Europe as a whole. That first multinational assembly has become the European Parliament, with members democratically elected from each country and aligned in a melange of political parties and groupings ranging from far right to far, far left.

As Schuman had foreseen, the growth from a coal and steel trading organization with six members to an economic, political, and cultural union of half a billion people did not happen all at once, or according to a single, comprehensive plan. For the first three decades or so of the community's existence, there was considerably more movement toward union on the economic front than in the area of shared governmental duties.

In the years following the Schuman Declaration, the European Movement took the continent by storm. To the hungry, chilly, deprived millions still suffering from the last war and worrying increasingly about the next one, the ideal of a "common European home" had enormous appeal. The "Idea of Europe" spread across the Atlantic and found forceful support in the United States—partly for the same pacifist, ideological reasons that made it so attractive to Europeans, and partly out of sheer realpolitik: for Washington, a unified Western Europe could be a strong ally in the struggle against the Soviets and their Eastern bloc. "Far from resenting the rise of a united Europe," President John F. Kennedy explained in 1962, "this country welcomes it—a New Europe of equals instead of rivals, instead of the old Europe torn by national and personal animosities." Just like Churchill, Kennedy saw the new United States of Europe as a sort of latter-day replica of the United States of America. As the Europeans struggled to come up with a mechanism for governing a continent, Kennedy said, "the debate now raging in Europe echoes on a grand scale the debates which took place among the American states between 1783 and 1789." In some instances, in fact, the debates were almost precisely the same, including the difficult question of how to balance the authority of large states with small ones in a federal union.

Initially, Europe's founding fathers hoped to build their new continent in many spheres at the same time. Just as Schuman's Coal and Steel Community was planned as both an economic and a political union that would necessarily force joint action in defense as well, the New Europe was supposed to develop as an economic, governmental, legal, and military combination. In fact, those four strands did not progress together. Schuman's famous prediction—"The single Europe will not be made all at once, or according to a single comprehensive plan"—turned out to be exactly right. Beginning with the six-nation coal-and-steel combination, the economic integration of Europe moved ahead faster and further than did the legal, military, or political track. For more than thirty years, in fact, the industrial and financial "community" was the heart of the European project; it wasn't until the last decade or so of the twentieth century that the member nations made real progress in forging a pancontinental governmental structure.

There were several reasons why European integration advanced most quickly on the economic front.

For one thing, the development of political structures to govern a collection of sovereign states was difficult—just as it had been for the American states in the 1780s—because nobody knew quite how much sovereignty the individual members would surrender to the collective whole. Many of the founding fathers of united Europe—Monnet, Schuman, Spaak—were eager to form a "supranational" government that would effectively take over control from the nation-states and their parliaments. The political leaders of the nation-states, predictably, were less willing to cede national power to a central governing body. While Monnet and his ilk were dreaming out loud about a federal government for all Europe, leaders like Charles de Gaulle envisioned a *Europe des patries*—a Europe of cooperating, but not submissive, nations. As John F. Kennedy foresaw, it would take decades of debate to resolve these issues—or, more precisely, to begin to resolve them. To this day, Europeans are arguing about the relative powers of the individual countries and the overall union.

In contrast, Europeans had fewer scruples about cooperation in finance and industry. Since the Industrial Revolution, the nations of Europe had in fact led the world in devising international agreements necessary to make commerce and industry work across national borders. The International Postal Union, the International Conference for Promoting Technical Uniformity in Railroads, the International Meteorological Association, the International Congress of Actuaries, the International Association of Accountancy, the Committee for the Unification of Maritime Law—all these were European projects, with the lesser industrial powers like the United States and Japan admitted more or less as a courtesy. That's why the global standards of weight and measurement are maintained to this day in Paris. That's why the system of international timekeeping, necessitated by the advent of high-speed railroads and steamships, is based on an imaginary line that runs through London— the Greenwich Meridian.

Moreover, industrial leaders saw fairly quickly that a single market spanning the continent would greatly expand business opportunities. As the job of clearing away the postwar "rubble heap" and the rebuilding of shattered cities proceeded, the separate economies of Germany, France, Italy, the low countries, and Britain all soared. The twenty years following the war were described just about identically in many languages, from Britain's postwar miracle to Italy's *miracolo* to Germany's *Wirtschaftswunder*. The confidence that came from that hefty industrial rebirth, together with the strong economic success of Monnet's Coal and Steel Community, made it easier for the separate nations to contemplate a single, borderless European market.

The major motivations for economic integration, though, were developments far from the European mainland.

Across the Atlantic, the American industrial juggernaut raced ahead with the postwar boom, and the United States displaced all the great economies of Europe to rank firmly as the richest nation on earth. This was a jarring change for European countries that had ranked as the richest in the world for centuries. The United States, once a reliable customer for European industrial production, now emerged as a formidable competitor. If France, or Germany, or Britain hoped to regain their prewar economic dominance, they could only do so by working together. By itself, Great Britain couldn't begin to match the industrial might of the United States; but working in a combination with the other great industrial and financial powers of Europe, Britain—or at least, Britain-in-Europe—could again be a contender.

The emergence of the United States as the world's leading industrial nation was hardly a surprising development. The global development that did surprise the Europeans, though, was the end of the Age of

Empire. Even a statesman as insightful as Winston Churchill failed to see it coming. When British liberals argued, at the end of World War II, that the colonial era was a relic of history, Churchill huffed and puffed and issued a famous denial: "I did not become His Majesty's First Minister to preside over the liquidation of the British Empire." How wrong he was.

For five hundred years—ever since the intrepid fifteenth-century Portuguese explorers were dispatched by Prince Henry the Navigator—the nations of Europe had been conquering, Christianizing, governing, and looting vast areas of the world. They contested openly with each other for the title of greatest imperial power, and that dubious honor passed around freely. Political theorists have often noted the reverse correlation between the size of the "mother country" and the reach of its empire: the smaller the homeland, it seemed, the bigger the colonial horde. For about a century, Portugal, a postage-stamp principality at the edge of Europe, ran the world's largest empire. The Netherlands, another vest-pocket nation, had a turn at the top of the ladder, as did Spain. Next came Britain, a compact island not much larger than Portugal. Despite the early embarrassment of losing its chief American colony to a revolution, the island nation collected the largest global empire in history and held on to most of it for the better part of two centuries.

Over the centuries, eight European nations became major players in the game of empire. And then, in less than a single human lifetime, the game abruptly came to an end.

- Germany lost its African colonies in the peace settlement following World War I.
- Italy lost Abyssinia (now known as Ethiopia) with its defeat in World War II.
- Spain collected an empire that covered most of Central and South America and scattered places in Asia. The Spanish Empire was essentially over by the end of the nineteenth century,

although Spain to this day still asserts a claim to some slivers of African land on the northern coast of Morocco.

- The Portuguese Empire, roughly one hundred times the land area of Portugal at its greatest extent, was the earliest European colonial regime, and the latest. Portugal lost its African colonies in the mid-1970s, and finally gave up its last handful of Asian soil, Macao, in 1999.

- The Dutch Empire, at one point fifty-five times bigger than the Netherlands, was taken over in 1942 by the Japanese, who carefully studied European colonial methodology and then bested their teachers in the first months of World War II. The Dutch organized local resistance movements in Indonesia to fight Japan, telling these native fighters that they were battling for "liberation." As soon as Japan surrendered, Dutch governors showed up again in Jakarta to reassert their authority. But the Indonesians, now sold on the concept of liberation, were no longer willing to be colonists. The Dutch departed for good in 1950.

- Belgium controlled a swath of Africa roughly eighty times as big as Belgium, but lost its last foreign holding in 1960, when the Belgians could no longer hold back the freedom fighters in the Belgian Congo.

- France, with foreign colonies twenty times as large as France itself, fought and lost a series of colonial wars following World War II. Paris gave up in Southeast Asia in the 1950s; the north and central African colonies peeled off in the 1960s.

- The British Empire, on which the sun never set, was already shaky before World War II, and fell apart fairly quickly thereafter. Like the Dutch, the British had recruited local fighters to overthrow the Japanese conqueror in East Asia—and then found these locals resistant to British control as well. The power and success of Gandhi's revolt inspired not only India but a dozen other British colonies to demand their independence. In 1997, when the British finally handed the island of Hong Kong back to China, the scene of the Union Jack being hauled down over the last real colony sparked national celebrations in China, and national trauma in the U.K. The "liquidation of the British Empire" was complete. It was a blessing, in a sense, that Churchill did not live to see that last colonial flag come down.

Whether set forth in the blunt British rationale—"the white man's burden"—or the elegant French formulation—*mission civilisatrice*—the official European explanation for these centuries of European domination tended to be that the colonial rulers just wanted to help. A more cynical, and probably more accurate, summary of the imperial impulse can be found in the mnemonic device used by generations of freshmen cramming for the final in European History 101: the colonists were driven by gold, God, and glory. The colonies provided a cheap, reliable source of profitable commodities—not just gold, but silver, iron, coal, corn, coffee, tobacco, palm oil, citrus—and they made a lucrative captive market for manufactured goods from the ruling power. But selfishness was not the whole story. The missionary impulse was also strong for most of the European colonists; there were few who doubted that spreading the one true faith to "lesser breeds without the law" was an admirable calling.

Finally, and perhaps most important of all, there was patriotic glory. A colonial empire was crucial in terms of national prestige; by the second half of the nineteenth century, no self-respecting European power felt complete unless it held dominion over palm and pine in some distant corner of the planet. The lust for colonial glory was most evident in the aftermath of the Franco-Prussian War in 1870. Having suffered the ignominy of defeat, Paris set out to find something its army could conquer. Over the next thirty years, the French grabbed a series of new colonies in Africa as well as the region that came to be known (in the West, at least) as French Indochina. These colonial holdings almost certainly cost the French far more, both in francs and in blood, than they ever produced. But nobody paid much attention to that minor shortcoming. By extending its tendrils across the map of the world, France had once again proven itself to be a great power.

Even today, when the Age of Empire is generally viewed as a lamentable chapter in world history, the glory years of foreign domination can still evoke satisfying memories for the nations of Europe. The capital cities of all the former imperial powers are cluttered with heroic statues marking the conquest of one province or the defeat of a rebellion in another, and many Europeans clearly like seeing those bronze and marble memorials of their former global sway. When the mayor of London, Ken Livingstone, proposed that the statues of British colonial heroes in Trafalgar Square were out of place in twenty-first-century Britain and should be replaced with more up-to-date figures—Livingstone even suggested a statue of Gandhi—the idea was shouted down in short order. In 2003, some four decades after Belgium surrendered its colonies, I went to Brussels' legendary nightclub, the Ancienne Belgique, to hear an African jazz singer named Barly Baruti. Introducing himself, Baruti told the audience that he came from "a country that now calls itself the Democratic Republic of the Congo. Before that, it was Zaire. Before that, it was the Republic of Congo. And before that, it was the Belgian Congo." With this reminder of the days when their nation owned a hunk of central Africa, the Belgian crowd burst proudly into applause.

The loss of empire, then, brought with it not only the loss of a key trading market but also the demise of a certain stature, a certain sense of importance on the world stage, that had marked Europe's long colonial era. Looking for a new source of trading income and a new platform from which to reclaim their former global eminence, the former colonial powers found both gold and glory in their new European Union.

As we have seen, the first postwar venture in economic cooperation, the European Coal and Steel Community, turned into a runaway success, partly because of Jean Monnet's adroit leadership and partly because a continent rebuilding itself after a horrific war was a perfect place to sell vast quantities of coal and steel. By the mid-1950s, with the community racing ahead, the six member nations (France, Germany, Italy, Belgium, the Netherlands, and Luxembourg) were ready, indeed eager, to expand their cooperative endeavors. The creation of the Common Market—formally, the European Economic Community—in 1957 put the six on a path toward a single trade market with no internal tariffs and common laws on taxation, wages and hours, workplace safety, and so on. Because France in the 1950s already had a national law requiring equal pay for men and women, the French demanded that the other five members do the same; thus the Common Market's regulation on gender equality became a key model for the burgeoning feminist movement in the United States and other countries. The Common Market also endorsed a French-style farm subsidy program, with revenues from industrial growth guaranteeing steady prices and income for farmers in all the member nations.[2] The European Economic Community, and its continuing drive toward "ever closer union," was so successful that other European nations came knocking at the door. At first French strongman Charles de Gaulle—who tended to see a united Europe primarily as a tool for advancing the interests of his own country—blackballed the outsiders. He vetoed the applications of Norway, Britain, Denmark, and Ireland. Norway, bolstered by the promise of immense wealth from newly discovered oil reserves in the North Sea, decided not to renew its application, and has remained outside the EU ever since. Britain was finally admitted in 1973, along with Ireland and Denmark. After Greece, Spain, and Portugal threw over their dictators—a popular democracy with a free market and guaranteed civil liberties was a requirement for entry—they, too, were admitted. With the addition of Austria, Finland, and Sweden, the original six had become fifteen by 1995, comprising most of the major nations of Western Europe and five of the world's ten richest nations.

For all the EU's economic success, the humanistic impulses that had driven its founding fathers were still paramount; the continent-wide conviction that working together was better than fighting against each other remained the strongest bond pulling Europe together. The moral aspect of European unity was powerfully revived by the historic transformation of 1989–91, when the Soviet Union collapsed and its unwilling satellites in Eastern Europe were suddenly freed. The end of the cold war happened so quickly that people and politicians on both sides of the iron curtain were left up in the air about its meaning. For one man, that metaphor was literally true: cosmonaut Sergei Krikalyev, who blasted into Earth orbit in 1991 to board the Soviet space station. Within weeks, he was a spaceman without a country. While poor Krikalyev was circling the planet, the Soviet Union had ceased to exist. When he returned to Earth in early 1992, the landing zone at what had been the USSR's space center was in an independent nation, Kazakhstan.

Gradually, a new sense of possibility began to emerge from chaos. The collapse of the Soviet empire, and the creation of more than a dozen newly independent states on European soil, inspired a new vision for European leaders—the dream of a continent completely united, from the Arctic Circle to the Azores, from Galway Bay to the banks of the Volga. As in the first days of European unity after World War II, religious figures played a key role in promulgating this ambitious idea. A spiritual leader from the Eastern bloc (Poland) whose work had taken him to the west (Rome) was a key advocate of bringing the eastern states into the western union: "Europe has two lungs," Pope John Paul II preached. "It will never breathe naturally until it uses both of them." The rapid reunification of Germany, which went forward virtually without dissent despite an enormous fiscal burden for the prosperous West Germans, served as a model and an inspiration. "We are all Germans, after all," said the West German chancellor. In the same sense, the people of east and west were all Europeans, after all.

Since the days of Jean Monnet, European leaders had been arguing about the right way to expand the community of nations. The question came down to "broader" vs. "deeper." Advocates of a deeper expansion wanted the existing nations to expand the authority of the combined European government into new areas of policy first, and then reach out to new members. The "broader" school called for sweeping more and more of Europe into the union first, and then adding to the powers of the collective entity. The collapse of the Berlin Wall more or less resolved this question by propelling both views forward. In the 1990s the EU became both broader and deeper. On the "deeper" side, the member states agreed to the common currency, the single central bank, borderless travel, uniform food and health regulations, and numerous other changes that increased the power of the EU government in Brussels and decreased the power of the national members to govern these issues individually. At the same time, the fifteen members opened their arms to their eastern cousins to make their union broader by taking in new member states.

Candidate countries had to accept endless conditions. Any would-be EU member was required to guarantee its citizens a popularly elected government, the full range of civil liberties set forth in the far-reaching European Convention on Human Rights, and a free-market economy. The applicants also had to agree to give up their national currencies in favor of the euro, and to incorporate some 80,000 pages of EU law—a package known as the *aquis communitaire,* or "common agreement"—into their own statute books. They had to accept most aspects of the generous European welfare state, the EU's tough environmental laws and Western-style protections for criminal defendants, and they had to promise visa-free entry for anyone coming from another EU country. Most of the candidates, particularly those shaking off fifty years of Communist rule, were delighted to commit to these changes. The civil liberties requirement posed a serious problem to Turkey, which applied time and again for membership and was turned down on grounds that its human rights record was not up to EU standards.

In May 2004, ten new countries were formally inducted into the European Union. Seven of the new members—the Czech Republic, Estonia, Hungary, Latvia, Lithuania, Poland, and the Slovak Republic—were former Soviet satellites. Slovenia was the wealthiest of the new nations formed when Yugoslavia split up. The final two members were small island nations in the Mediterranean, Malta and Cyprus. They were all eager to join the club; nine of the new members held referenda before signing up, and EU membership was approved by comfortable margins in each country.

To accommodate the newcomers, the EU expanded its list of official languages to include Czech, Latvian, Estonian, and so on, creating a fairly ludicrous situation in which every official meeting and most official documents had to be rendered simultaneously in twenty different languages. If nothing else, the European Union has been a fantastic employment boon for interpreters and translators. The union did not, however, change its flag to mark the expansion. The familiar design, a circle of twelve gold stars on a deep blue background—it was created in 1987, when the union had twelve members—did not expand to twenty-five stars. The notion of adding a star for each new member of the union was contemplated for a while, but adding a star was considered the American approach to flag architecture, and the United States of Europe is not inclined to take its cues from the United States of America.

The expansion to twenty-five member nations finally pushed the EU to take a long, hard look at its governing institutions, which had not changed in their basic outline since Jean Monnet first chaired a six-nation community of coal and steel producers. The EU set up a constitutional convention, with 105 delegates from twenty-eight countries (the twenty-five members plus three applicant countries not yet admitted), to design a new architecture for pan-European government. As we'll see in appendix 2, the constitution sparked some bitter disputes. Final ratification was stalled for many months by an argument—familiar to anyone who has studied the disputes that wracked America's convention in 1789—over how to allocate power among the big and the small member states. But in the end the convention did a reasonably good job.

The chairman of this rather unwieldy body was the former French premier Valéry Giscard d'Estaing, a smooth charmer with a sharp sense of history. M. Giscard constantly compared his convention to the representatives of thirteen confederated states who had gathered in Philadelphia in 1787 to write a constitution for the new United States of America.

The European newspapers loved this comparison, and regularly illustrated their stories about the convention's discussions with the somber Junius Stearns oil painting of 1787, *George Washington Addressing the Constitutional Convention*. Giscard's initial draft even proposed that the EU formally change its name to the United States of Europe, but this idea was rejected in the end—probably because it sounded too American.

In 2002 and 2003 I attended several sessions of Europe's constitutional convention (it was formally titled the Convention on the Future of Europe). I found Giscard's comparison to be apt. For an American, the questions at issue sounded like clear echoes of the debate two centuries earlier in Philadelphia. How much power should go to the central government, and how much should be retained by the individual states? How could the interests of small states be protected in a Parliament likely to be dominated by the delegations from much bigger nations? Which decisions should be made by the professional bureaucrats, and which should be entrusted to a popular vote? Many of the delegates spoke far too much, and many of the meetings went on far too long. But whenever I dozed off from sheer boredom, I snapped out of it by reminding myself that tedious arguments in a decorous debating chamber in Brussels were certainly preferable to the bloody disagreements that had killed so many million of Europe's young men not far away, in Flanders fields.

The growth of the union, from the original six to the current twenty-five, has been accompanied by the rapid growth of a new European government in Brussels, with strong controls over business, finance, and commerce across the union. The European nations have a joint trade office; since the EU leads the world in both exports and imports, their combined clout is at least as strong as America's in the World Trade Organization. The EU and its members have developed a sort of useful schizophrenia about these international groupings. When the issue is sheer size, the EU offers itself as a single market with a single government, representing nearly 500 million people and a collective GDP in the range of

$11 trillion. But when it comes time to cast votes, the EU members suddenly become separate countries, with twenty-five separate votes to cast on behalf of the European position. At home, the member nations have set up a joint patent office, a common portfolio of consumer protection, credit, and banking laws, a common bankruptcy code, continent-wide merger and acquisition rules, and a pan-European food safety commission. The EU has a single competition czar who regulates antitrust matters in all member nations. This official is one of the most powerful figures in global business, a fact that another great business leader, Jack Welch, learned painfully (see chapter 4).

Meanwhile, the "Eurocrats" in Brussel are building an ever wider and deeper catalog of regulations governing European industry and finance. The flood of European regulations has sparked a backlash in parts of the continent, particularly among those who are philosophically or politically opposed to the idea of a single Europe. Although European countries generally don't have the healthy disdain for government common in the American heartland, the Eurocrats have begun to generate the same sort of feeling. Some Europeans just love to hate Brussels, in the same way Texans or Alaskans love to hate Washington. For that reason, you have to bring a healthy sense of suspicion to many of the stories of ridiculous regulatory excess that commonly show up in the Euroskeptic, or conservative, branch of the mass media.

After extensive digging, I can confidently report that the alleged European regulations governing the shape of toilet bowls, requiring that fishermen wear hairnets, and banning square gin bottles—all cited in breathless exposés in the British press—have never existed. On the other hand, there really is an EU regulation governing the size of condoms (although it is not true, as the British papers gleefully reported, that the Italians lobbied to have the dimensions reduced). There are rules limiting the noise level of power lawn mowers. There is a required methodology that all member nations must follow when calculating their gross domestic product (GDP). Regulations govern the hidden police cameras that catch people speeding on European roads. Rules guarantee the comfort of animals in transit to slaughter yards, and govern the maximum permit-ted curvature of cucumbers sold anywhere in the European Union. The minimum legal length of bananas that Europeans can buy is set at 14 centimeters, or 5½ inches. Another rule sets a minimum of 27 centi-meters for the "grade" of bananas, whatever that is.

And then there is EU Directive 80-181-EEC, the pan-European reg-ulation that made greengrocer Steve Thoburn a national hero—a reluc-tant one, but a hero nonetheless—in Great Britain.

In the rusty shipbuilding town of Sunderland, England—the ancestral home of George Washington—Steve did a bustling trade hour after hour at the tiny market stall he ran, "Thoburn's Fruit and Veg." The place is a veritable EU of greenery: Steve sold Dutch leeks, Spanish peppers, French apples, British spinach, and Greek olives, all neatly stacked and marked with country of origin and price per pound in Steve's firm hand. "I label everything," Steve explained. "I want me customers to know what they're buying."

An intense but likable thirty-something with curly hair and a gold ring in his right ear, Steve was caught red-handed weighing and selling bananas by the pound. He was charging 34 pence (about 55 cents in U.S. money) per pound. This was a bargain price, by English standards, but the sale was a blatant violation of EU Directive 80-181-EEC, a regula-tion requiring that fresh produce sold in any EU country must be priced and weighed in metric measures—that is, liters and kilograms. Under a statute incorporating EU trade regulations into British law, Steve was charged with violating the Weights and Measures Act. Prosecutors said this was simply a matter of enforcing the law; Steve, though, saw an offi-cial conspiracy against small business. "They're after me because all I have is this little market," he said. "Anybody in this town can still go to McDonald's and buy a Quarter-Pounder. Why doesn't that have to be a 113-Grammer?" (In fact, McDonald's outlets throughout Europe are required to list the metric proportions of all their food and drink items.)

Anyway, Steve went on, the women of Sunderland had always bought bananas by the pound, and they wanted to continue. Steve Thoburn was determined "to give me customers what they want." Accordingly, he stubbornly refused to replace his pound-and-ounce scale with a metric version, even when the town prosecutor indicated that Thoburn's Fruit and Veg could face fines equal to $6,000 if convicted on the two pending counts.

Britain's national newspapers had a field day with the story—they dubbed Thoburn the "Metric Martyr"—and Euroskeptics across the nation adopted him as the symbol of their anti-Brussels campaign. On a chilly January day, Steve went on trial in Sunderland Magistrate's Court; the judge declared that the case centered on "the most famous bunch of bananas in British legal history." Inside the courthouse, Steve was represented by a high-powered defense lawyer who had been hired by a national Euroskeptic organization and imported from London to argue the case. Outside, a noisy crowd was waving flags, banners, and bananas. Their posters read: "Metric Martyr on trial here! Hoot to support!"

Some passing motorists did hoot their horns that morning, but many others drove past silently. Even in Sunderland, an insular, self-contained city in the north of England, feelings about Brussels and the European Union were mixed. It was easy, of course, to build up an indignant head of steam against arrogant foreign regulators, daft government rules, and prosecutors determined to turn a pound of bananas into a federal case. On the other hand, there was hesitation in the city about attacking the European Union. At the dawn of the twenty-first century, the EU had become crucial to Sunderland's well-being. The few contracts still being awarded at the aging, inefficient shipyards along the river Wear were largely funded by EU grants to local fishermen and shipping companies. And the largest single employer in Sunderland these days is a new Nissan plant, located there specifically to give the Japanese auto maker a European presence. By building its cars in an EU nation, Nissan can export to any other EU member country free of tariffs, duties, and regulatory hassles.

Even Steve Thoburn was ambivalent. When I went up to Sunderland to meet the Metric Martyr, Steve complained that he was thoroughly uncomfortable with that title, and with the way his case had been turned into political fodder for the anti-EU campaigners. "I don't give a toss about politics," Thoburn said, carefully arranging matching hillocks of red and green peppers on his market shelves. "I've never cast a vote. I have nothing against metrics. If somebody come into me premises and says, 'C'mon, luv, give us a kilo of bananas,' I'd sell it to her. But nobody ever asks for that."

Steve had no particular problem with the European Union, either, or with the Eurocrats, or with Brussels. In fact, the day I dropped by Thoburn's Fruit and Veg, the special offer of the day was none other than brussels sprouts. "Oh, I love brussels sprouts," Steve told me, holding a firm green specimen between thumb and forefinger. "You put this on the roast platter on Sunday, and that's the king of veg."

Despite the efforts of that high-powered London lawyer and his political backers, the Metric Martyr was convicted on two counts in the town court. The Euroskeptics then launched a series of high-profile appeals, promising to go to Britain's highest court, or even to the European Court of Justice, which can overrule the top British judge. All that seemed likely to delay a final decision in the case for years. Steve Thoburn, with his fines on hold while the legal battle went forward, did his best to get back to the business of selling fruit and vegetables. When customers said, "C'mon, luv, give us a pound of bananas," he did exactly that. His message to the European Union was simple: "Leave a bloke alone so he can give his customers what they want."

For many Europeans, though, both business owners and their customers, the ethic of standardization at the heart of Europe's regulatory regime has paid significant dividends. No matter how vast its international structure may be, any corporation can benefit from a strong, profitable home market, and the twenty-five-nation common market of the EU gives European countries unfettered access to the largest single trade market on earth. As we'll see in chapter 5 of this book, uniform rules and pancontinental technical specifications emanating from Brussels have helped make European companies world leaders in several key industrial areas. In some cases, such as passenger aircraft, providing that kind of advantage over American industry was a key rationale for Europe's unified stance—a strategy that American competitors often recognize too late.

But the boldest and most far-reaching act of economic union—the change that made the European Union a tangible daily reality for more than 300 million people from the Arctic Circle to the Azores—took place on January 1, 2002. That New Year's Day was known in Europe as E-day, because that was the day when Austria, Belgium, Finland, France, Germany, Greece, Ireland, Italy, Luxembourg, the Netherlands, Portugal, and Spain adopted the euro as their common currency.

Each of the new euro nations held noisy, splashy celebrations on New Year's Eve to greet their new money. Fireworks filled the frigid night sky, and bands blared in celebration. At Willy-Brandt-Platz in Frankfurt, a statue of the euro symbol five stories high was unveiled, and a pop group offered the world premiere of a jaunty number called "With Open Arms (EuroWorldSong)." At an elaborate sound-and-light show in Brussels, the EU's finance minister told a cheering crowd that the arrival of the euro was "the most important event of mankind's monetary history"—an exaggeration of absurd dimensions, perhaps, but a comment that captured the mood of a continent that night. Newspapers went wild, with full-page greeting cards welcoming the currency and odes of fond farewell to the outgoing money. ("Arrivederci, amica lira," read the headline in the Italian sports daily *La Gazzetta dello Sport*.) The obituary columns of the Paris daily *Libération* included a report on the life and death of "the late French franc." Several British papers hit on the perfect January 1 headline to greet the new arrival: "Happy New Euro." Even the respected, sober French newspaper *Le Figaro* got into the act, changing its name for one day to *Le Fig-Euro* and adopting a permanent new price of one euro per day (a price cut of about 11 percent from the former daily rate of seven francs).

As the final minutes of 2001 ticked away, Europeans left their New Year's parties and lined up, in tuxedos and evening gowns, outside ATM machines to get their hands on euros. Near the place des Martyrs in Brussels, I met Phillipe Bruseau outside the Kredietbank a few minutes past midnight. Sounding just a little embarrassed at himself, this decorous gentleman asked me to take a photo as he withdrew euro notes from the bank machine for the first time. "How many thousand times have I gone to the ATM?" he said. "But this time, it's history." M. Bruseau seemed downright surprised when he pushed the buttons and four crisp, never-folded twenty-euro bills came out, like clockwork. "I had convinced myself they couldn't make it work," he said. "But they did it! How did they make it work?"

That overnight switch to the euro was not merely an historic milestone in the emergence of a United States of Europe. It was also a formidable achievement. It was by far the largest currency conversion in world history, and it went off right on schedule, without a hitch. How did they make it work?

THREE

The Almighty Undollar

"The introduction of the euro," wrote Robert Mundell, an American Nobel laureate in economics and one of the world's leading experts on currency unions, "is one of those ephochal events that can only be understood in the context of long periods of history." The history that Professor Mundell had in mind was that covered in the last chapter; his point was that the crisp new euro notes that appeared in January 2002 amounted to a significant piece of history folded up in every European's wallet. And the launch was epochal, Mundell explained, for two reasons.

In the first place, nothing like it had ever been attempted before. New currencies have been introduced from time to time in many nations, but there had never been a multinational conversion on a continental scale involving so many millions of people, so many wealthy countries, and such well-established, healthy currencies as those the euro replaced. The project involved seven years of planning, and even then most of the euro nations arranged a safety valve in case things went wrong; they allowed people to use both old and new currencies for a couple of months to smooth the changeover. Only the Germans, with their consummate faith in the technocrats at the Bundesbank, were willing to go cold turkey. The euro became Germany's sole legal tender effective at midnight on January 1, 2002; from that moment, the deutsche mark was no longer accepted. As it turned out, the Germans got it right. The extended dual-currency periods in the other euro nations proved unnecessary. Europeans took to their new money so readily that 95 percent of all transactions in the twelve euro countries were being carried out in euros by January 5. Every bank account, every contract, every financial instrument, was denominated in euros less than a week after the introduction.

The other epoch-making aspect of the united Europe's new currency was the challenge it presented to the planet's dominant form of money, the almighty dollar. From day one, the euro had more daily users than the U.S. dollar. As the unit of exchange for a monetary zone that includes two of the world's five richest countries (Germany and France) and four of the top twelve (Germany, France, Italy, and Spain), the euro became the world's second-most important currency on the day it was launched. But the Europeans have larger ambitions than that. The euro was specifically designed to challenge the global hegemony of the U.S. dollar as the world's preferred reserve currency and as the standard unit of exchange for international financial transactions. The common currency is "an assertion of Europe's desire to create a monetary system that serves its own interests rather than accept a framework set up to work to American advantage," argues a best-selling book by the British analyst Will Hutton. "With the euro, the EU now has the weapon with which to fight back."

While it may have been epochal for Europeans to adopt a single currency, it was not unprecedented. At various earlier eras of European unification, there were currency unions covering much of the continent. A Roman tribune, trader, or tax collector circling the Mediterranean rim in the third century AD would have used the same denarius as his coin from the frosty moors of southern Scotland to the palmy shores of the Greek isles. Charlemagne decreed common coinage in AD 800 for his multination kingdom, which he called the Holy Roman Empire even though it was not Roman, not an empire, and far from holy most of the time. The Hanseatic League, a Baltic Sea trading area that flourished in the fifteenth century, issued a standard currency that spread across Germany and all of Scandinavia. Napoleon III created a "Latin Monetary Union" with six members—France, Belgium, Switzerland, Italy, Greece, and Bulgaria—but it flourished for less than twenty years. A Scandinavian Monetary Union, involving most of the Baltic nations, did slightly better, operating from 1872 to 1914.

The concept of a common European currency to help build financial and political connections across a united Europe emerged yet again in the earliest days of the post–World War II European movement. Jean Monnet was advocating the creation of a single currency even before the birth of his European Coal and Steel Community. Monnet's friend Jacques Rueff, a key French economist of the postwar era, declared in 1949 that "Europe will become united through its money, or not at all." As the economic union grew, the pressure for a monetary union grew with it. Still, the idea met with considerable resistance, among governing elites and the man on the street alike. The proud ancient nations of Europe were willing to surrender some elements of national sovereignty to build their continental union, but it was something else entirely to surrender revered national symbols that dated back centuries or millennia.

The Greek drachma was the oldest currency on earth, mentioned by Xenophon and Aristophanes in the fifth century BC and a reminder to every Greek citizen of the glorious heritage of Periclean Athens. The French franc had an equally noble lineage. It was first minted in 1360 as a ransom payment to win the freedom of King Jean le Bon ("John the Good"), a hero of the Franks who was captured by the English at the battle of Poitiers. The Dutch guilder—the name drawn from an Old German term for "gold"—was another fourteenth-century coin. The Spanish peseta and its ancestor, the peso, dated back to 1497. Italians had been using the lira since the days of Michelangelo. The deutsche mark, successor to Hitler's reichsmark, was a mere child compared to other currencies, having been first minted by Allied occupying armies in 1948. But it was a cherished form of money because the strength of the mark symbolized the Germans' postwar economic miracle.

In short, the established currencies of Europe carried historical and cultural meanings that made them hard to give up. This reaction is easy to understand; even those Americans most supportive of the North American Free Trade Association might balk if the governors of NAFTA proposed that the United States give up its *e pluribus unum* greenback in exchange for a new NAFTA peso. In Europe, it took decades of building unified institutions before the people of the EU were ready to think about unifying their money.

As Europe became more and more unified, the arguments for a common currency became increasingly persuasive. A key point was the symbolic role that a single European money could play. For Churchill and several other founding fathers, the United States of America was always the model for a future United States of Europe, and the dollar was viewed as the most familiar emblem of the U.S.A. Even the economists saw the symbolic importance of shared money. "The euro is much more than just a currency," said Wim Duisenberg, the Dutchman who was the first head of the European Central Bank and thus a man who would seem to be more concerned with financial than symbolic implications. "It is a symbol of European integration in every sense of the word."

There was political and emotional appeal as well. The Irish were eager to jettison their pound as a way to demonstrate their independence from the old imperial master, Great Britain. The Greeks wanted to use the euro in large part because their traditional rival, Turkey, could not. The people of Portugal and Luxembourg, small countries with money that nobody else wanted to bother with, wanted to have a currency that had some clout in the world. And all over the continent, advocates of "ever stronger union" and a more powerful central government in Brussels saw the single currency as another step toward a single European state.

But money is mainly an economic instrument, and the primary reasons for the common currency were economic in nature. On the most basic level, it cost the people of Europe a lot of money to use all those different kinds of money. In the era when each country had its own currency, travelers had to make a currency exchange every time they crossed a border—and pay a fee to a bank with every exchange. Currency exchange rates go up and down, of course, but the so-called forex, or foreign exchange business, was conveniently arranged such that the traveler always lost on the transaction, and the banker always gained.

Consider how costly it would be if an American who flies from Baltimore to Boston were required to convert Maryland dollars to Massachusetts dollars before leaving the airport—and to pay a bank five cents for every Massachusetts dollar received. The next day, heading back to Baltimore, the traveler would have to trade in her remaining Massachusetts money for Maryland dollars—and pay the bank another fee for the privilege. It's obvious that these expenses add up quickly; before the euro, the EU estimated, the average European traveler paid about $15 in exchange fees for each border crossing. On a continent where you can easily pass three national borders in a trip of 100 miles, that was expensive. This burden was even more costly for businesses, which had to pay the transaction cost of currency exchange for each cross-border purchase. With the coming of the euro, though, the transaction cost fell to zero for any trip or trade within the twelve-nation euro zone. With euros in her pocket, a Finn can travel to Florence with a stop in Frankfurt along the way and never even glance at the *bureau de change*. The EU has estimated that elimination of currency exchange expenses saves the euro nations about 0.4 percent of GDP each year—a total savings greater than $10 billion annually.

A more important benefit for the business community was the elimination of exchange rate risk. This risk applies in any international transaction involving different currencies; it's the chance that the yen, for example, will fall disastrously in value just after you've agreed to accept payment for your product in yen. Let's say, for example, that a maker of cashmere goods in Scotland agrees to sell 5,000 sweaters to a clothing store in New York. The Scot needs to get 100 British pounds per sweater to turn a profit. So he offers them to the New York retailer for $180 apiece. That's a good deal for the Scot, because $180 will convert to 110 pounds, a solid profit on each unit sold. But then, before the first sweater is delivered, some quirk in the international forex markets sends the dollar tumbling downward; now the $180 price converts only to 90 pounds. The Scotsman will take a loss on each sweater sold. That's exchange rate risk. Of course, there's a chance that the dollar will go up in value vis-à-vis the pound. Then the Scotsman makes out fine—he gets more pounds for each sweater—but the New York retailer takes a hit. That, too, is exchange rate risk. Over centuries of international business, traders learned how to insure against exchange rate losses by hedging foreign currencies; but that adds another layer of expense to every transaction. For the European nations, routinely selling and buying across international borders, exchange rate risk was a daily business burden. The common currency lifted the burden.

The euro provided a boon to buyers by providing price transparency. Before the common currency, consumers in Ireland routinely paid about 13.4 pounds for a bottle of vodka. The same bottle was priced in Spain at 998 pesetas. As it turned out, the price in Ireland was three times as high. But this was hardly obvious except to a vodka drinker who happened to know by heart the pound-peseta conversion rate. Once that bottle was priced in euros in both countries, Irish consumers, and consumer magazines, could see that the same bottle cost 6 euros in Spain but 17 in Ireland. For consumers, that kind of knowledge is power. They will pressure retailers to match the price elsewhere. In fact, they did. Vodka prices in Ireland fell dramatically after the introduction of the euro. A similar "price convergence" developed across the euro zone in numerous other areas, including utility rates, recreational equipment, pharmaceuticals, and automobiles.

The same phenomenon—price transparency leading to price convergence—has been evident in a key economic indicator called the Big Mac Index. Before the euro, prices for McDonald's trademark burger—essentially the same product, with the same ingredients, everywhere it is sold—varied by as much as 75 percent across the eurozone, from roughly $3.55 in Finland to about $2.00 in Greece. Two years after the euro was introduced, there were still national differences in McDonald's menus, but prices had converged dramatically. The average Big Mac price was 2.71 euros (roughly $3.30), and the difference between Finland and Spain had dropped from 75 to 15 percent.

Despite these political and economic motivators, the path to euro was neither straight nor smooth. The elimination of import tariffs among the six Common Market nations in the 1960s prompted the formation of the European Currency Unit, or ecu, basically a bookkeeping measure to help keep track of multicurrency business deals. As trade among the member nations increased, it became increasingly important to minimize the exchange rate risk that plagued buyers and sellers. To do that, the community created an exchange rate mechanism (ERM) that was supposed to make sure that no European currency could rise or fall sharply against any other. This ERM, later renamed the European Monetary System (EMS), was a limited success at best. To Euroskeptics, the struggles of alphabet-soup experiments like the ecu, the ERM, and the EMS proved that any effort to link or combine Europe's many moneys was doomed to fail. To Europhiles, the experience proved the opposite: that halfway measures were doomed to fail, and complete currency union was essential.

At the end of the 1980s, the member nations appointed a committee to decide which of these diametrically opposed views was correct. The result was more or less preordained; the group was chaired by a committed Europhile, Jacques Delors, and stuffed with his backers. Sure enough, the *Delors Report,* issued in April 1989, called for the launch of a common European currency before the end of the twentieth century, and recommended that a single central bank be created to regulate monetary matters among all nations using the currency. Unlike thousands and thousands of other weighty reports issued by various blue-ribbon commissions over the decades, this one produced concrete results. For one thing, the common currency was indeed created, following almost exactly the calendar set out in the *Delors Report.* For another, the endorsement of a single currency prompted one of the great treasures in the lengthy annals of xenophobic headlines in London's tabloid press. The *Sun* responded to the Delors recommendation with a front-page banner that said it all for the Euroskeptic camp: "Up Yours, Delors."

The Delors proposal was formally adopted by the EU member nations in the Maastricht Treaty (named for the small Dutch city where it was signed) in 1992. On the theory that a "community" was probably too small an entity to have a world-class currency of its own, the same treaty formally changed the name of the European Community to the European Union. The treaty established a three-stage schedule for rollout of the new European money. The first phase, in 1994, saw the creation of the European Monetary Institute to design and create the new money, and to decide which countries would be permitted to use it. The second stage, set to begin on January 1, 1999, was the new currency's birth as an official monetary instrument, but only in "virtual" form, for securities, business transactions, and bank accounts. The third stage, three years later, would be the launch of coins and bills, to be followed shortly by the official demise of the traditional currencies.

Somewhat miraculously, the Delors schedule was adhered to precisely, with the first coins and bills spilling out of cash machines a few seconds after midnight on January 1, 2002—exactly in accord with the schedule laid out a dozen years earlier. Before the money could be issued, though, some important fiscal regulations had to be set in stone. If a nation chronically operates in debt, piling budget deficit upon deficit and funding the red ink through borrowing, that performance tends to weaken its currency on the forex markets. But if six or eight or twelve nations were going to share a currency, each country wanted to be sure that the others would not run up big debts, and thus weaken the common money. And so the EU created a series of rules to try to enforce fiscal responsibility on each country using the currency. Under this Stability and Growth Pact, nations using the euro cannot run a budget deficit greater than 3 percent of GDP. That way, each nation in the currency zone is responsible for maintaining the integrity of the currency on world forex markets.

The Stability and Growth Pact set a rigid standard for modern governments—so rigid, in fact, that even the world's richest nation would not meet the test. In George W. Bush's fourth federal budget, the United States had a deficit that reached 4.8 percent of GDP, far beyond the European limit. For that matter, it is not clear whether the European nations can meet the test either. At various points in recent years, Italy, France, and Germany have all skated increasingly close to—and sometimes beyond—the 3 percent barrier. So far, the EU has not dared to invoke the harsh fiscal penalties that are supposed to be triggered when the pact is violated.

Beyond that, a single currency zone required a single central bank to set the basic interest rates and control money supply—the same role the Federal Reserve serves in the United States. This job was assigned to a new institution, the European Central Bank. There was broad agreement among the EU members that the ECB should be closely modeled on the central bank that had won the most admiration in the half century since World War II—the German Bundesbank. Accordingly, the ECB set up its headquarters in Frankfurt, Germany's financial capital, just down the street from the old premises of the Bundesbank. And just like the Bundesbank before it, the ECB has gained a reputation in its early years as a ferocious inflation fighter. It has kept the eurozone's interest rates high—far above the levels the Federal Reserve has set in the United States—even when many of the member nations could have used a dose of lower interest rates to lift them out of economic doldrums.

The huge decision to jettison the continent's historic currencies and move ahead toward a common money was followed by a series of smaller, but equally difficult, decisions required to implement the big new idea.

First, Europe's money needed a name. Naturally, there were countless suggestions, but most of the ideas proposed for this supranational currency had suspiciously nationalistic roots. Italians proposed the "florin," harking back to the famous coinage of medieval Florence. Greeks argued that "drachma" had the virtue of an unrivaled longevity. The French pushed for the name "ecu," a French word used for both a thirteenth-century French coin and the European Currency Unit of the 1960s.

There was also a suggestion that each country keep its own currency's name, but preface the term with "euro." Thus the common currency would have been called the "Euromark" in Germany and the "Euroschilling" across the border in Austria.

After years of such suggestions, the member nations agreed unanimously in 1995 that the continental currency should take its name from the first four letters of the continent's name. The word *euro* not only served as a reminder of the basic point but was also a name that just about every European could pronounce—although not the same way. The sound varied from "yoo-rah" in Ireland to "yu-ro" in Spain to "oy-rho" in Germany and Austria. For amounts smaller than one euro, the fractional denomination is "cent"—from *centum,* the Latin word for 100. There are 100 cents per euro.

The coming of the common currency had far-reaching economic and political effects, but the choice of a name had a grammatical impact as well. For one thing, Europe's money underwent a gender change. In most European languages, the national currency—including the Italian lira, the Spanish peseta, and the German mark—had been a feminine word. But the new common noun, *euro,* was made masculine in most of the languages (in Greek, *euro* is neuter). There was also grammatical controversy over the plural. By official EU decree, the plural of *euro* is supposed to be formed in the English way, by adding a final *s*—i.e., *euros.* The Italians, however, ignored this dictate and used a Latinate plural, *euri,* that sounded more natural to Italian ears. A battle of the wills ensued, which ended only when the Eurocrats in Brussels ordered the Italian Finance Ministry to shred all copies of that nation's fiscal 2002 budget because it used the prohibited plural form. In their next budget, the Italians abjectly surrendered, using *euros* and swallowing whatever objections they may have had to English-style pluralization.

To compete on equal terms with world-class currencies like the dollar, the pound, and the yen, it was clear that the euro would need a world-class graphic symbol, something as striking and as recognizable as $, £, and ¥. European leaders handed this important task to Jean-Pierre

Malivoir, a Frenchman and a longtime Eurocrat who held the crucial job of "chef d'mission Euro"—that is, Euro mission chief—in Brussels. The experts told M. Malivoir to hire one of the continent's leading graphic design firms to come up with a pan-European equivalent to the dollar sign. But the mission chief, a thrifty sort, couldn't bring himself to pay the million-dollar fees that such firms tend to charge on major projects. So he sat down at his cluttered office in a Brussels office park and created, on his own, a marque that is destined to be one of the most recognized graphic symbols on earth.

"What we knew," the soft-spoken M. Malivoir told me later, "was that an important currency needed a symbol with the kind of instant recognition that your dollar sign has. I had noticed that the dollar, the yen, and the pound sterling symbols all had the parallel straight lines. Well, there was a starting point. I took the Greek letter epsilon, because an epsilon is an E, and E is for Europe, you could say. I took epsilon and imposed two parallel lines. Then we sent it out to citizen panels all over the eurozone, and they liked it. Voilà! We had our symbol." Although M. Malivoir saved the EU a sizable design fee by creating the symbol in-house, he never got any monetary reward for it. "Oh, there was no bonus or anything," he said calmly one day as we walked past a six-foot-high stainless steel model of his creation in downtown Brussels. "But you only have one chance in a lifetime to do something this big. That is reward enough for me."

Designing the euro symbol was one thing; designing the actual money proved to be considerably more complicated. After centuries of insults, invasions, and conquest, Western Europe was replete with ancient enmities and lingering animosities that made it impossible to design money the way individual nations had been doing the job for centuries. Nobody was willing to have another country's general, queen, or national hero on the currency. After all, that general or monarch may well have invaded and ravaged the country next door a few centuries back. There was so much stored-up national resentment that the moneymakers couldn't even agree on universal figures like Shakespeare, Mozart, or Picasso. The

EU's own founding fathers, statesmen like Churchill and Monnet, were also persona non grata on the euro. Famous historic structures like the Parthenon, Notre Dame Cathedral, and the leaning tower at Pisa were taboo as well.

"It was totally forbidden to use any people or any familiar buildings," recalls Robert Kalina, an engraver in the Austrian central bank, who was chosen to design the euro notes. And yet the notes had to evoke "a feeling of the shared heritage of Europe."

Kalina solved this vexing problem by turning to architecture. For the seven notes, he produced designs in seven colors drawn from seven major architectural periods in Europe's long history, following this scheme:

Euro note	Era	Color
5-euro	Classical (Greco-Roman)	gray
10-euro	Romanesque	pink
20-euro	Gothic	blue
50-euro	Renaissance	orange
100-euro	Baroque-Rococo	green
200-euro	Iron and glass	yellow
500-euro	Twenty-first-century postmodern	lavender

"To give symbolic meaning to the pictures, we used doors and windows on one side of the note, to show openness," Kalina explained. "The reverse side shows bridges, to show our connections." Kalina worked more than a year on his seven new bills, and succeeded admirably in producing a European currency that serves as an accurate graphic mirror of European culture. Despite the taboo on depicting actual structures, Kalina produced a handsome set of images that really look like Europe. To anyone who has traveled the continent, the arches and bridges seem instantly familiar. Even if you know that the graceful iron suspension bridge on the back of the 200-euro note is a composite, it feels like a bridge you've seen in Europe somewhere.

In fact, Kalina's 5-euro bill has been criticized for being too realistic. The handsome three-tiered Roman-style bridge arching across the note looks strikingly similar to the famous Pont du Gard, a spectacular three-tiered arching bridge the Romans built across the Gard River near Nîmes, France, in the first century AD. Civic leaders in Nîmes have made the most of the similarity; they boast proudly that their bridge, still standing at the end of its second millenium, is a symbol of both old and new Europe. Nîmes now invites tourists to stuff some 5-euro notes in their pockets and visit the real Pont du Gard. Herr Kalina, the designer, begs to differ: "It is the same style, but not the same bridge."

But while the euro notes were strictly supranational in character, the new euro coins allowed some degree of national chauvinism to intrude on the pancontinental spirit of the currency. Like the new series of U.S. quarters that honor the fifty states, the coins have one common face—with a stylized map of Europe amid stars and stripes—and one face specific to each country. All of the coins, no matter where minted, are legal tender in each of the euro countries. There are eight euro coins, worth 1, 2, 5, 10, 20, and 50 cents, 1 euro, and 2 euros.

This meant that Europeans could still have their own kings or symbols or national slogans on their money, even after the demise of the franc, lira, and so on. The opportunity, naturally, prompted excited debate in most eurozone countries: What should we put on our coins? In the end, though, the national designs turned out to be fairly predictable—at least to those who knew the look of pre-euro coinage. Ireland's euro coins have the familiar Celtic harp; Austria has the edelweiss; Germany has Berlin's Brandenburg Gate. Dutch coins show Queen Beatrix, and the Belgians feature King Albert. The French have some coins with the face of Marianne, the beautiful but fictional representation of rural youth (by national law, the Marianne figure must be "young and feminine, with determined features"), and some with the slogan that had appeared on every franc since the time of the French revolution: "Liberté, egalité, fraternité." Italy's coins show deathless Italian art, including Leonardo da Vinci's

"Vitruvian Man" and Sandro Botticelli's *Birth of Venus*. The Austrians made a coin with Mozart on it, and Spain memorialized the quixotic Cervantes. Italy's central bank authorized the Vatican to mint euro coins of its own, and these naturally bear the likeness of Pope John Paul II.

For my money, the cleverest coins are from Greece. The national side of the Greek euro depicts a famous, or perhaps notorious, moment in Greek mythology: when the king of the Olympian gods, Zeus, took the form of a white bull and raped a comely maiden. For those not up on their mythology, the coins include the name of the woman: Europa, the comely nymph who would give her name to a continent. And so Greece, the poorest by far of the eurozone countries, issued a pan-European coin that shows Europe (or at least Europa) under the domination of a Greek god.

The manufacture and delivery of this brand-new money—about 600,000,000,000 euros in cash was required for the initial rollout that began on New Year's Day—turned out to be the biggest logistical exercise Europe had seen since World War II. There were about 51 billion new coins to mint and ship, and some 14.5 billion bills to print and distribute—with massive precautions, of course, against theft along the way—to governments, banks, stores, and ATM machines in every corner of the continent. Somebody who obviously had time on his hands computed that if all the bills were stacked in a pile, they would tower fifty times higher than Everest; the total weight of the new coins was heavier than twenty-four Eiffel Towers. It was not just the money that had to be changed. Every price tag, postage stamp, and parking ticket in twelve countries had to be remade. Every cash register had to be reprogrammed. The makers of Monopoly, a popular game in every euro country, had to produce millions of euros worth of Monopoly money.

To keep the euro out of the hands of counterfeiters as long as possible, the European Central Bank rejected the idea of handing out the new bills before they became legal tender. That meant that the 14 billion euro bills all had to be in place and ready to use at the same time—that is, by the close of business on December 31, 2001. By mid-December, virtually every delivery van in Europe—not to mention tens of thousands of military vehicles—had to be pressed into euro duty to get the bills and notes where they had to be. After considering numerous scenarios, the central bankers decided that the best way to hand out the new money to ordinary people was to do it in the course of ordinary business. That is, anybody who made a bank withdrawal, from a teller or a cash machine, from January 1, 2002, onward would get the money in euros. Any retail customer who paid for his purchase in francs, escudos, and so on would get his change in euros. That put the distribution burden primarily on banks and shops, and it was a major undertaking. Shops turned their backroom storage areas into makeshift vaults to hold the new money they would be using in January. Some banks had to shore up their aging floors to bear the weight of the old coinage being handed in together with the new euro coins to be handed out. In mid-December, the French banking employees' union, Force Ouvrière, responded to the pressure in totally predictable fashion, threatening a nationwide strike on January 2 to protest the extra workload the new currency had imposed.

Beyond the chore of getting the euro to its users, there remained the formidable task of getting them to use the euro. In the months leading up to the great currency exchange, top Eurocrats were seriously worried on this score. Surveys taken just nine months before E-day showed that only about half of all the people in Europe were aware that their money was going to change on the following New Year's Day. In Greece, only about one in three people had even heard of the euro. These polls offered disturbing proof that there really was such a thing as the "democratic deficit"—the charge, leveled regularly by Euroskeptics, that ordinary European people felt no connection to the European superstate growing up in Brussels. But the immediate problem was more pragmatic than an argument among political scientists. Early in 2002, the franc, the mark, the lira, and so on were going to disappear—but the millions who used these moneys every day didn't seem to know it. To deal with this alarming level of ignorance, the EU and the individual governments launched a massive, multimillion-euro marketing drive to create awareness of the historic currency changeover just down the road.

The striking thing about the advertising campaigns selling the common currency was how little they had in common. The various national marketing efforts reflected not so much the unity as the lingering diversity of a continent that still cherishes its individual languages, traditions, cultures, and cuisines. In fact, many of the national ads played right into long-established stereotypes. The French, true to form, featured beautiful women. The Greeks invoked the Parthenon; the Italians, the commedia dell'arte. The devout Portuguese called in Catholic priests. The Irish ads were funny. The Germans, *natürlich*, created no-nonsense commercials featuring authority figures sternly setting forth the rules that would be followed. Along the shores of the Mediterranean, Spain, Italy, and Greece all took the Latin approach, with TV ads that were heavy on romance, music, and passion.

The TV commercials run by the Finnish Central Bank involved a mixture of the Nordic and the sunny South. The ads starred a friendly truck driver who explained how much cheaper and easier it would be for him to crisscross the continent once he didn't have to change currencies at every border. For some reason, though, the truck driver delivering this thoroughly practical message, in Finnish, was a Spaniard, who clicked his castanets and sang the complete commercial in a rollicking Mediterranean tenor.

The French national ads used a variety of attractive, fashionable women to make the euro pitch. For the final push, the campaign featured a strikingly pretty high-school girl named Lise, who stole the hearts of every teenage male in France as she explained how she would get her euros on the morning of January 1: "either from an ATM machine or as change for my baguette down at Uncle Dominique's boulangerie."

The playful Belgians sold the euro through a vicious assault on a piggy bank. Commercials in Belgium showed a girl—several years younger than Lise—who was having a chat with her cherished old piggy bank. "Don't worry, little pig," she said as she patted the porcelain figure with her hand. "I will have to get all the francs out of you on January 1 to trade in for euros. But it won't hurt." As the camera panned back from this tender scene, the viewer saw that in her other hand the girl was holding a hammer, ready to smash the piggy bank to smithereens.

Beyond the airwaves, governments, schools, and companies in the euro countries pulled out all the stops to alert the citizenry to the big change as it drew near. The Bank of Ireland sent a free pocket calculator—with a special key just for converting the Irish pound to euros—to all 1.4 million Irish households. Microsoft and Apple offered tens of millions of free upgrades to their operating systems so that computers across Europe could display M. Malvoir's euro symbol; Web sites in every country offered free downloads of fonts with the euro sign. Most of the twelve euro countries supported a transcontinental competition called "Be a Euro Superstar," a euro-knowledge contest for schoolchildren. A typical question was, "What is the capital of Slovenia?" (People intelligent enough to be reading this book, of course, already know that the correct answer is Ljubljana.) The first prize didn't seem terribly appealing—it was a trip to Frankfurt to spend New Year's Eve with Wim Duisenberg, the head of the European Central Bank—but the bank said millions of children took part. By the fall of 2001, many European cities had set up huge clocks at the heart of town—generally, beside the central railroad station—ticking off the days, hours, and minutes until the euro was to arrive. When I saw an elaborate countdown clock on the town square of Klagenfurt, Austria, I told the mayor how impressed I was that the city had taken the trouble to remind Klagenfurters of the fundamental change heading their way. "Well, it wasn't really much trouble," the Bürgermeister replied. "We put the clock up there in 1999 to count down to the millennium, so we figured we might as well use it again."

In addition to the distinctive campaigns mounted by individual countries, the European Central Bank spent some $70 million on a continent-wide awareness drive of its own. The bank's ads evoked shared elements of European culture, from ancient ruins to modern soccer games, from lederhosen-clad hikers at alpine lakes to smiling couples at outdoor cafés enjoying one of the continent's all-time favorite snacks, french fries with mayonnaise. The tag line was the same in each country, except for linguistic distinctions: "The Euro, our money"; "Der Euro, unser Geld"; "El Euro, nuestra moneda"; "De Euro, ons geld"; "L'euro, notre monnaie." In the end, these national and transnational educational efforts paid off. By the last week in December, polls throughout the euro zone showed that 90 percent or more of all Europeans knew that their francs, schillings, and escudos were headed for the last round-up sometime in the new year.

The transition from old money to new was smoothed somewhat because the changeover on January 1 was not completely a "big bang" kind of thing. Public employees—a sizable chunk of the workforce in every European nation—had been paid in the new currency for months before the switch, through direct deposits to their bank accounts. Well before January 1, the vast majority of European bank and brokerage accounts had already been recalibrated. A German, for example, who deposited 10,000 marks into his bank account in November 2001 would find on his December monthly statement that his balance had increased by 5,112.92 euros. Another helpful factor was Europe's global lead in the technology of plastic money. For several years now, Europeans have used cash cards—similar to the prepaid farecards on U.S. subway systems—for a much broader range of purchases than Americans do. From the morning baguette and espresso to the last taxi ride home at night, the standard transaction is not the exchange of currency but rather the quick swipe of a card. For that kind of business, a reprogramming at headquarters was the only transition required.

Despite all the time, money, and ingenuity devoted to the changeover, there was a palpable sense of foreboding among top Eurocrats as the clock ticked down to the birthday of the new currency. The director of the Dutch National Railway warned commuters to plan for two extra hours of travel time each day until the clerks and machines could get used to the change. Italian bank clerks joined their French brethren in threatening to strike. On the eve of the great transition, a senior official at EU headquarters in Brussels, Gerassimo Thomas, offered a fairly downbeat assessment of the days to come: "We are pretty confident that we will definitely have the situation under control by the second or third week of January, but we need to prevent too many bad personal experiences from happening at the start."

And then, when the bells and fireworks greeted the New Year and the New Euro at midnight on January 1, 2002, there was amazing news all over the continent: Everything worked. The ATM machines spit out the long-awaited money like clockwork, and the big crowds that lined up to get their euros in the post-midnight chill displayed a happy, celebratory mood—as the media dubbed it, a mood of "Europhoria." Bars and restaurants that stayed open late for the celebrations took payment in francs, Finn marks, or deutsche marks and made change in euros, exactly as the planners had foreseen. Shortly after dawn's first light on New Year's Day, a Belgian named Patrice Mercier stepped away from a newsstand in central Brussels, counting the change from his purchase of that morning's *Le Monde* and a pack of Winstons. He had paid in Belgian francs, but received the change in euros. He was astonished. "This is exactly what the government has been saying: You pay in the old currency and get change in the new one," M. Mercier said. "But I guess I didn't really expect it to happen. *Mon dieu,* it worked!"

In fact, the biggest currency exchange in the history of the world proceeded in almost perfect fashion. When the euro went to work on January 2, the first business day of the new currency regime, problems were minimal, and acceptance of the new currency was universal. Railway stations in Holland and elsewhere reported business pretty much as usual, with lines at the ticket booths not much longer than on any other day. The French and Italian bankers' strikes fizzled. Butchers, bread makers, and bartenders found ways to cope. On the evening of January 2, when I ordered a stein of dark red Belgian beer in a tavern just off the Grand Place, Brussels' medieval market square, the barmaid stumbled just briefly as she presented the bill. "Let's see, the Trappiste Rochefort beer, that used to be 130 francs," she said. "So today it costs—no, wait a minute—I'm sorry—where's my calculator?—oh yes, that will be, let's see, 3 euros and 2.226 cents."

The result was a much faster transition from old money to new than anybody—except the Germans, with their no-margin-for-error approach—had predicted. The two-month "dual currency" periods in the other eleven eurozone countries turned out to be far longer than any country needed. In less than two weeks, the legacy currencies had basically disappeared from commerce. (Much of the old paper currency was burned as fuel, or turned into agricultural compost; the legacy coins are probably still sitting today in abandoned purses and wallets in the dresser drawers of 100 million homes.)

Among individual consumers, the change to the euro produced both winners and losers. Among the bigger winners were successful contestants on the French version of *Who Wants to Be a Millionaire?* Producers decided they had no choice but to award the top prize in euros—even though 1 million euros was the equivalent of 6.56 million French francs. Somehow, *Who Wants to Be One-Sixth of a Millionaire?* didn't have the necessary ring to it. On the other hand, church leaders in some jurisdictions were worried. The 1-pound coin that the Irish traditionally drop in the collection plate each Sunday gave way to the 1-euro coin, which is worth 21 percent less. The Roman Catholic hierarchy in France passed out flyers urging parishioners to give two 1-euro coins each Sunday instead of the single 10-franc coin that they had traditionally put in the plate; otherwise, the bishops warned, the church could lose about 35 percent of its weekly collection. Consumers in general seemed convinced that retailers were using the new money as a tool for price-gouging—that is, that the stores would round up any price in the process of conversion. In fact, major retail chains like Spar—a Europe-wide version of 7-Eleven—promised that they would always round down when converting prices to euros. Still, reports after the first year of the new money suggested that there had been an inflationary spike in European retail prices. As with most economic statistics, the experts offered competing explanations of this development. Some economists said that price increases accompanying the switch to euros were responsible for the inflation. Others said precisely the opposite: that the price transparency resulting from a common currency had forced high-cost manufacturers and retailers to lower their prices, and thus held inflation to a lower rate than it would have reached otherwise.

Even before the further expansion of the EU, the euro began spreading beyond the original twelve countries officially using the currency. Smaller European principalities like Monaco, Montenegro, Liechtenstein, and Vatican City switched to the euro when their bigger neighbors did. Andorra, a tiny alpine ski mecca perched high in the Pyrenees between France and Spain, became a single-currency country for the first time in its long history; previously, Andorra had used both French francs and Spanish pesetas. The Swiss, surrounded by euro nations, kept their franc but began accepting the euro as if it were a currency of their own. A few scattered outposts that were still in colonial status also adopted the new currency. Thanks to the international dateline, the first retail transactions using the world's newest currency actually took place on the Pacific atoll of New Caledonia, a French protectorate where the new year dawned twelve hours ahead of the mother country.

On the other hand, three active members of the European Union took no part in the gala New Year/New Euro celebrations, having decided to stay out of the common currency, at least for the time being. The British pound, the Swedish kroner, and the Danish kroner are still legal tender in those countries, even though their governments continue to participate in virtually all other common endeavors promoted by the European Union.

The reasons are partly economic—the view that interest rates and monetary decisions are better made at home, rather than by the European Central Bank in Frankfurt. This argument rings true in Britain, where the Bank of England seems to most people to be a better and more familiar steward of monetary policy than the ECB has been. The economic rationale is a little harder to justify in Denmark. Denmark has officially tied its interest rates to those set down by the ECB; that is,

Danish monetary policy is effectively set in Frankfurt, not Copenhagen. But while they have given up their monetary independence, the Danes don't get any of the advantages that would come from joining the common money. So why do they stay out? The real opposition to the euro in the holdout nations is not so much economic as it is emotional and political.

When British Euroskeptics stand up before cheering crowds and promise to "keep our queen on our pound in our pockets," the appeal is to the people once known as "little Englanders"—the bloke down the pub who doesn't speak any foreign language, doesn't much like foreigners, and doesn't much want to use any of their money. The one Briton who has been able to soar above that attitude, who can convince his countrymen that their place is at "the center of the Europe and the center of the world," as he puts it, is Prime Minister Tony Blair, an arch-Europhile. In the fall of 2002, after the successful launch of the euro on the mainland, all the pundits predicted that Blair was ready to launch a nationwide campaign for a pro-euro referendum. Then the war in Iraq intervened. The voters' trust in Blair plummeted, and whatever dream he might have had of a euro referendum in Britain was stuffed deeply away on the back shelf.

While euro opposition in Britain tends to be a right-wing position, the left have led the anti-euro movements in both Denmark and Sweden. The basic argument was that the Stability and Growth Pact that comes with euro membership—the rule limiting a country's budget deficit to 3 percent of GDP—would be a threat to the Scandinavian countries' beloved welfare systems. The fear is that the European Central Bank might order Stockholm or Copenhagen to limit their generous health care, pension, and education benefits to reduce the deficit. This argument could well be right, and it prevailed with both electorates. In a Danish referendum in 2001 and a Swedish ballot in 2003, the voters in both countries said no to the euro, even though the prime ministers and most of the political establishment in both countries campaigned for a yes. In Sweden, the anti-euro advocates adeptly sidestepped the charge that they were anti-EU as well by blanketing the nation with their bumper-sticker slogan: "Yes to Europe, No to Euro."

The Swedish referendum on the euro had a tragic outcome: the nation's foreign minister, Anna Lindh, campaigning hard for the pro-euro side, was approached a few days before the election by a disheveled man with a dagger in his hand. He stabbed her repeatedly, and she died a few hours later. Police later arrested a suspect, but were never able to determine the exact relationship between the euro campaign and this lethal assault.

At some point, it seems safe to predict, the British, Danes, and Swedes will have to change their minds about the euro and join up with their fellow Europeans. Meanwhile, the currency is scheduled to be adopted by all ten of the European countries that joined the union in May 2004. Having watched in dismay as the holdout nations stayed out, the EU made it a condition of membership that new applicants must commit to the common currency. They will make the switch one by one, as their internal economies qualify for membership. By the end of the first decade of the twenty-first century, the euro will be the coin of the realm for about half a billion people, from the Atlantic coast of Ireland to the Russian border—even if the holdouts continue to hold out that long. Another half-dozen countries have made initial applications for membership in the EU and could be in the union by 2010 or so. Beyond that, Turkey (with about 5 percent of its land area in Europe) and Russia (with about 20 percent) could become EU member states, and thus euro states. This would mean a euro serving an economic union with three times the population of the United States of America, and considerably higher total GDP and trade figures. For the Europeans, the dreams of grandeur, the hope of creating "the weapon with which to fight back" against the might of the U.S. dollar, are likely to come true.

It's unlikely that many Americans lie awake at night worrying about the threat to the almighty dollar posed by Europe's new anti-dollar. But perhaps they should. The emergence of a new currency backed by some of the richest nations on earth and used as the medium exchange for the planet's wealthiest trading bloc could pose a serious threat to the dollar's vaunted stature as the world's preferred reserve currency. Just two years after its launch, the euro was already forcing Washington to pay higher interest rates to central banks around the world to induce them to buy U.S. Treasury bonds. This means that, at a time when the U.S. deficit was rising to new records every year, the mere existence of the euro was making it more costly for Americans to finance that debt. Corporations and governments that once had to maintain large reserves of U.S. dollars won't have to do that anymore now that the euro offers a reliable alternative. Some international transactions that used to be routinely priced in dollars are now being denominated in euros—which means that Americans, not the other guys, have to bear the transaction costs of currency exchange. In short (as we shall see in chapter 9), the European Union's common currency could undermine some of the benefits of financial dominance that Americans have enjoyed, and taken for granted, since the end of World War II.

Those few American pundits and politicians who have focused on the euro have generally gotten it wrong—as Dr. Kissinger was honest enough to admit back in the prologue to this book. A week before the euro's picture-perfect launch, the estimable George Will called Europe's new currency a "momentous milestone," but added a caveat: "It will not work." On the eve of E-day, economist Arthur Laffer told readers of the *Wall Street Journal* that Europe should be praised for its historic currency innovation—and then assured the American audience that the EU currency was likely to lose value steadily against the dollar on global markets. In fact, the euro rose about 60 percent against the dollar in the first two years after it replaced the old currencies. Heading toward the third birthday of its launch, the euro was the strongest currency on earth. (Not all Americans underestimated the new money, however. The *New Republic* said just before the launch that the euro "could easily prove the most important economic event of the decade.")

For Europeans, in contrast, the euro's status as a challenger to dollar dominance is genuine. On that New Year's Day when the currency was launched, the European Commission's president, Romano Prodi, spoke of the new money with another of his Italian metaphors. "The euro is just an antipasto," Prodi said. "It is the first course, but there will be others. The historical significance of the euro is to construct a bipolar economy in the world. The unipolar world is over. There are two poles now: the dollar, and the euro."

For Prodi, of course, a "bipolar" currency world was just one facet of the broader effort to create a "bipolar" world in every respect—to see the European Union as a global superpower of American dimensions. For Americans, who are already citizens of a superpower, this might not appear to make much difference. So the Europeans have grandiose ambitions for their new form of supranational state. So what? Does it make a difference to us?

Any American still asking those questions might want to place a call to a prominent American who learned all too well that it does make a difference. That would be a businessman named Jack Welch.

FOUR

Welch's Waterloo

Jack Welch learned the hard way.

By the turn of the twenty-first century, you might have thought that Jack Welch had no more lessons to learn. After two stupendously successful decades as chairman of General Electric, Welch had become a shining star of the corporate universe, studied in all the business schools and admired, quoted, and emulated by his fellow CEOs around the world. With a ruthless focus on the bottom line, he reported eighty consecutive quarters of profit growth, through good times and bad. A ferocious cost-cutter, he insisted on economies in every corner of the giant company—every corner, that is, except the chairman's office. During his two decades at the top, Welch took home hundreds of millions of dollars in salary, options, bonuses, and benefits. Indeed, he created a lifestyle of Babylonian splendor for himself at the company's expense. Among much else, General Electric gave Welch a multimillion-dollar apartment in Manhattan. The place was staffed with maids and butlers and routinely stocked with vitamins, fresh flowers, and fine wine—and all those niceties, too, were paid for by the company.

Eventually, this gargantuan compensation would come to embarrass both Welch and his company, serving as Exhibit A in the media's case against corporate greed and excess. But as long as Welch was running things, GE's board and stockholders felt he was worth every million. Under his leadership, after all, General Electric was the most valuable corporation on earth.

Accordingly, when Jack Welch announced his plans to retire in the fall of 2000, General Electric's stock plunged, even though the news had been anticipated for months. A few weeks later, when Welch made the completely unanticipated announcement that he was not retiring after all, the stock soared on the news.

The reason for Welch's sudden reversal was a golden business opportunity that he put together, literally overnight, just weeks before he was scheduled to ride off into the sunset. On a Thursday afternoon, Welch heard a rumor that Honeywell Corporation, another industrial titan, was up for sale. By Saturday evening Welch, his lawyers, and his bankers had squeezed out the original buyer and put together a proposal for GE to buy Honeywell instead. Honeywell happily accepted—and why not? GE's offering price of $45 billion meant that the purchase would be the biggest industrial merger in history. "This is the most exciting day in the 118-year history of General Electric," Welch told reporters when he announced the GE-Honeywell engagement. The transaction was so important, and the regulatory approvals required were so complicated, that the chairman would delay his retirement to manage the merger. The stockholders were thrilled to have Welch back on top, and the chairman, too, was delighted with this unexpected turn of events. This mega-deal was to be Jack Welch's last major contribution to his company, and to corporate America.

Except the deal didn't work out. Welch's final swing of the bat turned into a spectacular flop, a costly and humiliating failure that would be followed by a steep decline in Welch's fortunes—his reputation, his marriage, and his sumptuous lifestyle. The proximate cause of this disaster was the multinational entity in Brussels called the European Union—or, more specifically, a group of bureaucrats in Brussels who outsmarted and outmaneuvered Welch and his high-powered legal team at every turn. But the larger reason for Jack Welch's expensive debacle was a matter of timing. In Europe, Welch came up against a force more powerful than the most powerful corporate chieftain. He ran headlong into the path of the great historic movement we've read about in this book—the unification of Europe. As Jack Welch learned the hard way, it is a phenomenon that Americans cannot afford to ignore.

When Welch announced his merger plans before a media throng that October morning in New York, it may not have been obvious that the creation of a new kind of supranational state embracing some two dozen countries across Europe would have any impact at all on a merger between two American companies. None of the corporate types at the GE-Honeywell press conference even mentioned the European Union, and no reporter asked about it. In fact, the European concept of "pooled sovereignty" was to prove decisive in scuttling Jack Welch's last big deal. As part of a broader transfer of power to the central European government, the nations of Europe have set up a single office in Brussels that controls antitrust policy for all the member countries of the European Union. As with the rest of the EU, its antitrust division—formally, the Directorate-General for Competition—is determined to set its own stamp on antitrust policy, and to see the rest of the world honor the rules that Europe has created for its own rich markets.

One area where Europe is particularly determined to stand on par with Washington is in business regulation—as Jack Welch learned the hard way. Brussels has no intention to step aside and let the U.S. Justice Department set the global antitrust agenda. Similarly, the European Union is determined to stand up to U.S. corporate power—even the power of a legendary CEO who heads the world's richest company. For that matter, Brussels was flexing its regulatory muscles long before Jack Welch sought approval for his merger. By the time the GE-Honeywell deal arrived in Brussels for consideration, the Directorate-General for Competition had already squelched business plans proposed by such titans of American business as Microsoft, Intel, and Coca-Cola. In 2000, the directorate killed the WorldCom/MCI–Sprint merger before U.S. antitrust officials even got around to ruling on it.

Despite that track record, it is clear in retrospect that Jack Welch and his expensive phalanx of lawyers and financial advisers had no clue that the unified Europe, with its global ambitions, might be a problem. In the intense rush of deal-making leading up to "the most exciting day in GE's history," and in the weeks of work that followed, the experts working for GE and Honeywell concluded that there would be no antitrust obstacles to their planned merger. When Welch announced the deal at the October press conference in New York, he predicted that all regulatory approvals would be granted by the following February. Asked specifically about antitrust problems, Welch was characteristically curt and confident: "This is the cleanest deal you'll ever see," he assured the assembled reporters. The man had no idea what was coming.

As we saw at the beginning of this book, many Americans who were supposedly experts in international affairs consistently underestimated the scope of the revolution sweeping Europe. So it was not terribly surprising that the scrum of tough, no-nonsense business types running General Electric and Honeywell would miss it as well. During the years when Europe was getting its collective act together, Jack Welch had been busy making one of America's oldest corporations bigger and richer than ever before.

When John Patrick Welch Jr. studied high school geography in Salem, Massachusetts, just after the end of World War II, he saw a world where the United States had emerged as the financial and industrial giant. Once-mighty Europe was a shattered and hungry continent where both the winners and the losers of the war were dependent on huge sums of American aid. Friendly, outspoken, and determined to be at the center of events—his high school class voted him the title of "noisiest"—Welch was popular in school but not a top student. As a senior, he didn't get into either of his preferred colleges, Dartmouth or Columbia; he ended up down the road at the University of Massachusetts. He eventually took a Ph.D. in chemical engineering, and landed a job with a manufacturer of industrial plastics.

Welch's first—and last—employer was General Electric, a firm far better known for its dynamos, transformers, refrigerators, and lightbulbs than for plastics. General Electric was the oldest manufacturing firm in the electric industry. The company traced its lineage back to Thomas A. Edison himself; at one point in the 1880s, it was known as "The Edison General Electric Company." It is the only firm on the Dow Jones Industrial Index that has been part of that select list of manufacturing giants since the index was begun in 1896.

The plastics operation in Pittsfield, Massachusetts, where Welch initially landed was a minor backwater of GE's far-flung manufacturing empire. But the ambitious, hard-driving young chemist made enough of a splash there to move up rapidly through the corporate hierarchy. By the age of forty, a point when most GE executives might still be hoping for a vice presidency somewhere down the road, Welch was openly campaigning to become the company's next CEO. When he was chosen for the job, in 1981, at the age of forty-four—the youngest chairman in the company's long history—he immediately began a shakeup that lasted for the next twenty years. He had immense faith in his own seat-of-the-pants judgment, and considered a quick response to events much more valuable than long-range planning. "To sit around and draw up five-year plans is absolutely a waste of human effort," he declared.

Many Welch disciples went on to brilliant and lucrative careers at General Electric or other corporations. Because Welch believed in paying handsomely for hard work, many of his underlings became seriously rich—as did long-term GE stockholders. Anyone smart enough to buy $10,000 worth of General Electric shares on the day Jack Welch became chairman and then leave it alone would have had an investment worth more than $600,000 on the day he retired. That was about three times the gain of the Standard & Poor's 500 Index over the same period.

Still, the Welch years weren't good for everybody at GE. He was ruthless about cutting jobs—well over 100,000 people were forced to leave GE in his first decade at the top. The press, in turn, was ruthless in reporting on the mass layoffs he engineered. For years, a man who loved the limelight couldn't stand to read his press clippings. The media kept bringing up all those layoffs. Somewhere along the line, Welch acquired a nickname he absolutely loathed: "Neutron Jack," after the bomb that kills humans by the thousands but leaves the buildings standing. Even those who survived at Neutron Jack's GE spent their careers under intense pressure; one union leader observed that Welch "squeezes his people dry, like lemons."

Welch thought the nagging fear that your job might be the next to go was a useful motivator. He insisted that each of his top managers fire the worst 10 percent of their subordinates each year, and was astonished when some of them actually tried to protect loyal underlings who were on the borderline. A tough negotiator, he was determined to emerge on top in every transaction—personal as well as business. When his first marriage broke up and he began a new romance with a successful New York lawyer, he got her to agree to give up her career so she could share his schedule of constant travel. The new Mrs. Welch also agreed, under pressure, to take up golf.

The chairman was equally unsentimental about product lines. For the first fifteen years or so of his regime, he enforced a rule that GE would only compete in businesses where it was No. 1 or No. 2 in the market. Consequently, he dumped about 350 of the sprawling company's units, including GE's trademark color TV business, semiconductors, air-conditioning, and the GE toasters and coffeemakers that had brought the company into every American kitchen. After GE was convicted in a series of criminal cases involving false accounting on defense contracts, Welch sold the defense business.

But Welch's greatest success—and the key to the enormous growth in sales and profits during his tenure—came in buying new companies to add to the GE fold. Over twenty years, he merged some 900 outside firms into General Electric. The corporate shopping spree had considerably more to do with the "General" aspect of Welch's company than with the "Electric." He bought TV networks and department stores, chemical, plastics, and ceramics makers, a brokerage firm, and an outfit that sold health insurance for dogs and cats. Confident that he and his team could manage almost any company in any line of business better than the people they bought it from, his strategy was to move fast and snap up the target before other potential buyers could get organized. "Speed, simplicity, self-confidence"—that was the mantra.

Not every acquisition was successful. Welch paid nearly $4 billion in 1988 to buy Montgomery Ward, a century-old retailer with millions of loyal customers from coast to coast. After a dozen years of that superior GE management, Ward slumped into bankruptcy and was left for dead. Overall, though, the mergers added significantly to earnings—and in fact became a necessary crutch to sustain the Welch promise of higher earnings every quarter. By the late 1990s, Welch was making acquisitions worth about $15 billion each year, which is to say he spent about $300 million per week, on the average, buying companies. Necessarily, the central rule was to act fast: buy now, study the geography later. With billions in the bank, GE could afford to hire the world's best lawyers and financiers to work out any problems that showed up after the first quick deal was made.

That was the scenario that Jack Welch followed in the fall of 2000 for his last and most disastrous deal, the attempted acquisition of Honeywell. It was an overnight success that turned into an extended failure. The story began on October 19, 2000, an otherwise uneventful Thursday, when a little-known medical equipment company called Wipro was to be listed for the first time on the New York Stock Exchange. The firm had partnered with GE on several projects, so Wipro asked Welch to show up on the trading floor to bring some hoopla to the occasion. At first, the idea worked perfectly: the celebrity CEO was engulfed by cameras, microphones, and reporters shouting questions. But suddenly, late in the trading day, the media flock swooped across to another corner of the floor to cover a breaking story. As curious as the next man, Welch wandered over to see what was happening. The excitement was focused on Honeywell, a normally unexciting industrial stock that had been in the doldrums for months. In less than an hour, it had abruptly leaped by

30 percent—nearly $10 per share. There was only one possible explanation: a mega-merger was in the works.

A reporter stuck his mike in Welch's face and asked him to comment on market rumors that United Technologies, a GE competitor in several fields, had made a surprise offer to buy out Honeywell; several others burst out with related queries. But by the time the press got to the most important question, Welch was way ahead of them.

"What's GE going to do about it?" a reporter shouted. Racing off the floor, Welch called over his shoulder: "We'll have to go back and think about it." In fact, he was already thinking about what to do; within minutes of hearing the unexpected news, Welch was on the phone plotting with his lawyers, bankers, and board members as to how GE could muscle aside United Technologies and take the prize for itself. Two helicopters full of GE executives dashed from corporate headquarters in Connecticut to New York to do the paperwork. Welch called the chairman of Chase Manhattan and told him to put the investment bankers to work at once on a huge deal. How huge? the banker wondered. Welch wasn't sure, but rumor had it that United Technologies was offering $40 billion for Honeywell, and GE would have to do better than that.

It was classic Jack Welch, the very essence of speed and self-confidence—but Welch's bold move very nearly wasn't speedy enough. On Friday morning, when he placed a call to Honeywell's chairman to discuss a GE counteroffer, Welch was told he was too late. Honeywell's board was already meeting in executive session to accept the United Technologies proposal; the deal was done. A less determined man might have folded his cards at that point and gone on to a well-earned retirement. Jack Welch, however, stormed the corridors, raging at his underlings to find somebody, anybody, at Honeywell who could interrupt that board meeting. Eventually, he found a secretary on the GE side who knew a secretary at Honeywell; the two women conferred. A few minutes later, a note scrawled in Jack Welch's hand was faxed to Honeywell headquarters and slipped into the boardroom: General Electric would be willing to pay a hefty $5 billion more than the United Technologies offer.

That proved irresistible. By the afternoon of October 20, less than twenty hours after Welch heard that Wall Street rumor, he had capped the biggest merger agreement in the history of American industry—and found time along the way to rescind the retirement notice he had issued months before.

It was a triumphant day, except for one lingering shadow. Amid the hullabaloo of lawyers and bankers and board members, Welch never got around to telling his wife that the retirement she had been looking forward to for so long was now to be delayed. When he finally broke the news at a dinner with friends that Friday night, Welch recalled later, "she didn't take it well."

Welch had an inordinate fear that the business press might not take it well, either. The story of GE's unexpected grab of a mighty industrial titan, the last-minute maneuver that made a multibillion-dollar deal, was of course great copy in itself. But Welch was obsessed with the thought that the reporters would find a personal agenda at the heart of the transaction. When GE and Honeywell held a press conference to announce finalization of the merger, Welch spent much of the session protesting— perhaps protesting too much—the notion that he had bought Honeywell just to delay his retirement. Welch gruffly promised a punch in the nose for any reporter who wrote that. "This is not a story of the old fool who can't leave his seat, who loves the job so much he can't go home," he said. A few seconds later, he came back to the same point: "It ain't anything to do with being sixty-five and hanging on," he said. A minute later, he was back again: "There is a lot of psychobabble out there to the effect that, 'Is this guy hanging on to the building?' Don't write that story. That story is stupid."

The story that Welch wanted to see in print was rather his assessment of what a "great match" the two companies would make. Although both companies made plastics, chemicals, electrical machinery, and aircraft engines, Welch kept saying that the product lines were not overlapping. A merger of two huge companies both making the same products would naturally raise eyebrows among antitrust regulators, but that wasn't the case with GE and Honeywell, Welch argued. GE made large jet engines, while Honeywell made midsize and small jet engines. The products were "complementary," not competitive. That's why Welch's highly paid lawyers and economists had assured him that "there would be no problem at all" getting government regulators to approve the huge deal.

On this point, Welch and his army of experts were half right. With a tailwind from a new, business-friendly Republican administration in Washington, the biggest industrial merger in history sailed easily through the approval process. The Justice Department's Anti-Trust Division gave the merger a formal seal of approval with only minor conditions. That was good news, but it hardly prompted anybody to break out the champagne in the GE boardroom. By then, it had become clear that the two firms had another government to worry about—one that was far less willing to provide smooth sailing for two huge American companies. This obstacle came as a surprise—to Jack Welch, at least. "The last thing I ever expected," Welch recalled after the deal had collapsed, "was a long antitrust review by the European Commission."

But that's what he got. Within days of the official announcement of the merger, Welch was told that he would need to go to Europe to lay out his plans before the Directorate-General for Competition. What with one thing and another, Welch put off the trip for months; thus it was not until the following January, over a long lunch in Brussels' Quartier Européen, that Jack Welch came face to face with his nemesis: a decorous, scholarly, eminently proper Italian named Mario Monti.

If Jack Welch was the very model of the modern corporate general, Monti was the archetype of a new governmental creature spawned by the movement toward common government on the continent: the Eurocrat. The son of a banker from a suburb of Milan, Monti studied economics, first in Italy and then at Yale, and went back to Milan to teach monetary theory at Bocconi University. He went on to become president of the university, training a corps of young economists from all over Europe in the key principle—free trade across international markets—underlying the movement toward economic union in Europe.

Although his quiet manner suggests nothing more than a polite, deferential academic, Monti is in fact a figure of fierce determination who has never let the status quo stand in his way. Like many Italian economists, he was frustrated that the central bank, the Bank of Italy, maintained no measure of Italy's money supply. While his academic colleagues issued learned papers and angry columns condemning the bank, Professor Monti filled the gap himself. He gathered the data as best he could and began issuing a newsletter with his own quarterly estimates of money supply; quickly, the "Monti M1" and the "Monti M2" gained acceptance as quasi-official figures. This shamed Italy's central bankers into producing their own official tally.

In his college classes, and in his regular economic column for a national newspaper, Monti championed free-market ideals throughout the 1970s and '80s, when state ownership and heavy regulation were the norms throughout Europe. He was one of the strongest continental champions of the privatization movement that Margaret Thatcher pioneered in the 1980s. But his most passionate cause was the unification of Europe. Growing up amid the industrial rubble left behind after World War II, he could see clearly that Italy was never going to be a global economic force again—unless it combined with its neighbors to build a pancontinental economy. Dr. Monti pushed vigorously for a borderless, Europe-wide market. If American manufacturers in New York could ship their goods to California or Florida without paying tariffs, he argued, it made no sense for a company in northern Italy to be hit with import duties for shipping goods a few miles down the road to France or Austria. He recognized that powerful international corporations would require powerful regulation—but the regulators, too, he argued, should operate on a Europe-wide basis. Customs laws, competition rules, antitrust regulation, and taxes should also be common across national borders, he said. And because of the enormous clout that a trading bloc the size of Europe would hold, Europe's unified business regulations would become the world's regulations.

For two decades, on those occasions when conservative parties emerged on top in Italy's roller-coaster politics, the prominent free-market academic was almost always offered cabinet jobs in Rome. Monti turned down all those offers, on the grounds that he was having a larger impact training the next generation of Euro-business leaders at Bocconi. But when he was asked, in 1995, to join the European Commission—effectively, the European Union's executive branch—as cabinet minister in charge of financial integration, customs, and common taxation, he could not resist the chance to practice the pan-European ideals he had always preached. After four years as commissioner for the internal market, Monti was offered an even better Brussels post: director-general for competition.

By taking over as Europe's antitrust czar, Mario Monti became one of the most powerful economic regulators on earth. The source of that power was a basic element of European unification, something we will see at work throughout this book—the idea of "pooled sovereignty." That is, each of the EU's member nations gives up some of the normal powers enjoyed by sovereign nations and hands the authority to Brussels instead. As chief of the Directorate-General for Competition—or "DG Comp," as it is known in Euro-business circles—Monti regulates mergers and acquisition, pricing, and business practices for virtually every industrial nation in Europe. The governments of Germany, Britain, France, Spain, and the other European countries no longer have this power; it resides in Brussels. In theory, Monti's decisions are subject to review by the other ministers in the European cabinet, or by a vote of the heads of state of the member nations. In practice, his reputation and stature are so imposing that almost nobody second-guesses Mario Monti.

On top of that, DC Comp has a formidable battery of enforcement measures. When Monti is on the trail of a company suspected of price-fixing or similar violations, he can authorize his agents to walk into any company office—or, sometimes, into an executive's home—and dig through the files to seize documents that could help with the prosecution. Because the investigators frequently enter the premises early in the morning, before any employees are around to get in their way, these wide-ranging searches are known as "dawn raids." (In a nice touch, one Euro-business reporter who writes a regular column on Monti's activities has adopted the byline "Dawn Raid.")

But for all the dawn raids and the rejected mergers and the heavy fines—he hit the German giant DaimlerChrysler with a €70 million fine for charging different prices in different European countries for the same auto model—Monti hardly fits the image of the fire-breathing regulatory dragon. The director-general for competition is a quiet, gray-haired scholar, so mild and unassuming that when you see Signor Monti wandering down the long halls of the European Commission headquarters, he looks like a tourist who has become separated from his group and gotten lost. To a lot of his fans in Brussels, pitting Mario Monti against a veteran corporate dynamo like Jack Welch seemed almost unfair—like sending Mr. Rogers up against Rambo.

Yet there was a fist of iron inside Monti's velvet glove, as Welch learned on that first visit to Brussels. Crossing the Atlantic in a corporate jet with a phalanx of antitrust lawyers in tow, the GE brass decided that the best tactic for their first presentation to Monti would be to use General Electric's strongest weapon: Jack Welch himself. With his personal charm and persuasive skills, Welch would make the case for the merger, face-to-face. So the American CEO and the European regulator met for a long, private lunch. Welch flashed his friendly, casual smile, stuck out a hand, and said, "Mario—call me Jack." Monti pulled quickly back into his shell. "Mr. Welch," he replied in his accented but precise English, "we have a regulatory proceeding under way. I feel the proper approach would be to keep things on a more formal basis. You can call me Sgr. Monti." From that icy moment, "Mr. Welch" realized that he could be facing trouble in Europe.

And the deal was, in fact, in trouble. Welch and his lawyers quickly found that the DG Comp team had spent the months before this first meeting doing extensive homework on GE and Honeywell. The Europeans knew considerably more about the two American companies than the Americans knew about European merger rules. As it turned out, before Welch ever got to Brussels to plead his case, Monti had a team of investigators in the United States talking to competitors of GE and Honeywell—including United Technologies, the firm that Welch had pushed aside when it was minutes from completing its own buyout of Honeywell. The Europeans came away primed with inside information about the parties to the proposed merger. At one point in the talks, Monti's economist asked Welch and his staff about a piece of high-tech aircraft electronics manufactured at Honeywell's plant in Redmond, Washington. The GE team responded with blank stares; they had never heard of that particular Honeywell product until the EU regulators described it to them.

In typical fashion, Welch fought back hard to make up for GE's stumbling start. He spent the first half of 2001 shuttling across the Atlantic, battling to convince the Europeans that the deal made sense. He was confident; after all, he had successfully sold hundreds of mergers to the antitrust authorities in Washington. In fact, though, the GE team made a fundamental tactical blunder in its approach to the negotiations.

Welch et al. concluded that the way to get a merger approved in Europe was the same approach they had used so often in the United States. When the trust-busters in Washington expressed concern about diminished competition for a particular product line, Welch would promise to sell that product line to some competitor, so it would be out of GE's control. In the GE-Honeywell case, for example, Welch promised Washington that he would sell the Honeywell unit that made helicopter engines. It was a minor concession on the company's part but a significant achievement for the Justice Department and its antitrust division. Welch referred to these divestiture agreements as "givebacks," or "goodies." He had learned from experience that U.S. regulators loved to stand up on the day a merger was approved and boast about how many millions of dollars worth of divestiture they had squeezed out of mighty General Electric. Welch got his acquisition, the regulators got their "givebacks," and everybody went away happy.

The problem was that European antitrust regulators were not interested in harvesting a portfolio of small divestitures from big companies. The Europeans were concerned with bigness itself—the fear that a company with an overwhelming presence in certain markets would use its sheer size to drive out competitors, and then drive up prices for consumers. The GE-Honeywell merger was a classic example of the difference in antitrust theory on opposite sides of the Atlantic. Welch was certain his merger would be approved, because GE and Honeywell had "complementary," rather than overlapping, product lines. GE made the engines for big commercial jets, but not the avionics (that is, the electronic control mechanisms). Honeywell made avionics, but not big engines. And Welch was prepared to offer lots of "goodies" to sweeten the deal.

In Washington, these distinctions were good enough. But in Europe, the combination of two giants both marketing to the commercial aircraft industry was a significant concern in itself, regardless of the specific products involved. The fact that GE's huge lending division often financed deals for European plane builders and airlines only heightened the concern. As Monti told Welch directly at several of their meetings, DG Comp was worried about that kind of corporate power and its impact on competitors. What if GE designed jet engines that required the use of Honeywell avionics—and thus roped in customers who could no longer turn to other suppliers for avionics? That kind of "bundling" would hurt European avionics manufacturers and customers as well. Welch was never able to allay this fear (possibly because tie-ins like that were the reason he wanted the merger in the first place).

As winter turned to spring, the American executives and the European regulators forged ahead on different paths. Welch continually increased the basket of "goodies" he was willing to give up to win European approval of the deal. Monti, unimpressed by these offers, continually talked to competitors and customers, most of whom vigorously opposed the deal. Welch was frustrated. "I couldn't believe the stuff we were putting on the table," he said later. "Two-point-two billion dollars' worth of divestitures eventually. And they were just ignoring it." In mid-June, when Welch made his last trip to Brussels for a final round of "give-backs," Monti showed no interest. The next day, waiting in his hotel suite in Brussels, the CEO received a personal phone call from the director-general. The merger proposal would be presented to the European Commission in two weeks, Monti said. DG Comp would recommend disapproval. "The deal is over," Monti said quietly. "Now I can say to you, 'Good-bye, Jack.'"

To Welch, of course, the deal was not yet over. He was a fighter, and there were still those two weeks remaining to fight for a positive vote in the EU cabinet. That led to his second major blunder. From Brussels, Welch placed a call to Air Force One, which was ferrying George W. Bush and his staff to attend the European Union summit in Sweden that same week. Welch told the White House chief of staff, Andrew Card, that he needed political help. The president would be meeting with the leaders of all European Union nations—effectively, Mario Monti's bosses—in a couple of days. American pressure, Welch insisted, must be brought to bear. Foolishly, the White House agreed.

As he traveled across Europe, Bush dutifully complained about Monti's decision both privately and publicly. He was "concerned," the president told a news conference, that American businesses might not be "treated fairly" by EU antitrust officials. The result was a storm of outrage among the assembled Europeans—not at Mario Monti, but at Jack Welch, at GE, and at George W. Bush. Welch's appeal for U.S. political pressure, and the president's response, was exactly the wrong way to deal with the European Union. (As we'll see throughout this book, it was a mistake the Bush administration would make over and over again.)

The various EU heads of state had differing views of their new continental union and its role, but there was one point on which every European could agree: Europe is no longer the weak little sister who can be pushed around by swaggering Americans. The last thing Europeans were willing to stand for—particularly at a time when corporate America was awash in charges of executive crime and dishonest accounting—was an American president lecturing them on the right way to regulate corporate behavior. Even the mild-mannered Mario Monti went ballistic—or at least, as ballistic as anyone had ever seen him. He summoned the entire Brussels press corps to a press conference and issued a fiery denunciation: "These deplorable attempts to trigger political intervention . . . from other countries have no place in our decision-making process, and they will have no effect on us whatsoever." The director-general even dared to suggest that Bush's engagement on the GE side brought to mind the often-dubious relationship between government officials and big business in his native Italy.

This final mistake annihilated whatever hopes Welch might have had to reverse Monti's decision. When the European Commission met in July, the GE-Honeywell decision was no longer a simple question of antitrust. It had become a fundamental test of Europe's backbone, its willingness to stand up to American pressure. And since the only losers in the case were two companies headquartered in Connecticut and New Jersey, U.S.A., it was easy to show the necessary backbone. The commission voted 20–0 to support Monti's negative recommendation. Jack Welch's final corporate venture had ended in abject failure.

When Welch brought the bad news home to his board of directors and his country, there were predictable reactions. U.S. senators raced angrily to the TV cameras to complain that Europe had no right to impose its own antitrust rules on two American corporations. The secretary of the Treasury argued that the European Commission, "not elected by anybody," was "meddling outside its jurisdiction." That contention had some appeal on the GE board; irate directors asked Welch why an Italian in Brussels should have the final say over a merger born and bred in the United States: "To hell with Europe, Jack. Let's do it anyway."

Welch, the realist, rejected all these fantasies. The power that gave Europe the authority to say no, he explained, was plain enough: sheer market power. The unification of the continent has produced a single market bigger than the United States or Japan. American companies can no longer say, "To hell with Europe," because they need access to that huge European market. When a sympathetic interviewer on MSNBC (a network that Welch had started during his CEO days) began griping about EU regulation of American companies, Welch cut him short: "We have to do business with Europe, so we have no choice but to respect their law," he said. Then he added, in the tones of a man who has learned a hard lesson, "That really is just the way the world works now."

When the dust settled and the huge deal was abandoned, there was a reckoning to be made. Both General Electric and Honeywell had devoted much of their corporate energy and talent for nearly a year to completing the merger, and all that expenditure was wasted in the end. Stock prices for both companies swooned; GE shares went from $60 just before Welch began chasing Honeywell to $33 when the deal fell apart. There were also hefty bills to pay. General Electric has declined to reveal how much it spent in outside fees on the Honeywell deal, but the estimates provided to board members ran to about $50 million in legal fees, and another $25 million or so to Chase Manhattan and other banks and investment houses involved in the deal. The bankers' bills came in considerably lower than they would have been if the deal had been completed. But the total fees were still formidable.

For both Jack Welch and Mario Monti, the GE-Honeywell case proved to be a turning point.

Welch, having already delayed his departure past GE's mandatory retirement age, had little left to do but pack up the office and turn the company over to his hand-picked successor, Jeffrey Immelt. His exodus fell far short, though, of the joyful victory lap he had envisioned. By ending his career with failure on a global scale, Welch had become a tainted figure, vulnerable now to criticism and second-guessing from the fickle media and a business community that had previously put him on a pedestal. No longer the paradigm of the executive world-killer, Jack Welch was just another American executive who had failed to spot the major challenge to American might that was growing on the European continent. Welch didn't like what was happening to his reputation, but he understood it: "If this deal had come along in the middle of my career, it would have been another swing and miss. Coming at the very end, after I had postponed my retirement, the loss of GE's biggest deal seemed to loom larger."

Part of the problem was the zeitgeist: After the billion-dollar debacles at Enron, WorldCom, and their ilk, the very notion of a celebrity CEO was suddenly suspect. The investment industry and the business press took a long, hard look at the bookkeeping practices of major corporations; General Electric and Jack Welch were not exempt. With GE's share price falling, reporters and analysts focused on a single line in the company's balance sheet: a $14 billion item listed, mysteriously, as "All other current costs and expenses accrued." A GE spokesman noted that the same line item could be found on the books for any year in the past decade; but in the post-Enron world, unexplained expenditures of $14 billion looked dubious at best. In this suspicious new atmosphere, even General Electric's stellar record of continuous earnings growth—eighty quarters without a single downturn!—spawned distrust. How could any company do that? Had Jack Welch cooked the books? "Commentators who marvelled at his 20 years in charge now tut and shake their heads," the *Economist* noted tartly.

Reeling from these attacks, Welch made his problems vastly more complicated through a personal mistake. A few months after his retirement, the editor of the *Harvard Business Review* offered Welch a chance to answer the critics: the review would publish a long reprise of the GE-Honeywell deal, with Welch offering his interpretation of each step along the way. This project required a series of lengthy interviews with the review's editor, Suzy Wetlaufer. Welch got along well with her—so well that the couple were soon romantically involved. It didn't take long for Jane Welch, the lawyer who had given up her career and taken up golf in order to marry the CEO, to realize that her husband had found another woman. It didn't take long after that for the media to catch up with Welch's marital problems.

Now Welch was snarled in both corporate and personal scandal. Falling back on his basic rule of business—"speed, simplicity, self-confidence"— he looked for the swift, simple solution. He recommended a divorce lawyer to Jane Welch and urged her to wrap things up quickly. Mrs. Welch had different ideas. She hired a tenacious, high-powered Manhattan divorce specialist and launched a vigorous battle to win a sizable chunk of the Welch wealth. Jack Welch resisted. After months of legal back-and-forth, Mrs. Welch launched her weapon of mass destruction: she put together a detailed affidavit listing every one of the perquisites and privileges that General Electric was providing for its ex-chairman. All these company-paid benefits, she said, had left the couple accustomed to an "extraordinary lifestyle," which Jane Welch expected her husband to provide for her after the divorce.

This document, which came to be known as the "perks affidavit," was one of scores of legal papers filed with the clerk of the Superior Court in Bridgeport, Connecticut, on a Thursday afternoon. It was dutifully stamped and stuck away in the accordion file labeled "Welch v. Welch." Somehow, financial reporters immediately learned about the Welch affidavit; the next morning's newspapers contained extensive accounts of the millions and millions that General Electric was shelling out to keep its former chairman comfortable.

Jane Welch's affidavit showed that GE had guaranteed the couple lifetime use of a $10 million apartment in the Trump International Tower on Central Park West, and invested $7.5 million to furnish it to Jack and Jane's satisfaction. All the food, flowers, alarm systems, cell phones, drinks, vitamins, and household goods the couple could consume were billed to the company. For Jack, the sports fan, General Electric provided season tickets to two different baseball teams as well as the New York Knicks; he was given box seats for the tennis championships at Wimbledon, Paris, and Forest Hills. For Mrs. Welch, the music fan, GE funded season tickets to the Metropolitan Opera. The company paid Welch's dues at numerous golf clubs around the country, and provided free transportation, by jet or limousine, wherever he wanted to go. The "perks affidavit" went so far as to detail the couple's travels at company expense; they ran about $290,000 per month.

At a time when the nation was already up in arms about corporate corruption and executive gluttony, this precise accounting of the endless bounty showered on one ex-CEO hit the business world with explosive force. At this point, Welch's old pals in the corner offices of corporate towers began turning on him. Their message was clear: Pay Jane whatever she wants, and bring this embarrassing sideshow to an end. "The Welch case . . . threatens to keep the image problems of the CEO class before the public," the *Wall Street Journal* noted on its front page. "Increasingly, the refrain heard whispered in board rooms is: Why doesn't he settle?" Eventually he did, and Jane Welch reportedly walked away with several hundred million dollars. General Electric, for its part, revealed that it was facing an "infomal investigation" of Welch's platinum parachute by the Securities and Exchange Commission; on the same day, Welch and GE jointly announced that the company would terminate Welch's range of perks, saving stockholders some $2.5 million per month. As a footnote, GE decided to open a large office in Brussels, with some two dozen lobbyists on the staff to keep track of the European Union and its increasingly ambitious efforts (which we will see in chapter 9) to regulate American business operations.

If Jack Welch's star descended sharply following his brush with the European Union, Mario Monti's shone ever brighter in the European skies. The mild-mannered Eurocrat who humbled America's most high-powered corporate chieftain became something of a hero—not just in Brussels but among Europeans in every corner of the continent who wanted to see the EU take its place beside the United States as an equal player on the world stage. Monti, of course, played down any suggestion that he had emerged on top in a one-on-one with Jack Welch. In an interview a few months after the deal was rejected, Monti adapted his business-professor persona. The real problem, he said, was a management failure: the failure by GE's management to study Honeywell's financial situation sufficiently before leaping into the deal. Once Welch, et al. learned the truth about Honeywell, Monti speculated, they may have wanted to back out of the deal, and the European Commission served as a neat excuse. (For what it's worth, Welch spurns this suggestion and says he was expecting to win approval right up to the moment he learned of Monti's rejection.)

Monti was a key force in the establishment of the International Competition Network, or ICN, an organization that is supposed to promote enforcement cooperation and policy coordination among antitrust officials of the EU, the United States, Canada, Mexico, Australia, and Japan. Monti became an enthusiastic champion of this global antitrust affiliation. He was by far the most enthusiastic champion, in fact, since the plan met lukewarm acceptance from his counterparts in the United States and Japan, who suspected that the ICN was a mechanism designed to make EU competition policies—that is, Mario Monti's competition policies— the global standard for antitrust enforcement. Back in Brussels, Monti, in his quiet, studious way, denied that he was trying to get tough on the United States or American companies. Still, he doggedly pursued a four-year investigation of Microsoft. In 2004, he hit the American software giant with a $600 million fine and ordered the firm to rewrite its flagship product, the Windows operating system. Microsoft complained, but complied.

But if Mario Monti was a reluctant, even apologetic combatant in the transatlantic antitrust battles, he became an admired figure precisely because of those battles. There was a strong clique of Monti fans in academia, including Norman Davies, an expert on Eastern European history at Oxford. "The notion of a European regulator in Brussels who can make the Americans tremble in their boots is fairly attractive to us," Davies said with a chuckle. "It used to be the Americans who were telling everybody what to do. Now the tables are turning.

"If you are Germany or France or the U.K," the professor went on, "you can't help looking at American power, American economic might, and thinking, 'That's a rather big elephant over there.' But if your individual country becomes part of a unified European economy, then you think, 'Goodness—we could be even bigger.' And Mr. Monti is the personification of that thought."

In the late 1990s, as he approached retirement after decades in the classroom, Norman Davies also learned a lesson—a thoroughly pleasant lesson—about Europeans' growing sense of allegiance and connection to their own continent. A rather big elephant of his own creation—a comprehensive European history, a 1,365-page text priced at $40—struck a popular chord and became a runaway best-seller in several languages. Professor Davies struck it rich. And deservedly so.

Davies, of course, had analyzed why it was that his history text became an international best-seller. "There were many points along the way when you really couldn't be proud to be a European," he said. "But I think today, at the start of a new century, Europeans are proud of where they stand and how much they have achieved. And this huge EU establishment is part of that. It's not any longer going to be whether France is the winner, or Germany, or the U.K. The competition now is different, first because it is peaceful, and further because it is global. And Europeans are becoming confident now that Europe is going to be the winner."

FIVE

L'Europe Qui Gagne

or, I Can't Believe It's Not American Butter

Let's conjure up a typical American couple—we'll call them Bill and Betty Yankee, of Syracuse, New York—heading out on a summer weekend for a typical American vacation. It will be a short vacation, compared to European-style holidays (as we'll see in chapter 6), because the Yankees are typically hardworking Americans who rarely take more than a few days off at a time. The Yankees plan to leave Friday and make a road trip to visit their son Bob in Chicago. They'll spend one night at Bob's place, and then set out early Sunday for the long drive home. They want to be back home in time for work Monday morning.

Bill is a maintenance man at Niagara Mohawk Power Corp., the electric utility serving about 1.5 million customers across upstate New York. Betty is a sales clerk at Casual Corner in the Syracuse Mall. Frankly, the couple is a little stretched at the moment, but they both badly need a break, so Betty has gone to the Household Finance outlet in the mall for a $750 loan. The day before the trip, Bill takes the family Jeep into Jiffy Lube for an oil change and then fills the tank at the Amoco station down the street. Early Friday morning, they pop a Dave Matthews CD into the car stereo, stop at Dunkin' Donuts for breakfast—Betty skips the doughnut and sips a can of Super Slim Fast instead—and then start driving west. Except for another fuel stop, this time at a Texaco station, they stay on the road most of the day, snacking on Baby Ruth, Power Bars, and various flavors of Snapple. To keep their dog Yank happy on the road, Bill has a few cans of Alpo in the back seat.

After a long drive, the couple stops for the night at a Holiday Inn. Bill has a Miller Lite and smokes a couple of Lucky Strikes to soothe his nerves. Betty, a fan of historic fiction, curls up with a bottle of 7Up and a great new novel by Helen Scully that she ordered from the Literary Guild. The next morning, they fill the tank at a Shell station and drive on to Chicago. Betty doesn't let Bill smoke in the car, so he chews a wad of Bazooka bubble gum instead. As they approach the city, Betty calls Bob on her cell phone—both mother and son use the Verizon network, so the call is free—to say that they'll soon arrive.

At their son's house, the Yankees present the gifts they've brought along—a new Brooks Brothers necktie for Bob and a pair of Ray-Bans for his wife, Barb. Barb, a copywriter at the Leo Burnett advertising agency, proudly shows a portfolio of the new ad series she has created for her chief client, Dial Soap. Barb had to work that Friday, so she didn't have time to make dinner; instead, she pops a few Lean Cuisines into the oven. It's not fancy, but she does offer three different flavors of Ben & Jerry's for dessert.

After a pleasant Sunday morning with their son and daughter-in-law—Bob is excited because his newspaper, the *Chicago Sun-Times*, has run his story on the front page—Bill and Betty set out for the trip home. They gas up at a Total station and drop in at a Stop & Shop to buy a couple of big bottles of Dr Pepper for the long drive. Unfortunately, the traffic is heavy, and it becomes obvious the Yankees are not going to get home at any decent hour that Sunday. So they stop at a Travelodge and watch part of *A Beautiful Mind* on pay-per-view before they drift off to sleep. Well before dawn the next morning, they set off again and made it back to Syracuse in time to go to work.

It all sounds like a thoroughly American vacation, full of American places, products, and services. In fact, this long weekend was about as

American as apple strudel. Despite the familiar American brand names, just about every product and service the Yankee family bought or used on this trip came from European-owned companies.

Household Finance, the venerable American loan company that advanced the money for the trip, is now a branch of HSBC, the big British banking firm. The family Jeep, of course, is made by a subsidiary of Germany's DaimlerChrysler. The Amoco gasoline they bought—a brand name that used to be an acronym for "American Oil Company"—is now a product of the British petroleum firm BP. Shell and Texaco stations in the United States are both run by the Netherlands oil company Royal Dutch Shell. Total is a subsidiary of France's oil giant, elf/Total. Jiffy Lube is also a Dutch-owned firm.

The Dave Matthews Band is one of America's most popular rock groups at the dawn of the new century, but Dave's record label is owned by BMG, the music arm of the German publishing giant Bertelsmann. Dunkin' Donuts is the property of Allied Domecq, a British beverage conglomerate. The diet drink Slim Fast belongs to the Dutch-British packaged goods company Unilever. Baby Ruth is made by a subsidiary of the Swiss food and candy titan, Nestlé, as are Power Bars and Alpo dog food. Snapple is owned by Britain's Cadbury-Schweppes. The Holiday Inn chain belongs to the hotel/motel holding company Six Continents, which happens to be the biggest owner of hotel rooms in the United States but is a British firm based in London. Miller Lite is one of several American beers owned by SAB Brewers, a multinational operation with headquarters in Britain. The Lucky Strike brand belongs to British-American Tobacco (a completely British company, despite the name). The Bazooka gum that Bill chews to ward off cigarette cravings is now a product of Cadbury-Schweppes, as is Betty's favorite American soda pop, A&W Root Beer.

That Helen Scully novel Betty read is published by The Penguin Press, a subsidiary of Pearson, the British firm that also publishes the *Financial Times* (not to mention the book you're reading now). But that's hardly surprising in publishing circles today; such kingpins of American fiction as Tom Clancy, John Grisham, and Philip Roth are all published by European-owned companies. The Literary Guild is part of Bertelsmann's global literary empire. The Verizon cellular phone network is an American subsidiary of the British giant Vodafone, the world's biggest operator of cellular networks. The gifts that Bill and Betty brought to the young couple in Chicago are both respected American brands that now belong to Italian owners; Ray-Ban is a branch of Luxottica, SpA, and Brooks Brothers is part of a broad network of fashionable stores owned by Italy's Retail Brand Alliance. Lean Cuisine is a Nestlé product, and Ben & Jerry's belongs to Unilever.

Right through the last day of their trip, the Yankees were consistent supporters of European-owned products. The Stop & Shop where they stopped and shopped is part of the U.S. grocery business of the Netherlands' Royal Ahold NV; Dr Pepper belongs to Cadbury Schweppes. The Travelodge motel chain is part of the portfolio of Britain's Compass hotel group. The Oscar-winning movie *A Beautiful Mind* was produced by a Hollywood subsidiary of the French media colossus Vivendi, which has also been a major operator of pay-per-view television in the United States.

It's only fitting that the Yankee family is constantly buying from European companies, because all four of the Yankees, like millions of other Americans today, are employed by European-owned firms. Niagara Mohawk is one of several American power utilities owned by Britain's National Grid. The fashion shop where Betty works, part of the thousand-unit Casual Corner chain, belongs to the same Italian firm that owns Brooks Brothers, Retail Brand Alliance. The Leo Burnett agency belongs to a French group, Publicis; Barb's client at the agency, the Dial Corporation, is a subsidiary of Germany's Henkel Group. Even a product as localized as the *Chicago Sun-Times* is owned by a holding company of the London media magnate Conrad Black (and has become a central focus of a bitter corporate battle between Lord Black and his fellow British investors).

. . .

As the Yankee family vacation suggests, an endless web of European connections is woven through corporate America today, touching consumer
products, retailing, finance, services, transport, and heavy manufacturing.
This broad pattern of European ownership reflects a tidal wave of investment sweeping across the Atlantic from Ireland, Britain, France, the
Netherlands, Belgium, Germany, Italy, Scandinavia, Spain, and, on a
smaller scale, from Eastern Europe as well. The long economic boom in
the United States and Europe of the 1990s drew hundreds of billions of
dollars from European investors into American corporations. Of course,
wealthy people around the world like to invest in American business, but
European multinational companies, banks, and investors are by far the
top source of foreign capital coming into the United States, as Commerce Department figures demonstrate year after year. For the year 2000,
Europeans provided more than 65 percent of all foreign investment in
the United States. The Europeans' strong currency has made it even easier for the Dutch, Germans, Italians, and so on to snap up American
properties; investments priced in dollars these days look extremely cheap
to an investor wielding the mighty euro on world markets.

This unprecedented crescendo in European ownership is testament to
the appeal of the American economy. But it also demonstrates the fiscal
power and the global reach of European multinationals and investment
firms. Not since the colonial era, when Britain, France, and Spain each
claimed imperial sway over segments of the broad land that would
become the United States, has so much of the American economy been
under the control of Europeans—or any other foreign interest, for that
matter. The European acquisitions are not, perhaps, well known among
the general public in America. In Europe, though, the growing roster of
familiar American products now in European hands is widely recognized, and cheered, as evidence of a phenomenon known as "L'Europe
Qui Gagne"—that is, "Europe, the Winner."

It would take most of this book to list all the "American" companies, retail chains, and brands that are actually European products today, but here's a tally of some familiar brands in European ownership:[1]

Brand	Corporation	Country
DKNY	LVMH	France
Sunglass Hut	Luxottica	Italy
Brooks Brothers	R. B. Alliance	Italy
Archway Cookies	Parmalat	Italy
Hellman's Mayonnaise	Unilever	Netherlands
Mazola Oil	ABF	U.K.
Libby's Pineapple	Nestlé	Switzerland
Hawaiian Punch	Cadbury Schweppes	U.K.
Taster's Choice coffee	Nestlé	Switzerland
Captain Morgan's Rum	Diageo	U.K.
Snapple	Cadbury Schweppes	U.K.
Random House	Bertelsmann	Germany
Kent Cigarettes	BAT	U.K.
Kool	BAT	U.K.
Viceroy	BAT	U.K.
Case Tractors	Fiat	Italy
Plymouth, Dodge, Chrysler, Jeep	DaimlerChrysler	Germany
Dove Soap	Unilever	Netherlands
Vaseline	Unilever	Netherlands
Pennzoil	Royal Dutch Shell	Netherlands
The New York Post	News Corp.	U.K.
Allfirst Bank	Allied Irish Banks	Ireland
Alex Brown (broker)	Deutsche Bank	Germany
First Boston (bank)	Credit Suisse	Switzerland
Bird's Eye frozen food	Unilever	Netherlands
Los Angeles Dodgers	News Corp.	U.K.
Armour Corned Beef Hash	Henkel	Germany

This kind of monetary clout is a classic example of "soft power" at work, and the flow goes both ways. The Europeans have clearly built up the kind of corporate empires and banking fortunes that give them the wealth to purchase major chunks of another country's retail and industrial base. But there is power on the American side, too—the power to create products and globally recognized brands that draw investors and their billions toward the United States. The result is that some of the products that seem most familiar to American consumers—from Snapple to Slim Fast to Bazooka to Ben & Jerry's—are in fact European products today. The people who design, build, advertise, and sell these products work for European companies, and their employment fate is ultimately in the hands of investors and corporate boards scattered all over the New Europe.

The two biggest institutional food companies in the United States—Britain's Compass Group and France's Sodexho—serve billions of meals to Americans every year, quite likely including the meals at your company's lunchroom or your children's school cafeteria. In 1970 an American company, Philadelphia-based Aramark, controlled the American market and was thus the biggest institutional feeder. Then the British and French moved in with hundreds of millions of investment dollars and superior management; by the beginning of the twenty-first century, both European firms have twice as much of the U.S. market as Aramark can claim.

Motown Records was bought by a French company. Britney Spears's label, Zomba, belongs to the German media giant Bertelsmann. Following the burst of food-company investments in the late 1990s—one clever industry analyst dubbed it the "European pantry raid"—such classic American treats as A&W Root Beer, Squirt, Country Time Lemonade, Welch's grape juice, RealLemon, Chicken Tonight, Dreyer's Ice Cream, and even I Can't Believe It's Not Butter are now European-owned. Quaker State Motor Oil sounds like it comes from Pennsylvania, but the company is part of the Royal Dutch Shell petroleum empire. Dozens of U.S. banks and financial firms are wholly-owned subsidiaries of

European giants like Royal Bank of Scotland, Allied Irish Banks, Credit Suisse, and Union Bank of Switzerland.

For that matter, you can't even rely on the word "America" in the brand name any more to determine if a product is American. The Radio Corporation of America (RCA) belongs to Germany's Bertelsmann. The *American Heritage Dictionary* was published by a subsidiary of the French media firm Vivendi. If you book a cruise on the SS *Pride of America*, your money will go to the owner of that huge ship, Norwegian Lines (perhaps because of the patriotic name, the Norwegians even managed to get U.S. government funding to build the *Pride*). The U.S. Shoe Corporation belongs to an Italian shoemaker. The Chef America line of frozen foods belongs to Switzerland's Nestlé. There may be nothing more American than apple pie, but Mott's Apple Pie Filling, along with Mott's apple sauce, apple juice, and so forth, are British-owned today.

Not every euro-invasion of American business has been a success story. And there has been one genuinely spectacular failure, involving a short but ambitious Frenchman whose dream of creating a global empire turned into a Wall Street Waterloo.

The hero and the villain of this cautionary tale is Jean-Marie Messier, the son of a rural accountant, who was educated (tuition-free, of course) at ENA, the civil service college that has trained most French prime ministers and presidents. In the 1980s, just as the privatization movement was building steam, he landed a job in the prestigious privatization ministry in Paris and watched with fascination as various local entrepeneurs took over state-run water companies, power utilities, and transit lines all over Europe. In 1994, when he was thirty-seven, the former civil servant talked his way into the top job at one of those privatized water companies, Generale des Eaux. Never one to underestimate himself, Messier quickly decided that running a local water company was a waste of his formidable talents. With backing from major French banks, he went on an acquisition spree, first buying up other utilities and then stretching his reach toward the high-tech world.

Messier bought telephone networks and cable TV companies and launched a start-up called Vizzavi, which was supposed to become a European version of online portals like Yahoo! or Google. At first the French government, and the business press, loved him; he was dubbed "le Napoleon du divertissement." If anything, the chorus of praise increased when the new Napoleon started aiming at the United States. His holding company, renamed Vivendi, bought the venerable New York publishing house Houghton-Mifflin. Further acquisitions included the Home Shopping Network, the Sci-Fi Network, and a chain of American theme parks. The French water company became, briefly, the owner of the U.S.A. Network. But Messier outdid even his own stellar reputation in December 2000 with his biggest adventure in *divertissement:* Vivendi spent $34 billion to buy the recording and movie operations of Universal Studios. Messier was now a kingpin of Hollywood and the pop music world. He was the boss of a hundred thousand people, including the likes of Russell Crowe, Shania Twain, and Bono. An unabashed disciple of the Jack Welch school of management—and management perquisites—the hard-charging Frenchman moved to a lavish penthouse just a few blocks from the Welch apartment in Manhattan. In classic Welch style, he managed to get his company to buy the place for him and pay all the expenses.

Even after the events of September 11, 2001, when most other media companies warned of drastic revenue cuts ahead, the newly named Vivendi Universal continued to report that all was well. It wasn't. By July 2002 the unpaid debts, the mysterious transfers, and the misleading corporate accounts had caught up with "le Napoleon." At the age of forty-seven, Messier was fired. Like his mentor, Welch, the ex-CEO negotiated a hefty golden parachute when he walked away. But eighteen months later, the American Securities and Exchange Commission, under fire at home for failing to crack down on corrupt American CEOs, cracked the whip at the Frenchman instead. The SEC forced Messier to donate his entire $20 million severance package to investors who had suffered from his failed acquisitions. And the glitzy American media empire Vivendi had accumulated came back into American hands when the board sold most of the pieces to General Electric.

Despite a few disasters like that, European investors have generally made out just fine on their U.S. properties. That success helps explain why they keep sending money across the Atlantic. But there is transatlantic investment flowing the other way as well, with American firms constantly reaching for the consumer base in wealthy European countries. Through names like McDonald's, Starbucks, and the Gap, U.S. investment is evident in virtually every European city. (You can also find Baskin-Robbins outlets all over Europe, but that "American" ice cream chain with its trademark thirty-three flavors now belongs to Britain's Allied Domecq.) The American presence is not restricted to American labels. Such familiar European car brands as Volvo, Jaguar, Aston Martin, and Land Rover are all owned by Ford Motor Co. today.

Even so, the United States is a net gainer, by hundreds of billions of dollars, from the back-and-forth investment. In 2000, according to Commerce Department figures, U.S. direct investment in Europe reached $650 billion; European investment in the U.S. was almost $900 billion. In economic terms, the big U.S. surplus in direct investment helps pay for the big U.S. deficit in international trade. The European-American Business Council says that Europeans are the top foreign investors in forty-four states, with Texas and California receiving the most funds. But every state and every major city has felt the rush of European investment money in the past decade or so.

Should Americans despair about the far-reaching spread of European ownership through the U.S. economy?

On one hand, the investment surge should be seen as a forceful compliment to the United States. If Europeans see our country as a better place to put their money than their own economies, that's a strong endorsement of the strength and promise of American ways of business. European investors themselves agree on that point. In a lovely sun-splashed office in London's snooty Mayfair neighborhood, I paid a call on Sir Ian Prosser, the natty, savvy Briton who turned an English brewing firm, Bass Ale, into the world's biggest hotel company, Six Continents. The CEO offered me a chilled ale—he gave me a choice, but of course I asked for Bass—and told me why he is pouring so much money into the U.S. market.

"Why invest in the U.S.A.? It's simple," Sir Ian said in his friendly way.

It's a great economy, and it produces great returns. It's a good place to make a return on your money, and that's what we're in business to do. It can be a countercyclical investment for a European country, because the two economies don't always move in parallel. If our European hotels are weak next year, there's a chance our American hotels will be the strong bit. Or vice versa. We are a European company, a British company, but there is no need to restrict ourselves by geography. Anyway, we learn a lot by doing business in the States. The U.S. is so competitive that we know the things we learn operating there will help us in all our other markets around the world.

If Europeans like us are keen to be in the U.S. market, that's a great thing for Americans. We bring in investment money, we create jobs, we improve neighborhoods. Believe me, our company pays a lot of property tax, a bundle, to your American states. Of course it's a tribute to the U.S. that so many European firms want to own businesses there.

What the foreign investor giveth, though, the foreign investor can take away. In the first years of the twenty-first century, more than 4 million Americans—people like our friends Bill, Betty, Bob, and Barb Yankee—worked directly for firms owned by European investors or companies. Perhaps twice as many were employed in support jobs surrounding those companies—for example, the miners and railway employees delivering coal to the power plants run by National Grid's Niagara Mohawk subsidiary. It's great to have those jobs, but some economists worry when millions of American jobs are dependent on decisions made in foreign boardrooms. As we'll see in the next chapter, it is hard—often impossible—for a European company to reduce payroll costs in countries like France, Italy, and the Netherlands, which make most layoffs illegal. A European company facing a slowdown might well find it easier to cut jobs at the American branch in order to reduce costs. Indeed, that's what happened when the British beer-and-whisky company Diageo got in financial trouble; at the annual meeting, the Diageo brass told stockholders that it would generate savings by shutting down hundreds of outlets of its big American subsidiary, Burger King. That meant thousands of American jobs were lost to shore up the bottom line of a British company. (Diageo subsequently sold Burger King to a consortium of American investors.)

Beyond that, the U.S. economy has become dependent on the steady flow of transatlantic investment to offset its own spendthrift ways. With a balance-of-payments deficit approaching $500 billion annually—which is to say, Americans import about $40 billion per month more in goods and services than they can export—the United States needs the foreign investment income to bring those dollars home. In essence, the U.S. economy is like an addict that needs a sizable fix every day. So far, the rest of the world—and primarily Europe—has been willing to feed America's addiction by injecting billions of dollars of investment into the economy each year. But there is, of course, always the risk that the flow could slow, or dry up completely.

There was a lot of fear along these lines, and orating, and anger, at the end of the 1980s, when Japanese companies made a series of high-profile purchases in America—not only "trophy properties" like the Rockefeller Center in New York and California's Pebble Beach golf course, but also famous corporations like Firestone and 7-Eleven. There was concern that corporate America was selling off the crown jewels. There was endless speculation along the lines that the Japanese would surely lay off their American employees before they would harm a Japanese worker back home. When Sony purchased Columbia Pictures, for example, the *Newsweek* cover story showed the Statue of Liberty wearing a kimono, under the headline "Japan Invades Hollywood." Members of Congress demanded federal investigations to study the extent of Japanese encroachment into the American economy.

But the huge recent wave of European investment has spawned little or no adverse reaction among Americans. Maybe this is because Americans are more aware than they were fifteen years ago that it is beneficial for any nation—and particularly a country with a massive balance of trade deficit—to take in foreign investment. Maybe Americans now realize that the money pouring in is creating factories and stores and jobs. Or perhaps Americans are more comfortable with foreign ownership today than they were fifteen years ago because the current investment surge is coming from blue-eyed, Judeo-Christian Europeans and not from East Asia. (That's certainly the standard view in China and Japan, where it is simply taken for granted that Americans are too racist to be comfortable when an Asian buys the company they work for.) Or maybe most Americans just don't know how much of their daily commerce is done with European-owned firms.

The wealth and the spirit of enterprise that are pushing the European investment in American business reflect a transformation of the business climate that has made the New Europe a key player in the new high-tech economy. You can see and feel this palpable change in any number of university towns—Cambridge, England, or Lund, Sweden, or Tampere, Finland, or Brussels or Munich or Milan—where medieval campuses are finding room for new research laboratories in computing, communication, and biotechnology. Cambridge is Britain's capital of venture capital, with aggressive young bankers searching the continent for innovative start-up companies to support. Munich has a sprawling new neighborhood of biotech start-ups; Geneva, Milan, and Tampere are software centers. Helsinki launched the programmer Linus Torvald and his Linux operating system, the most successful competitor anywhere to Microsoft's Windows. Southern France boasts proudly of its "arc of innovation," stretching from Airbus Industrie's massive airframe assembly plants just outside Toulouse to the microchip fabrication labs at Sophia Antipolis, near Nice. There is so much technological innovation going forward in the sunny region south of the Alps that a crescent of Europe stretching from southern Germany and Austria through the top of Italy and into southern France and Switzerland reports the highest per capita income in the world.

For all its devotion to governmental programs and the welfare state, Europe stands ahead of the United States in the drive to privatize traditionally governmental operations. Passenger rail service, still the province of taxpayer-funded Amtrak in the United States, has been turned over to private companies in most of Europe. Some countries are handing over air traffic control and tax collection to the private sector. There is more competition, and better service, among mobile phone companies in most European countries than in the United States. Applications filed with the pan-European patent office have increased about 75 percent since the start of the century. The number of PhDs in leading-edge technical areas has increased at roughly the same rate. In several important consumer areas—wireless communications, smart cards (as an option to cash or credit cards), interactive television, and automated vending—Europe is already well ahead of the United States. In several state-of-the-art markets, from cell phones to giant new passenger jetliners, the most innovative new products are coming out of Europe now. In every western European country, there are more mobile phones per capita than in the United States.

In a sense, it should be no surprise that a high-tech, online, state-of-the-art economy would blossom, and indeed thrive, in Europe. The World Wide Web, after all, was invented in Geneva. As Harvard Business School professor Michael Porter has written, European students come out of secondary school considerably better prepared than their American counterparts in mathematics, chemistry, physics, and biology. Europe's top universities stand roughly equal with America's best in these technological fields. Connections between particular industries and particular universities are often stronger than anything seen in America; at Tampere, the engineering labs are essentially an extension of Nokia's research and development arm. Europe's pool of engineers with advanced degrees has been growing for a decade, while the American figure is basically flat. Europeans cloned Dolly the sheep. Europeans invented Viagra. "The mystery is why, with all those strengths, Europe has fallen so short of the U.S.," Porter noted. "It comes down to too much government intrusion, and ambivalence toward the capitalist system." But now, the professor says, that ambivalence is disappearing. Europe is determined to be a technologically advanced capitalistic economy at least equal to the United States.

The unification of Europe has played a key role in the continent's corporate renaissance. The emergence of a borderless, tariff-free supranational state with uncontrolled movement of goods, services, and workers has given European companies a home market that is bigger and richer than the United States. The single currency makes formerly complicated sales transactions more efficient. Mario Monti's hard-charging Directorate-General for Competition has imposed a strict discipline designed to keep markets and companies honest. The uniform regulatory apparatus across twenty-five national markets has permitted development of uniform sizes, packaging, and technical standards that mean a product designed for one corner of Europe will work for the entire continent, and its half-billion consumers. Many successful European entrepeneurs have said that the emergence of a new, united Europe was a key element of their corporate success stories.

Perhaps the greatest industrial success to emerge from the integration of Europe's markets is the cellular phone (or mobile phone, or "handy phone," as it is generally known in Europe). Three different European companies—Finland's Nokia, Sweden's Ericsson, and Germany's Siemens—came from far behind in the past decade to match or pass the American giant Motorola in market share for mobile telephones. And a British consortium, Vodafone, has emerged as the world's largest cellular network. This did not happen because European wireless engineers are more inventive than Americans, or because Finnish, German, and British telecommunications executives are better managers. Rather, Europe's rise to the top in mobile phones was a direct result of the pancontinental push for uniform technical and commercial standards. The European Council, the EU's cabinet, declared a formal policy in 1987 to create "a common network that will allow European users on the move to communicate efficiently and economically from any spot on the continent." At the same time, the United States was moving in the opposite direction, vigorously embracing telecom deregulation, so that every cell phone network could and did develop its own standard. By the mid-1990s the United States was scrambling to reverse policy and switch to the European approach. Europe's uniform standard had proven to be the smarter policy.

I got a lesson in the commercial value of common technical standards when I visited the world headquarters of Nokia, in the Helsinki suburb of Espoo. Nokia's chief technology officer, Yrjo ("It's Finnish for George," he said) Neuvo, told me how it came to be that all European mobile phones are built to meet the same technical standard, known as the GSM standard. "We have to go back to the first days of mobiles, when a wireless telephone was almost a small suitcase that you had to haul around in the trunk of a car," George began. "And just like the United States, the European companies were each experimenting with their own networks, their own standards. You couldn't really use your German phone to call the U.K. Then, in 1982, we needed to switch from analog networks to digital. Nobody really knew which digital approach would be ideal, and there was some feeling that we should do the same thing as the U.S. companies—create five or six different digitial standards, let them all operate independently, and see which one worked best. In fact, we didn't go that route, and that was lucky.

"The thing is, something was in the air. This idea of Europeanization, of building a common Europe, was moving forward in many areas: joint research projects, joint business ventures, the European court, the economic union, that sort of thing. So we said, 'Yes, let's do the same thing in mobiles. Let's make one telephone standard for all of Europe.' And we did. We just phased out all the different national standards and went to one Europe-wide system. Our group of engineers that created the system was called the Groupe Special Mobile, so we took that name, GSM, for the standard itself."

With a brand-new Nokia phone in his hand, the prime minister of Finland made the first GSM call on July 1, 1991. The system worked well; far more important, it worked everywhere—or at least, everywhere in Europe. The borderless phone system prompted more and more people to try cellular phones, and the numbers snowballed. Access to a telephone connection was officially declared to be a basic human right for all Europeans in 1993, a part of the comfortable European welfare state. Since then, European nations have had considerably larger rates of "penetration"—that is, the percentage of a population using cell phones—than any other part of the world. Many European nations today have more mobile phones than land lines. Some have more mobile phones than people. (This is explained by people like "George" Neuvo, who keeps one cell phone in his pocket, another in his car, and a third at home.) Europeans today can use "handy phones" to buy a Pepsi from the vending machine, to bet on a number in the lottery, to find out how many more minutes before the city bus gets to their stop. The GSM standard has been adopted by about fifty countries outside of Europe; the name, accordingly, was changed to "Global System for Mobiles."

All of which created a massive market for the likes of Nokia—a market where American telephone companies could not compete. Well into the 1990s, mighty Motorola led the world year after year in market share for cellular phones; by the turn of the century the Europeans, with their GSM technology, had sprinted ahead of the American leader. Nokia became the world's leading maker of handheld telephones and mobile telephone equipment. "The Americans made a commitment to deregulation," George said. "We Europeans went the other way, toward a common system, because the mindset was that all Europe should be connected."

For a smart business leader the unified European market for mobile communications was an opportunity just waiting to be taken. And Jorma Ollila grabbed it.

Mr. Ollila, a Finn who took a graduate degree at the London School of Economics and worked for a while as a banker in the city of London, was thirty-five years old when he went home to Helsinki in 1985 for a middle-management job at Nokia. Even then, Nokia was an important presence in Finnish industry, but it was a totally different company from the technology powerhouse we see today. The remnants of the old Nokia are still abundantly evident in Finland. You only need a brief walk around the glitzy shopping district in central Helsinki to see how Ollila and a small group of technology-minded managers—the men who leaped past the world's technological giants in the booming cellular-phone market—started with an obscure company from the forests of Finland. At the Esso station on the corner, there's a stack of snow tires on sale, each one emblazoned with the trademark "Nokia." A couple of blocks away, on the sporting-goods floor of the huge Stockmann's department store, there's a display of fishing boots. The trademark? Nokia. At a computer store across the street, you can buy a color monitor with that same label.

In fact, though, these products are no longer made by Nokia Oy ("oy" is Finnish for "corporation"). The former conglomerate has spent the past decade spinning off dozens of its traditional businesses to focus relentlessly on mobile communications. In an age of merger and acquisition, Nokia opted for attrition—and this unfashionable strategy has paid off handsomely. By moving faster than Motorola into digital networks and wireless Internet access, Nokia increased its lead year after year. By 2004, it was selling a third of all the cell phones in use around the world—double the market share of any competitor. Nokia sells 9 millon handsets a week, with more sales in the United States and China than in Europe.

When I went to visit Mr. Ollila, an intense but friendly man who seems to be curious about every line of business—he quizzed me fairly diligently about how my newspaper makes its income—he said that concentration on the thing it does best is the key to Nokia's global success. Although it was "extremely painful" to get rid of well-established, and profitable, business lines, he explained, "you could see in the 1980s that a great business was opening up. The single wireless communications standard would make all of Europe basically one market. And we hoped that if we could succeed in that market, we could take the European standard around the world." With a wry smile, Ollila admitted that "retired Nokia people tell me that I'm unholy, I'm a traitor, for selling off the fishing boots and the pulp and paper and the PCs. But we are now in one of the fastest-growing and fastest-changing markets in the world. To play that game, you have to be completely focused on what the market wants." Whatever the retirees may say, Nokia's long-term stockholders should be happy. Sales have been growing at about 20 percent annually over the past decade, and Nokia sailed fairly smoothly through the wireless crunch at the start of the century. When Ollila went to Nokia, at a time when the company was still selling tires, tissue paper, televisions, heavy machinery, and the like, its total sales were slightly over $2 billion per year. In 2002, as Ollila celebrated his tenth year as CEO, sales were well over $30 billion annually.

When Nokia started out, as a one-shack operation on the banks of the Nokia River in Tampere in 1865, it focused on timber. Fairly quickly, though, the company branched out: pulp and paper, rubber products—including Finland's favorite fishing boot—wire, radios, and eventually televisions and computers. For Finns, Nokia was a combination Kimberly-Clark, L. L. Bean, and General Electric. In the 1980s the conglomerate dabbled a little in communications products, including an early "mobile phone" that weighed twenty pounds and was mobile only if you hauled it around in the trunk of your car. In 1984 the company started making telephones for the Texas-based Radio Shack. (Fort Worth has been the heart of Nokia's U.S. operations ever since, although it has opened a large corporate office in New York for financial operations.) The breakup of the neighboring Soviet Union and the ensuing recession in Russia took a devastating toll on Finland's economy. Nokia suffered along with everybody else here. In 1992, when Ollila, then forty-one, was made the boss, the company was struggling in many of its basic lines.

"We realized that the key to recovery was to find something that took advantage of our know-how and gave us global, not just local, growth opportunities," Ollila recalls. "And the more we moved into mobile phones and the infrastructure for mobile networks, we understood that we had to concentrate almost completely on that business. It was very, very hard to sell the pulp and paper business, and the rubber products, because that was what Nokia had been about since the 19th century." Because the brand was so strong in Finland and Russia, Nokia licensed rights to other companies to use its name on tires, TVs, and a few other products. Gradually, though, the trademark will disappear from noncommunications products.

The company's phenomenal success has been a major tonic for Finland's national economy, which battled back from a killer recession sparked by the collapse of the Soviet Union at the start of the 1990s. In standard European fashion, the government set industrial goals for the nation, and strongly encouraged Nokia's shift toward technology. Focusing in on a few hallmark technologies was also a governmental priority. Finland's prime minister for much of the decade, Paavo Lipponen, explained the strategy plainly: "If you're a country of 5 million on a northern peninsula speaking a language that nobody else understands, you'd better concentrate on doing just a few things and doing them very well." The interplay between Lipponen's government and Ollila's company met the national need. "We badly needed a third leg, after forest products and metals, to support our economy," the precise, scholarly prime minister said. "And now we have it in communications."

Lipponen's government also helped out by deregulating the telephone business. Today Finland has one of the most competitive, and cheapest, telephone markets in the developed world. This has helped Finnish telephone customers embrace the new era of wireless telephony much faster than supposedly high-tech Americans. Finland reached a "penetration rate"—that is, the share of the population owning mobile phones—of 100 percent by the turn of the century, when the American rate was still below 60 percent. Finland was the first country—but will hardly be the last—to have more mobile phones than traditional land-line units.

To house a corporation that has had a dramatic impact on world communications, Ollila oversaw the creation of a dramatic new world headquarters on an inlet of Helsinki Bay in Espoo, Finland, a few minutes by car (or an hour by kayak) from downtown Helsinki. Nokia's managers have spent decades creating a workplace that feels like a laboratory or a college campus, and the Finnish architect Pekka Helin's building is a key element of that feeling. The starkly modern headquarters rises from a sun-splashed blue inlet of Helsinki Bay, and looks more like a greenhouse than an office building. Some Nokia employees come to work by kayak across the bay; in the long Finnish winter, they commute on ice skates. On a little thumb of land jutting out from the building, Nokia has set its corporate sauna, open to workers from the executive suites to the kitchen help. Along with these comforts on the job, Nokia of course provides the full range of European-style benefits, holidays, and pensions to its 35,000 European employees. Like other business leaders everywhere, Ollila regularly complains about high taxes—and in Finland, that leaves a lot of room for complaint—but he says the virtues of a European business style have been key to Nokia's success. "We work in partnership with our government here. Our technical people work as close partners of the regulators in Brussels. And we want the people who work at Nokia to feel we all are partners, not bosses and employees. Perhaps that is a European way of thinking, but for us, it works."

If Nokia became a world leader by building products that fit in a pocket, another corporate offspring of the European unification, Airbus Industrie, is now building a product so big it won't even fit at most airports. Europe's builder of commercial jetliners has essentially bet its future on the biggest passenger plane ever built, the new A380. This behemoth of the air will hold more than 550 seats (up to 600, in fact, on charter airlines that don't mind squeezing their customers sardine-style) arranged on two decks both running the full length of the fuselage, with elevators, restaurants, and movie theaters inside the plane. The plane is so big that Airbus has agreed to help fund the enlargement of airports around the world so that they can handle A380 operations. At most airports, the new plane will stretch over three boarding gates, and passengers will be distributed among the three in the hope that the giant jet can be loaded and unloaded as fast as normal aircraft.

Even before the first A380 was to take off, though, Airbus had completed a formidable achievement in the commercial jet business. Final figures for the year 2003 showed that Airbus delivered just over 300 planes to its airline customers; Boeing delivered about 280 in the same year. For the first time, Airbus had passed its American competitor to lead the world in market share. At the beginning of 2004, Airbus had an order backlog of 1,500 planes, about 25 percent more than Boeing. It was a remarkable business turnabout. Boeing had been the world leader in commercial aircraft sales for more than thirty years. In the last year of the twentieth century, Boeing delivered twice as many jets as Airbus. Four years later, it was in second place and struggling to catch up.

The arrival at Number 1 was duly celebrated at Airbus's drab, relentlessly industrial headquarters beside an oversize hangar at the Toulouse Airport in the sunny south of France. By surpassing Boeing, the European plane maker had done precisely what it was created to do. For Airbus is the corporate embodiment of a basic EU philosophy: the counterweight theory. Just as many Europeans hope to see the EU stand on the world stage as an equal counterweight to the American superpower, Airbus was designed specifically to provide a counterweight to Boeing in the international market for commercial jets.

Airbus Industrie was begun in 1967 as a somewhat awkward shotgun marriage of four struggling European aircraft makers in Britain, German, France, and Spain. Nobody knew if the plane maker would ever turn a profit, but that wasn't the primary goal anyway. In welfare-minded Europe, the idea was to save the European air frame business, and the tens of thousands of manufacturing jobs it provides. In addition, it was hoped that a European plane builder could give national airlines— so-called flag carriers like British Air, Air France, Lufthansa, KLM, and Iberia—some relief from Boeing's monopoly pricing of large passenger jets. Finally, the combined aircraft company was seen as another link in the chain of a new, unified European economy—just like the European Coal and Steel Community after World War II.

With no prospect of a quick profit, the company was organized on a peculiarly European model. It began life as a *groupement d'intérêt economique,* a corporation with limited stockholders—in this case, just three: France, Germany, and Britain—that exists primarily for reasons other than paying dividends to its investors. In standard British fashion, a Conservative government in London subsequently had second thoughts about being involved in this EU operation and cut back the British share from 33 to 20 percent—a decision that would prove eventually to be a huge financial blunder, when Airbus started running up large yearly profits. Some thirty years after its birth, with the business firmly established, the corporate structure was changed. Today Airbus is owned by two private corporations—80 percent by the European Aeronautic, Defense, & Space Corporation (EADS), and 20 percent by British Aerospace, Ltd. It is not only a profitable business but such a successful counterweight to American industrial power that the new, unified Europe has become the global leader in jetliner production.

Airbus probably would not have succeeded if it had stuck to its original market niche, supplying the big flag carriers. Following the general trend of state-owned business in Europe, all of those airlines have since been privatized; some are defunct today, and others are struggling. Instead, Airbus went looking for new customers, and sold its planes all over the world; when a big American carrier, Eastern Airlines, placed a multi-jet order with Airbus in 1978, Airbus proudly touted the deal as a certificate of quality on Boeing's home turf. The European maker found an important new niche in the wave of low-cost airlines, particularly in Europe, that took off in the 1990s. A key element of the business plan for these no-frills carriers is to use only one model of jet; this system saves money on training, maintenance, and parts. Airbus figured out the new airlines' strategy faster than Boeing, and offered cut-rate prices to the cut-rate airlines when they started operations. By getting in first, Airbus essentially guaranteed that the new airlines would buy the same Airbus model over and over again when their fleets increased. As budget carriers like RyanAir and EZJet in Europe and JetBlue in the United States grew like crazy, Boeing could only sit aside and look on as its competitor rang up the sales.

Another key to the success of Airbus was a series of deliberately non-Boeing design decisions. The deliberately mundane name "Airbus" was chosen specifically to suggest a reliable, no-nonsense means of mass transportation. It was an airborne version of the business model perfected by Volkswagen (another plain-Jane name that means "the people's cart"). While Boeing pushed flash and dash, Airbus chose to build rather clunky but dependable flying buses with wide bodies (to fit more seats) and a standard cockpit that could be bolted onto any model. With the long-haul, transoceanic market in mind, Airbus worked hard to build planes that were more economical than Boeing's better-known models. Most important, the European company poured much more money into research and design than did Boeing. In the decade or so before it passed Boeing in world market share, Airbus routinely spent about 8 to 9 percent of annual revenue on research and development; Boeing was spending at about half that rate. While Boeing was building planes in factories that dated back to World War II, Airbus poured large sums into new, modernized production facilities around the continent, with final assembly centered at the massive complex in Toulouse.

When the European upstart began to emerge as a serious competitor, Boeing executives complained loudly that Airbus was essentially an EU welfare project, kept alive by massive government loans and subsidies. This was true. A U.S. government study in 1990 showed that Airbus had received outright payments of about $13 billion from various European governments since its founding, and another $26 billion in loans. The Europeans could hardly deny that national governments and the EU itself had propped up Airbus in its early decades; indeed, Europe is proud of it. The pattern of governmental support for European firms competing in global markets is a hallmark of EU operations, one of the key strategies Brussels is using to further the industrial counterweight campaign. Even a national champion like Boeing could not keep up with a competitor that was skillfully riding the wave of European unification.

Even though its complaints were accurate, however, Boeing was hardly a sympathetic figure when it came to griping about government handouts. The U.S. champion has received billions of dollars of its own in research grants, tax breaks, and noncompetitive contracts from Washington. It has been a major beneficiary of the Buy American Act, a federal law that requires the world's largest government to buy all its aircraft from a domestic source—i.e., Boeing. The flow of government money increased significantly after Boeing's merger with military plane builder McDonnell-Douglas brought in tens of billions of dollars worth of Pentagon contracts each year. In the same week that global 2003 sales totals were reported, with Boeing falling behind its European competitor for the first time, federal prosecutors in the United States announced a probe into private deals that Boeing allegedly made with a senior Pentagon purchasing official.

For Airbus, the government subsidies have decreased now that the company seems to be operating in the black. On the A380 project, Airbus itself and its subcontractors are putting up about three-quarters of the 10-billion-euro development cost, with Brussels and national governments supplying the rest. To keep its political support, Airbus has adroitly parceled out A380 fabrication work across the continent. This makes construction of the big jetliner one of the most complicated logistics operations since D-day.

The new plane's wings, nearly twice as large as any aircraft wing ever made before, are assembled in Wales. They travel by barge to Bristol, England, where the wheel assemblies are attached. This gargantuan hunk is then shipped by specially built tankers across the English Channel, barged up the Garonne River (clearing an ancient bridge with less than six inches to spare on each side), and then trucked to Toulouse. In a factory that stretches more than a quarter-mile, the wing structure is attached to the fuselage. Jet engines shipped in by cargo plane from Britain and Germany will then be attached. At that point, the bare airframe will be flown to another Airbus factory in Hamburg, where the seats will be installed and one of those interchangeable Airbus cockpits dropped into place. Then the plane is flown back to Toulouse for final preparation. By the time the first A380 is ready for delivery—Singapore Airlines, the first customer to sign up, promised to start transpacific A380 service in 2005—nearly all of the company's 48,000 employees in a dozen European countries will have played a role in its construction.

All this investment in a huge new model is a daring move, unmatched in the industry since Boeing bet the company on the 747 in the 1960s. The expenses of designing the A380, and creating the elaborate production facilities needed to build it, have been so high that Airbus won't make any profit until it sells the 250th plane. But the gamble seems likely to pay off. Two years before the first plane was to be delivered, Airbus had contracts for more than half that break-even number, a good omen for a new model in the aircraft business. The corporation's no-nonsense French CEO, Noel Forgeard, predicts sales of 400 or more A380s in the first decade of the new century. At the London Air Show, as his company settled into its reign as the world's leading supplier, Forgeard was optimistic: "We think Europe is going to be the center of aircraft innovation for a long time to come."

Even start-up businesses that don't receive loans or handouts from Brussels are benefiting from the economic integration of the European continent, and the risk-taking spirit it has inspired. "The EU just makes it easier to start a business," explained Dietrich Mateschitz, a man who ought to know. "The general mood is open to innovation. There is investment capital available. And when you have a product, you don't need to talk to two dozen different Food Ministries or Health Ministries to get it approved. This is all integrated now. Do you see the genius here? This means a business can get to consumers all over Europe, half a billion of them, without worrying about borders or currency problems or national approvals."

Dietrich Mateschitz ought to know all that because he started one of those thriving European businesses. Along the way, he placed a whole new product category on the supermarket shelf, added a new cocktail to bar menus all over the world, created tens of thousands of jobs, spawned hundreds of competitors, and made himself a billionaire, all within fifteen years. A big man with a big smile that beams out from his stubble of white beard, Mateschitz describes himself as "comfortable with risk," whether he is climbing a rocky cliff or helicopter skiing or mountain biking an impossibly steep trail in the Alps—or doing business. And this intensely confident Austrian ought to be comfortable with risk, because the biggest career risk he ever took paid off in spectacular fashion.

In the 1980s, Herr Mateschitz was a marketing man for a German pharmaceutical company, selling a toothpaste called Blen-dax in East Asia. The job involved countless overnight flights from Frankfurt to cities like Tokyo, Bangkok, and Beijing, and the corresponding jet lag, which Mateschitz came to despise. He was a salesman, after all; he needed to be at his peak of energy and enthusiasm to do his job right. But the long flights left him drained and worn for the first two or three days of each trip. He began to notice that taxi drivers in most big Asian cities were regularly sipping from small bottles of tonic. After one particularly exhausting flight, he asked the cabdriver to share the tonic. "Jet lag was gone," he recalls. "Suddenly, I felt so awake." Relating the story to me nearly two decades later, he still remembered the sheer excitement, the genuine passion, of that moment of discovery. "I found these drinks all over Asia, and there were huge markets for them. In the drugstores, there were racks and racks full of these bottles. I started thinking: Why doesn't the West have this product?"

In 1984, at the age of forty, Mateschitz quit his job with Blen-dax and poured all his savings into an energy drink. He started with the formula for a drink sold in Thailand under the name Kating Deng, which means "red water buffalo." Mateschitz tinkered with the name a little—he chose "Red Bull"—as well as the formula, the flavoring, the packaging, the message. Like the Asian tonics that had caught his attention, the product was a combination of stimulants: caffeine, an amino acid called taurine, and a sugar, glucuronolactone. In 1987, using his native Austria as a test market, Mateschitz put the sleek silver, red, and blue cans of Red Bull on sale. The label called it "a stimulant for body and mind." At first, stores didn't know what to do with a product sold as an "energy drink." There was no such product, and thus no market for it. But Mateschitz the marketing man solved that problem. "You don't drink Red Bull. You use it," the advertisements said. "You've got better things to do than sleep." "Red Bull gives you wings." Red Bull became a high-profile sponsor of continental sporting events, ranging from Formula One racing to the European "Flugtag" championships (that is, human-powered airplanes) and the national *Seifenkistenrennen,* Germany's version of the soapbox derby.

As Mateschitz had foreseen, there was a natural market all over united Europe for this new "smart drink": Generation E. The educated, borderless, vigorous, and fairly well-off members of Europe's youth culture spent long days on the ski slope or the running track and long nights at the downtown clubs, dancing and drinking until dawn. Accordingly, Mateschitz took Red Bull not only to sporting goods stores but also to the clubs and bars where Generation E hung out. By the mid-1990s, the drink of choice among Europe's clubbing set was the Vodka Bull, a half-can of Red Bull mixed with vodka. (You can also buy a Chambull, which is Red Bull with champagne, or a Bullmeister, which is Red Bull with the German liqueur Jagermeister, or a Bulgarita, which is Red Bull with tequila.) "Red Bull gives you wings any time, even in a night club," the company advertised. "Adding alcohol does not change Red Bull's properties." For young people starting to drag a little at 4:00 a.m. on the dance floor, the stimulant was precisely the needed thing.

With sales skyrocketing in Europe, Red Bull stormed into the United States in 1997, promoting a series of extreme sporting events and hiring the most popular man and woman on a college campus to serve as "Red Bull advocates." By the early twenty-first century, the company was selling more than a billion cans a year. The "energy drink" became an established category in the beverage business. The giants of the industry, including Coca-Cola and Pepsi, joined the parade that Herr Mateschitz had started. Well over 150 competing beverages came out—products that just happened to carry names like "Red Fox" and "Raging Lion" and "Wild Bull," and are often made with the same three stimulants Red Bull offers. Mateschitz belittles these "copycat" products, and with good reason: Red Bull's sales just keep expanding. In 2003, when Dietrich Mateschitz built a new corporate office building, he asked the architect to create a structure in the form of two erupting volcanoes, to reflect the product's explosive rate of sales growth.

Mateschitz placed the new headquarters of Red Bull GmbH in a breathtaking corner of the Austrian Alps beside a blue jewel of a mountain lake called the Fuschlzee. It is modern, dramatic, and ostentatiously casual. Young staffers in jeans and tank tops race across the marble floors with thick folders in their hands; a large black dog sleeps under the skylight outside the CEO's office. Herr Mateschitz himself follows the code, wearing checked shirts and jeans to work and joining in the beach volleyball games on the lakefront with his youthful junior executives. "We could have put our headquarters anywhere, so why not pick a place of extreme natural beauty?" he said, stretching an arm toward the glorious sun-washed peaks of the Salzkammergut, just outside his window. "Fuschl was just right for us. We can climb here, and ski, and ride our bikes around the lakes. And I can keep my planes at the Salzburg airport, only an hour away."

All of which makes Dietrich Mateschitz something of a type—the hardworking, hard-playing corporate founder who made himself a quick billion with a good idea and good marketing skills. To Americans, he is a type who might seem more at home on Wall Street or Silicon Valley than in a the mountains of central Austria. Mateschitz bristles at this suggestion. "Everyone is wondering that an Austrian got this idea first," he says, in his excellent but accented English. "This kind of thing, the start-up business, the global success, this seems so American, so Californian. That's what they are always saying. And I reply: Please do not forget that Europe, too, has its entrepreneurs. Do not forget that Europe is changing, that we have an entire continent now as our test market. Yes, Europe, too, has its innovators. And the Americans, with their copycat products, cannot stop us anymore."

The competition between the United States of Europe and the United States of America is particularly intense when you leave the planet and head to the realm of outer space. The EU, and some nonunion European nations, have funded the second-biggest space operation on earth. Given the ambitious goals of the European Space Agency (ESA), and the cost-cutting at NASA as the U.S. government fell deeply into debt at the start of the new century, the Europeans could be right when they say that the ESA will be the world's dominant space explorer in another decade or two.

The ESA has broad support across the continent. This is partly a throwback to the great European tradition of exploration that launched the age of empire six centuries ago. The space agency is popular as well because the opportunity to outshine the United States is a tempting prospect for many Europeans, and because the politicians running the agency have cleverly spread its multibillion-euro pork-barrel spending in a wide swath. The organization is headquartered in Paris, but it also runs a research and technology center (ESTEC) in the Netherlands, an operations center (ESOC) in Darmstadt, Germany, an astronaut university (EAC) in Cologne, a research center (ESRIN) in Italy, and banks of radio telescopes in England. Its rockets—primarily the Ariane-5 booster, the European heavy lifter that now dominates the global market in commercial satellite launches—blast off from a launch pad in French Guiana, one of the few remaining European colonies, on the northeast corner of South America.

Perhaps because of that zeal for surpassing American achievements, ESA has largely skipped exploration of the moon and aimed further out into the solar system—specifically, at Mars. On that far planet—about a year's travel, one-way, for the most powerful spaceship—ESA plans to top NASA. A European robot probe landed on Mars on Christmas Day of 2003. By 2011, the Europeans plan to send a sampling robot to the red planet to dig up some Martian soil and bring it back to Europe for analysis. (The United States also has robot explorers on Mars, sending back a flood of scientific data and spectacular pictures, but the American robots are not equipped to transport physical samples to Earth.) In the spirit of scientific partnership—or perhaps just to rub it in—the Europeans have thoughtfully offered to share some of the recovered Martian mud with American researchers. Sometime during the time period 2025 to 2033, the schedule says, a team of European astronauts will become the first men from Earth to land on Mars. (At which point they will presumably turn toward the camera, flick their thumbnails in their teeth, and say "Take that, NASA!")

ESA has launched some 200 satellites for various purposes; in addition to the Mars orbiter, there is a solar orbiter ("Ulysses"), a weather-predicting satellite ("Meteosat"), and a series of polar-orbiting satellites measuring environmental change, oil spills, and other pollution hazards ("Envistat"). For the most part, American scientists have cooperated with the Euro-satellite programs, and drawn useful data from them. But one ESA satellite project has been designed specifically to challenge American space supremacy—and has drawn an angry response from the Americans. That is "Galileo," a belt of thirty navigational and positioning satellites that will offer an improved version of the American GPS—or Global Positioning System—that is used all over the world.

The GPS system was developed by the Pentagon to help American military units find themselves anywhere on Earth; by tracking locations from a space satellite, a GPS reading can provide a much more reliable and faster geographic fix than any previous navigational method. The United States has provided a limited version of the GPS signal free to the entire world, prompting thousands of applications, from commercial jet-liners and huge oil tankers to the navigational screens in private cars and the wristwatch receivers that keep hikers from getting seriously lost in the woods. But GPS has its shortcomings, technical and political. The technical difficulty is that GPS—or at least, the public version that the Pentagon makes available for general use—is not precise enough for many applications. It is not useful for air traffic control, and it can't generally pinpoint a location closer than a few hundred feet. The United States has promised to improve resolution, but not until 2012 at the earliest. And GPS is not politically palatable to many potential users because it is a military project at heart; its signal is controlled by the Pentagon, a despised institution in much of the world.

Galileo's locational signal, called the Public Regulated Service, or PRS, has been designed to trump the American effort, offering resolution precise enough to find a bicycle, a well (oil or water), a school of fish in the vast sea, or a traffic jam on the expressway ahead. For military purposes, the system could spot a small nest of land mines or an approaching tank in time to warn nearby troops. The PRS service is scheduled to start testing in 2006, and reach full operational status by 2008. That provides Galileo a four-year monopoly on the improved technology before Americans can catch up; the European hope is that manufacturers and users of GPS devices today will switch to PRS service, and then people won't want to switch back to the American offering in 2012. Beyond that, the ESA plans to charge users for Galileo information, which is supposed to make the 4-billion-euro system a profit center for the EU.

The technical and political arguments against America's GPS and in favor of Europe's Galileo have been so convincing that China has agreed—in the face of tough American lobbying—to invest a quarter of a billion euros in the Galileo project. Israel and India, two close U.S. allies in most theaters, have also asked to become partners in the European system. The EU, the European Space Agency, and private European companies are already signing up future customers around the world.

The Pentagon has battled furiously, both in direct negotiations and in international conferences, to stave off the competition from Galileo. At one point, the U.S. tried to use its muscle on the International Telecommunications Union (ITU) to block the radio frequency Galileo wants to use. Since the Europeans and their business partners control more votes in the ITU than the United States does, Europe had more muscle, and the American effort basically failed. (The Europeans did agree that the

U.S. military can intrude on the PRS radio signal if it appears that a battlefield enemy is using the European system to spot Americans.) As Jack Welch learned, Europe usually fights back hard when the U.S. government seeks to reverse EU endeavors; accordingly, the Europeans are now treating the Galileo dispute as an elemental matter of sovereignty. Even Carl Bild, a former Swedish prime minister, a conservative (by Swedish standards, at least), and a man hardly known for strident anti-Americanism, sees it this way: "Galileo represents a litmus test for the EU in many ways. If Europe truly wishes to be taken seriously as a partner by the U.S. . . . it must demonstrate that it has both the will and the means to develop a presence in space."

Both on Earth and off it, the New Europe—*L'Europe qui gagne*—is pushing hard to be a partner and competitor of the United States. The United States of Europe, with its single currency and its common business regulations and its growing spirit of enterprise, is determined to win in international business battles. U.S. business executives are learning—as Jack Welch learned the hard way—that Europe is serious about competition on the world stage. American business leaders will have to respond in kind, bringing their own innovative skills and marketing talents to the global market.

Or perhaps an American might just want to sit back and try to ignore what's happening. We could head out to a bar and drown our worries. For this purpose, of course, we would hardly want to indulge in some European cocktail—no bottled French water, no Scotch, no Vodka Bull. The idea would be to settle in with a classic, born-and-bred American drink. Perhaps something like the trusty old Seven and Seven. Of course, this escape might not be a completely satisfying response nowadays. The fact is, both parts of that familiar American cocktail come from European companies now: Seagram's Seven Crown belongs to Diageo, the British beer and liquor firm, and 7Up is one of the flagship brands of Cadbury Schweppes.

SIX

The European Social Model

From the day our American family moved to London, we found a lot to love in Britain. The grand old palaces, the stunning new architecture in the big cities, the rolling rural downland, the lush green parks, the cheery village pubs, the charming street markets, the sweet voices of the boy choirs (and, more recently, girl choirs) in the majestic cathedrals, the roomy black cabs, the red double-decker buses, even London's crumbling, antique subway system—it all won our hearts. We found it much harder, though, to love the prices of things in the United Kingdom, with everything running about one and a half to three times as much as it costs in the United States. Adding injury to the insult was the stunning sales tax—a 17.5 percent tax tacked on to every purchase. Seventeen and a half percent! That's way above the combined city and state sales tax even in the most taxing American states, and more than twice as much as we paid back home in Colorado.[1] I kept wondering: Why do the Brits put up with a tax that high?

And then, barely a week after we arrived in London, our youngest daughter woke up with a painfully infected ear, bright red and swollen like a chestnut. We could guess the cause—it must have been that dubious ear-piercing shop in one of the charming street markets—but had no idea how to fix the problem. We had barely unpacked our suitcases and certainly hadn't had time to find a doctor in our new home. Feeling desperate, we piled into a roomy black cab and asked to go the nearest hospital. Within minutes, we were in the emergency (sorry, "casualty") ward at St. Mary's Hospital, an ancient, much-the-worse-for-wear institution just down the street from Paddington Station. After a quarter hour's wait there, a gentle nurse and an authoritative doctor took command of the case. They carefully removed the offending earring, reduced the swelling, treated the infection, and offered polite but firm instruction on the right way to care for pierced ears.

Our daughter—and her parents—felt an enormous sense of relief. I pulled out my checkbook (sorry, "chequebook") and waited for the bill. I knew this treatment was going to be costly—emergency rooms always are—but frankly, I was willing to pay for the excellent and reassuring medical care we had received. The nurse, evidently accustomed to American patients, smiled at my mistake. "You can put away your cheques," she said, crisply and proudly. "There won't be a bill to pay. We do it a bit differently here. In the National Health Service, we don't charge for medical treatment." With that, she sent us home.

Had the same minor medical crisis occurred in America, we would surely have received the same level of professional treatment. But we would have received something else along with it: a wad of bills. Having had a similar experience with emergency wards in the United States, I would expect that treatment like we got at St. Mary's in London would have brought bills of about $200 from the hospital, another $150 or so from the doctor, and another $100 from some lab technician. And I would likely have faced a three-month battle with an insurance company trying to get the bills paid. In Britain, there was no need to argue with the insurance company over the bill, because there was no bill (and consequently, no insurance company). As we left the hospital, my wife said quietly, "Now I see why we pay that 17.5 percent."

In the aging but efficient casualty ward at St. Mary's Hospital, our family had come face-to-face with something that evokes enormous pride among Europeans—a phenomenon they call "the European social model." This is an elaborate and expensive network of publicly funded, cradle-to-grave programs designed to protect everyone in Europe against the vicissitudes of contemporary life. Whether the threat to a person's health, comfort, or economic status is natural or man-made, the European social model is there to assist. In principle, this is not a foreign concept to Americans (or East Asians or Australians). If you topple off the tight wire of normal life in the United States, you will be caught by a "social safety net" that is supposed to provide some level of sustenance, shelter, and medical care. But in Europe, falling into the "safety net" is more like falling into a large, soft bed with a down comforter for protection against the cold and a matron standing by with a warm cup of tea to soothe the discomfort.

Access to the generous benefits of the social model is seen as a basic right of every European—and the word *every* is crucial here, because the social model is relentlessly egalitarian. At the same time, paying for the social model is seen as a basic responsibility of every European. And this widely shared sense of the government's social responsibility to everybody is another unifying force that makes Europeans feel they all belong to a single place—a place, they believe, that is definitely not American.

The responsibility for all to help pay is reflected in the tax structure that supports the continent's extensive welfare programs. European nations have the same panoply of corporate and personal income taxes, inheritance taxes, property taxes, and so forth as the United States, with the same type of exemptions that essentially exclude the poorest citizens from paying these wealth-based taxes. But the European countries rely much more heavily than most of the world on sales taxes—the Europeans call them value-added taxes—which are paid by just about anybody who buys anything. This system was created deliberately to make sure that lower-income people help pay for the social system. And do they pay! For an American, even an American who lives in a "high-tax" state like California, New York, or Washington, the VAT rates in European countries seem mind-boggling:

Austria	20 percent
Belgium	21
Czech Republic	22
Denmark	25
Germany	16
Estonia	18
Greece	18
Spain	16
Finland	22
France	19.6
Ireland	21
Italy	20
Hungary	25
Netherlands	19
Portugal	19
Slovakia	19
Sweden	25
United Kingdom	17.5

Which is to say, when we paid that heavy 17.5 percent VAT tax on our purchases in Britain, we were actually living with one of the lightest sales-tax burdens in all of Europe. When I was traveling around Europe, I wasn't surprised to see that the Scandinavian countries had high rates of VAT tax; they are rich, and they are famous for their high taxes. It was surprising, though, to find that even the poorest countries in the EU—Greece, Portugal, Hungary, and Slovakia—imposed sales taxes at rates that would start a taxpayers' revolt in most of the United States.

But if the burden is spread fairly equally, the benefits of the public welfare programs in the European social model are also distributed with a fairly even hand. To Americans, it is simply a matter of common sense that rich families get better medical care and better education than the poor; the rich can afford the doctors at the fancy clinics and the tutors to get their kids into Harvard. But this piece of common sense does not apply in most of Europe. The corporate executive in the back seat of the limo, her chauffeur up front, and the guy who pumps the gas for them all go to the same doctor and the same hospitals and send their children to the same (largely free) universities. It's not that the truly rich are resented, or hated, in Europe. People who have made billions in business—people like Stelios Haji-Ioannou, the budget-airline wizard from Cyprus (whom we will meet in chapter 8), or Britain's Richard Branson, or Austria's Dietrich Mateschitz (whom we've met in chapter 5)—are treated like heroes in their native countries. But no European would agree that a Stelios or a Mateschitz should get better health care or education just because they're rich.

This zeal for spreading the wealth fairly equally is reflected most dramatically in poverty rates. European nations certainly do have families living below the established poverty line (according to the definition preferred by the Organization for Economic Cooperation and Development, "poverty" means a family income at least 50 percent below the mean personal income in the nation as a whole). But they have a lot fewer poor families than the United States does. In America, about 20 percent of adults are living in poverty at any given time. In France, the comparable figure is 7.5 percent; it is 7.6 percent for Germany and 6.5 percent in Italy. Britain, with a somewhat leaner benefit system than its continental neighbors, has about 14.6 percent of its adults in poverty.

The helping hand of the social model is particularly evident when a worker becomes unemployed. Americans on the unemployment rolls tend to get a monthly government check, together with help in buying food and paying heat and light bills. At some level, when his savings fall low enough, an unemployed American worker may also apply for free government-supplied health care through Medicaid. In Europe, by contrast, a worker who is "made redundant"—that's the brutal British term for being laid off—will get a housing benefit, a heat and light benefit, a food benefit, a child care benefit, and a monthly unemployment payment that is almost always higher than the American standard. The European, of course, will have the same access as everybody else to the public health-care system. The American system, in which you lose your health insurance when you lose your job, strikes the Europeans as exactly backward. "I don't understand your approach to health care," a junior minister in Sweden's health department told me once. "It seems to me that your country takes away the insurance when people most need it."

Economists have a gauge to measure the relative generosity of unemployment assistance programs. It's called the replacement ratio—that is, how much of the worker's former income is replaced through benefits. In the United States, the figure varies from state to state, but overall a couple with two children and an income a little below average will have about 50 percent of earnings replaced by public assistance in case of unemployment. In France, the replacement ratio for the same family is 86 percent; in Britain, 83 percent; in Germany, 74 percent; in Sweden and the Netherlands, 90 percent.

This benevolent helping hand, funded by the taxpayers, tends to be described in the United States as a "welfare state," a phrase used derisively by American politicians to attack those who want to give away huge sums of public money. In Europe, too, the social safety blanket is known as the "welfare state," but in Europe people are proud of that term. I learned this on the campus of one of the world's greatest educational institutions, Oxford University. On a cold fall day, the students were holding a mass protest against one of Tony Blair's more daring government innovations: a tuition fee for college students. In Britain, as in most of Europe, nearly all universities are public institutions. Until 1999, university education was free in Britain, as it still is in most of Europe. To help balance his budget, Blair proposed a modest tuition fee, based on each student's family income, with a maximum payment of £1,000 per school year—about $1,500. Since then, Blair has raised the fee to a maximum of £3,000. Compared to, say, Princeton or Harvard (both running about $38,000 per year), this is a fantastic bargain. To Oxford students, it was an outrage, and that's why they were protesting. "Education Must Be Free," read the bedsheet banners draping from the leaded windows of the stately Gothic colleges.

Just for the sake of argument, I approached the student leading the demonstrations—Phillipa Warner Smith, the daughter of a lawyer from a tony London suburb—and suggested to her that education really isn't free. "Somebody is paying your professors," I said. "Somebody has to pay the light bill in the classroom." Ms. Warner Smith didn't flinch. "Education benefits society as a whole," she replied. "So the general society should pay the bursary." At that point, somebody turned on a microphone at the front of the crowd and a white-haired gentleman stepped up to give a speech. This turned out to be Tony Benn, a venerable leftist member of Blair's Labour Party, who took sharp issue with his prime minister on the subject of tuition fees. "Education benefits society as a whole," Benn declared, precisely echoing the student argument. "And government should pay for socially beneficial functions. This is an essential element of the welfare state that we have been building for the past century on this continent." The striking thing for me was the obvious pride in Benn's voice when he mentioned the welfare state, and the huge roar of approval from the crowd that greeted that term. "Protecting our welfare state," Ms. Warner Smith told me, "is probably the most important job that government has."

"Our welfare state"—that phrase nicely sums up the sense of ownership, the sheer pride, that Europeans feel toward their network of social support mechanisms. The social model is often cited as one of the basic elements that make a European country European. "Europe's welfare states," asserts the British analyst Will Hutton, "arise from . . . core European values and the European settlement. They define Europeanness. They are non-negotiable European realities." The Europeans argue that the generosity of their social model is the main thing that makes Europe different from other developed regions of the world. I heard the prime minister of Serbia, Zoran Djindjic, a Generation E member, make this point at a forum for Eastern European countries hoping eventually to be admitted to the EU. The session was a sort of beauty contest, to test whether the potential applicants were up to snuff, and Djindjic clearly passed the test. His great moment came when he was asked to give a Serbian view of what "Europe" is all about. "Modern societies are defined by three elements: political democracy, market economy, and social identity," the prime minister said in his smooth English. "It's in this third aspect—their attitude to social solidarity—that the Europeans seem to have an identity that is distinct from either Asia or America."

Citizens of the United States of Europe particularly like to brag that their social model makes them superior to the United States of America. "The simplest difference between the USA and Europe is that we have welfare states, and they do not," wrote the Irish political scientist James Wickham. Wickham applauds Americans' willingness to support charity and volunteer programs, but he argues that charity is not enough. "Social rights cannot depend on the voluntary goodwill of others. . . . The welfare state, enforced by law, is a defining feature of Europe."

Of course, the welfare state also forces Europeans to pay sky-high taxes. And the plush arrangements provided for people who are out of work may explain why Europeans who are laid off tend to accept their fate as a fairly permanent condition, rather than getting up and looking for a new job. But these problems tend to be ignored, except by a few marginal voices on the right, because Europe in general assumes the social model is preferable to what's going on in other parts of the world. "The reason why Europe compares so favorably with the US in respect of social and income mobility," Will Hutton says, "is that every European state sets out to offer equality of opportunity to all its people; the American neglect of the bottom 50 percent in the name of individualism is not reproduced in Europe."

The European social model involves a much bigger role for the public sector in daily life than Americans are comfortable with. The Public Broadcasting System (PBS) in the United States fills a fairly small niche in a TV and radio world dominated by giant private companies. In most European countries, by contrast, the public broadcaster tends to be largest and the most prestigious by far. Britain's BBC, funded by a tax of $170 per year paid by every home and office that has a television set, operates six TV and five radio stations. France's TFI, Germany's ARD, and Italy's RAI are more popular and more respected than any private network. Public transit systems are much more pervasive in Europe than in the United States, as are public art, public universities, and public medical systems. Public housing is so common in major European cities that it can't all be stuck away in a few big complexes. Instead, government-owned homes and apartment buildings are found in every neighborhood of every city and town. The inhabitants include not just the poor but a good proportion of the middle class as well.

Still, Europe's welfare state is not "European" in the sense that it is standardized or uniform across the EU. Brussels sets some minimal standards, but each country establishes its own menu of public assistance. Not surprisingly, considering its importance in everybody's daily life, the welfare state has been studied to a fare-thee-well by European academics. They divide the various approaches to state welfare into various categories: there's a Nordic model, generally covering the Scandinavian countries. There's the Rhineland capitalism model, developed in Germany and now common in Austria and the Benelux countries. There's a southern Catholic style, common in the Mediterranean nations. At the EU's eastern edge, the former Soviet states have largely maintained welfare programs inherited from Communist times. Britain, which is struggling to run a European welfare state with tax rates somewhat closer to the American standard, is in a class of its own. The Irish are more European than the Brits in this regard. Still, common features mark the social model across the continent.

Europe's welfare state begins at birth, with government payments to each newborn citizen and generous support for parents. In essence, the European governments pay new parents to leave their jobs temporarily and stay home. "We have made a fairly basic decision," Valgard Haugland, the leader of Norway's Christian Democratic Party and the cabinet minister for children and family affairs, told me. "We have decided that raising a child is real work. And that this work provides value for the whole society. And that the society as a whole should pay for this valuable service. Americans like to talk about family values. We have decided to do more than talk; we use our tax revenues to pay for family values."

In a small but comfortable two-bedroom apartment on a leafy green hill high above the ice blue Oslofjord, I came face-to-face with Norwegian family values. When a beaming blue-eyed girl with golden hair was born to Martin Aenstad and his wife Suranhild, Suranhild decided to leave her job as a secretary in downtown Oslo and stay home to raise her daughter, Serine. This cost her nothing. Suranhild was "hired" by the Norwegian government to be the mother of her baby. The state paid her a yearly salary equivalent to $18,800, or 80 percent of what she made as a secretary. With the savings on clothes and commuting, Suranhild came out slightly ahead.

Shortly after Serine's first birthday, Suranhild went back to her office job; her employers were required by law to take her back, in the same position. At that point, Martin took over the parental slot, taking a year's leave from his job as a junior engineer and drawing his paycheck as a father for Serine's second year of life. Sitting in his cozy apartment here, with eighteen-month-old Serine bouncing happily on his knee, Martin Aenstad told me that he felt no qualms about being a stay-at-home father. "I've had jobs, and now I'm raising my daughter. And I can tell you that being a house-father is hard work. At least when I was on the job, they gave me a lunch break. If Serine is hungry or crying or has a full diaper—well, you try telling her that Daddy needs a lunch break." Martin's pay was considerably lower than his wife had received, because the second year of parenting only draws a third of the worker's normal salary. But Martin knew that his old job was waiting for him when his year as full-time daddy came to an end. For her third year, Serine would go to a state-run child-care facility called a Kindergarten.

The United States pays a small percentage of its mothers a monthly stipend to help them raise and feed their children. The recipients are known as "welfare moms," and are generally stigmatized as women who can't find a real job. Norway, in contrast—like most other European countries—treats the monthly payment to parents as a salary. Income and social security taxes are withheld, just as with any paycheck. The payment is specifically designed for working parents, to encourage them to leave their jobs for a while and raise their children. Parents who don't have a job outside the home also get a monthly benefit for raising children, but it is considerably less than the "surrogate salary" provided those who leave a job to be full-time parents. In America, the White House and state governors routinely boast about how much their welfare rolls are being reduced. In Norway, the government takes pride in statistics showing that the number of recipients has been growing rapidly. For the past few years, the national parliament, or Storting, has been debating proposals to extend the plan to the child's third year.

With her baby chortling happily on her lap, Suranhild Aenstad told me that the parental-pay system is not perfect. For women like her, in their mid-twenties, the maternity-leave law makes it harder to get a decent job in the first place. "Women can suffer," she said, speaking excellent English. "We all know that some companies don't hire a woman if they expect you are going to take maternity leave in a few years." Cabinet Minister Haugland agreed that this is a problem. "Of course we have made it illegal for an employer to turn down a young applicant for this reason," she said. "But how do you prove it? They will never say they rejected somebody because of maternity leave."

Other European countries can't afford to pay as much for parenting as wealthy Norway does. Still, parental leave programs are standard, whether funded through state payments or by requiring employers to continue paying a salary while the employer is at home being a parent. Beyond that, European parents can expect a monthly benefit check from the government for the first eighteen years of each child's life. Health care and prescriptions are free for children up to a certain age, even in those countries that require a copayment from adults at the doctor's office. Education tends to be free, or at least extremely cheap by American standards, all the way through college. In Europe, the most prestigious universities are nearly all public, so the best college education in Sweden, say, or Scotland is available essentially for free to those who can gain admission. (At least, to those who come from EU member countries. American, Japanese, and Middle Eastern students at European universities pay handsomely for the privilege, and this flow of income from foreign students is one of the ways Europe pays for higher education.)

Once a European is educated, she moves on to the labor market and the broad array of employment rights that are considered a basic element of the social model. Wages are often not left to market mechanisms. They are set, either by unions or by government formulas, generally on a regional or sectoral basis, so that all auto companies, for example, pay all workers about the same weekly amount. As we have seen, mandatory programs of sick leave and family leave are far more expansive in Europe than the United States. Working hours tend to be restricted by law or union agreement. Italy and France have both made the thirty-five-hour week de rigueur. This doesn't mean that no worker can stay on for the thirty-sixth hour in a given week; rather, thirty-five hours is the point at which an employer is required to start paying overtime rates. This is supposed to encourage companies to hire more people—on the grounds that it is cheaper to pay a second man at the basic rate than to keep the first one on at overtime—but the economists don't agree on whether the laws have achieved that purpose. Holidays and paid vacations are generous; in much of Europe, a worker can expect five weeks of vacation from the first year on the job. British law mandates at least twenty-three days of paid holidays per year; France requires twenty-five days or more; Sweden, at least thirty. In contrast, the wretched overworked Americans have to get by with a meager four to ten mandatory paid holidays, depending on the state. The results of all this are evident in the OECD's ranking in average hours worked. In 2003, Americans worked an average of 1,976 hours; German and French workers averaged some 400 hours less. That is, Joe Sixpack works some ten weeks more in one year than his counterparts Jacques and Johann. Even British workers, who put in more time on the job than anybody else in Europe, work 200 fewer hours per year than

Americans do. And while they are enjoying those long vacations, European workers don't have to worry much about losing their jobs; in many European industrial sectors, layoffs are illegal.

It is conventional wisdom among American economists—and many of their continental counterparts as well—that this extensive coddling of employees who don't work all that much and can't be laid off is a key reason for Europe's relatively weak economic performance. In good times and bad, European countries tend to show lower gross domestic product (GDP) growth rates than the United States does. In good times and bad, unemployment rates for many European countries are far higher than in the United States. In the first years of the twenty-first century, U.S. unemployment rates ran near 6 percent; for Europe as a whole, the figure was about 9 percent. This lingering malady, marked by slow growth and high unemployment, is commonly known as Eurosclerosis. The reasons for it seem blatantly clear. A French employer who can't fire any employee is going to think twice before hiring any employee. A German factory that has to pay its workers for ten weeks of holidays and vacations out of each fifty-two is going to spend more, and produce less, than a U.S. factory that gets five more weeks of work from each hand for the same annual pay. The American system is more flexible, and accordingly more dynamic; jobs are more easily eliminated in the United States, but they are more easily created as well. To Americans, this all seems plain as day.

But there's another point of view. Europeans who support the labor protections built into the social model point out that many European companies do just fine, thank you, despite the rigid regulatory regime imposed on them. Volvo makes its cars in Sweden and the Netherlands, two of the strongest bulwarks of the welfare state—and yet Ford Motor Co. makes more money on its Volvo division than it makes from Lincoln and Mercury models it builds in the United States. Nokia's global work force is about 70 percent European, but it manages to stay far ahead of its chief American competitor, Motorola, which employs most of its people either in the United States or even cheaper labor markets. It was Germany's third-largest automaker, Daimler, that bought America's third-largest automaker, Chrysler—not vice versa. Over the past decade, employment has grown faster in Ireland, Denmark, and the Netherlands than in the United States, although those three countries are full-fledged backers of European-style labor perquisites.

The Europeans also challenge economic comparisons based on gross domestic product, the standard measure of a nation's wealth. When American citizens or governments spend money on deadbolt locks, barred windows, car alarms, police, and prisons, all that expenditure creates employment and adds to the GDP total. But does it make the United States a more desirable place to live than Europe, where there is less need for home security or prison guards? Those extra ten weeks of paid leave that a French worker enjoys have a negative impact on GDP statistics. But are Americans better off because they have to work ten more weeks per year? Martin Wolf, a conservative British economist who is generally critical of the excesses of the social model, admitted recently that he finds this question confusing. "Like many Europeans, I find the U.S. addiction to ceaseless work appalling," Wolf wrote. "I also dislike the determination of some European governments to force people to work fewer hours. But if Europeans want to enjoy some of their wealth in the form of greater leisure, why not?"

While the proworker policies of the European social model clearly make labor costs higher than in more laissez-faire societies like the United States, European employers have an advantage over their American competitors because of another key element of the welfare state: public health-care systems. Although the mechanisms and the finances of medical care vary significantly from one country to the next, all European nations have health-care plans that cover all citizens, with the government paying most (or all) of the bills. By many measures, these systems of "socialized medicine" work better, and more efficiently, than the mainly private American health-care system. The European countries have better public health statistics than the United States, and a higher rate of satisfaction among patients, even though they spend a much smaller share of national income on medical care. This chart, based on data from 2001–2, makes the point:

Country:	Nether-lands	France	Sweden	U.K.	United States
Health costs (% of GDP)	8.5	9.4	8.0	6.7	13.0
% paid by gov't.	70	77	84	84	45
Male life expect.	75	75	77	75	73

Some European health-care systems—notably those in France and Germany—use an insurance model for payment. Citizens join a plan and pay fairly small premiums, with government making up any shortfall. For someone who has a job, the employer is expected to pay a sizable chunk of the health insurance premium; for others, the government makes up the difference. In other countries, the state not only pays for, but also provides, medical service. Britain's National Health Service (NHS) is the prime example; Italy and Sweden use variations on the NHS system. The British are passionate about the concept of "free at the point of service," which is to say that you can "put away your cheques," as the nurse at St. Mary's Hospital told me, when you visit the doctor's office or the hospital. The payment comes through that 17.5 percent sales tax, and other taxes. The French, in contrast, make the patient pay a doctor's bill at the office, and then seek reimbursement from the national insurance plan.

In recent years, as the technology, and the cost, of modern medicine has increased, health systems have struggled with efforts to control costs. Just as in the United States, health care is rationed. New drugs are carefully reviewed before they are made available. If you are dying of heart failure, you probably get surgery right away. But if your problem is a painful knee or a cataract, you could spend months on a waiting list before you get to the operating table. Outside Britain, governments have begun to impose copayments for doctor visits. In Sweden, for example, the out-of-pocket fee is tied to the price of a movie ticket in Stockholm—about $12.

The advantage for European industry comes in avoiding the kind of health-care costs that pose an increasingly heavy weight pressing down on American companies. With the government picking up most of this burden—even in the Netherlands, with the biggest private-sector medical industry in the EU, the government pays 70 percent of health-care costs—the cost to employers is small, at least in comparison to the medical costs American firms have to pay. William Clay Ford Jr., the chairman of Ford Motor Company, says that fact is a key reason that a company like Volvo can compete on global markets; wages, pensions, and other benefits are more costly in Stockholm than in Detroit, but the huge saving on health insurance costs makes overall labor costs roughly equivalent. In the United States, more and more employers are responding to the sharp increase in health-care expenses by dropping medical insurance altogether for their employees (or at least for their blue-collar employees). In the spring of 2004, some 45 million Americans had no health insurance whatsoever. That option is simply unthinkable in Europe. The notion that everybody must have equal access to health care is a basic and incontestable fact of European life. Universal medical care is one of the things Europeans always mention, with pride, when they talk about the differences between the EU and the United States.

For these reasons, public health systems are entrenched in Europe and cannot be replaced by private medical care. Even if a conservative government swept into power somewhere, the "socialized medicine" system would be untouchable. Nigel Lawson, a former chancellor of the Exchequer in a Conservative British government, noted in his memoir that even an arch-Tory like Margaret Thatcher never dared take on the health service. "The NHS is the closest thing the English have to a religion," Lawson said. Political debate over the NHS in Britain tends to be predictable, even formulaic. The opposition parties complain that the health service is underfunded, that hospitals are leaky and crumbling, that citizens have to wait months or even years for surgery, that SOMETHING MUST BE DONE. In reply, Tony Blair stands up and says that the National Health Service is a national treasure, a shining jewel in the British crown, and his Labour Party, at least, has no intention of "turning it into a profit-making corporate endeavor as the Americans have done." Now, Tony Blair knows full well that nobody in Britain—nobody in Europe, for that matter—has any intention of creating an American-style health-care system. But Blair always falls back on this threat to end the argument.

As an American, I would rather see my country move in the European direction on health care than vice versa. I base this conclusion on our own family's experience with European-style medicine. After our initial experience with British health care in St. Mary's casualty ward, we stuck with the National Health Service all the years we lived in Britain. For our normally healthy family, the NHS did fine. Back in the United States, I work for a major corporation that offers an unusually generous package of health insurance benefits. But the availability and quality of the care we had in Britain were about equal to what we have at home—better, in one sense, in that British doctors still make house calls. We generally got to see the doctor on the day we called. The doctor's office (sorry, "surgery") down the street from our house had a notice warning, "The average consultation should last 10 minutes," which seemed rather brief. But once in the office, we never had the feeling that we were being rushed out the door. Looking at the waiting lists at British hospitals for major operations, and the long-term survival rates for cancer and other major diseases, I think I'd rather be in the United States than in Britain if somebody in my family contracted a serious disease. But for flu, colds, rashes, intestinal complaints, eye exams, and the occasional broken bone or sprain, the NHS doctors performed on par with any treatment we have had in the United States. And all for free.

Partly to save money, and partly because the threat of malpractice litigation is much lower for a British doctor, we found the NHS less inclined than American doctors to do tests and X-rays. The Brits wouldn't even give me an annual physical; my doctor explained that NHS economists had decided the savings did not justify the costs, at least for basically healthy patients. In the United States, a man my age is routinely given a PSA test to check for prostate cancer. I was never able to convince the NHS to do this for me. Even when I was sent to a neighborhood hospital for a blood test, the doctor declined to check the spot on the form calling for a PSA test as well. "We don't find it cost-effective," he explained. Of course, most patients would probably consider the test extremely effective if it spotted a cancer early enough to be treated. The determining factor, though, is what the NHS finds cost-effective.

For me, the best part of British medicine was the dog that didn't bark. There were no bills. We did pay for glasses and for dental care, which are not covered by the NHS except for particularly needy families. The adults in our family paid £6 ($9.50) for prescriptions; medicine was free for our children. But for all other treatment—even emergency ward visits and hospital stays—we never even saw a bill. This business of getting medical care for free can be habit-forming. Shortly after we moved home to the United States, I got a frantic call one day from one of my teen-agers. Her cross-country team required a blood test at the beginning of each season. While we lived in Europe, she took care of this every year at a place called the Royal Free Hospital, near our home in London. But once we moved home, she went to a U.S. hospital for the test. There, something amazing happened: they asked her to pay money! "Dad, they want $95 for this!" she said in shock over the phone. I explained that this seemed about the right price to me. "What do you normally pay for a blood test?" I asked. "Pay? I never pay," this distraught young woman replied. "In London, I just walked into the hospital, and they never asked me to pay."

In addition to protection of livelihood, family, and health, the Euro-pean social model also involves protection of civil liberties and individual legal rights. In this area, the social model is much more familiar to Amer-icans. In fact, the Bill of Rights that America's founding fathers added to the new Constitution in 1790 and America's federal court system were key models for the EU's founding fathers when they set up the initial supranational institutions in the late 1940s. Winston Churchill and Jean Monnet, two Europeans who understood and admired the United States, were instrumental in the creation of Europe's own bill of rights and its pancontinental courts.

From its beginning in 1951, Monnet's European Coal and Steel Community included a cross-border judicial arm to adjudicate international disputes. This "European Court of Justice" is still operating in Luxembourg. Its main job is to deal with disputes between countries, and to check the legality of actions of the EU government in Brussels. There is a separate European court to deal with issues touching individual liberties. When Churchill presided over the first Congress of Europe at the Hague in 1948, he drafted some British lawyers, led by Sir David Maxwell Fyfe (later to serve as chief British war crimes prosecutor at Nuremberg), to compose the European Convention on Human Rights. As Churchill said, it was a written guarantee of the basic freedoms the Allies had fought and died for in World War II. The document was eventually adopted by virtually every European country, including some that are not EU members. Although the convention was a British product from the start, the Euroskeptic Brits didn't get around to adopting it until 1998, when a pro-Europe prime minister, Tony Blair, rammed it through Parliament. Although many of the liberties it guaranteed came straight from English common law, the convention was the first written bill of rights ever granted to the English people. (Up to then, the English people had relied on judicial opinions to guarantee their civil liberties.)

To enforce the Convention on Human Rights, the 1948 Congress set up the European Court of Human Rights. Now headquartered in a dramatically modern courthouse in Strasbourg, this court acts something like a European supreme court. Citizens from any member country can bring a suit claiming their rights were violated. The Strasbourg court can, and regularly does, declare laws of the separate states to be invalid, and reverse the holdings of the highest courts of the member nations. Its mere presence, and the threat of an embarrassing ruling, tend to make the individual governments more sensitive to civil liberties than they would likely be without the court hovering over them.

When Mike Tyson went to Britain in the summer of 2000 to fight the European heavyweight champ, Lennox Lewis, the uncontrollable American boxer caused a furor at the weigh-in when he pointed at Lewis and roared: "I'm gonna rip out his heart! I'm gonna eat his children!" Coming from a man who had already eaten the ear of an earlier opponent, this unorthodox line of commentary shocked members of the British Boxing Board of Control. They responded by prohibiting Tyson from fighting in a British ring—a ruling that would have canceled the Tyson-Lewis bout and cost both fighters millions of pounds. But Tyson hired a famous British civil rights lawyer, who told the boxing council that punishing the American heavyweight simply for expressing his "views" would amount to a violation of his right to free speech under the European Convention on Human Rights. Faced with the possibility of a humiliating reversal from Strasbourg, the Board of Control backed down and let the Tyson-Lewis match go ahead. Unfortunately for Tyson, he proved a much less effective fighter than his lawyer. Lewis whipped him decisively, and Tyson's hopes to regain the heavyweight championship once more went down the drain for good. But at least his human rights had been protected.

The original 1948 text of the Convention on Human Rights has been amended and enhanced over the decades. Its current manifestation, approved in 2000, is a twenty-two-page document known as the Charter of Fundamental Rights of the European Union (or the Carta de los Derechos Fundamentales de la Union Europea, or the Charta der Grundrechte der Europäischen Union, or the Grundlaggande rattigheterna i Europeiska unionen, and so on in twenty languages). This charter has all the basic freedoms familiar to Americans. Article 10 guarantees "Freedom of thought, conscience, and religion." Article 20 states simply, "Everyone is equal before the law." Article 41 incorporates the same basic stance vis-à-vis government that forms the core of American administrative law: the right of all interested parties to fair notice and a public hearing before a government agency takes an adverse action. Freedom of speech, freedom of movement, the right to vote, the presumption of innocence, protection against double jeopardy, equal treatment of different races and genders, and freedom from torture and cruel punishment—all those familiar rights are set forth explicitly.

But the Charter of Fundamental Rights goes well beyond the range of civil liberties protected in the U.S. Bill of Rights, or most of the other constitutions around the world. To some extent, this stems from the particular situation of a multinational union. The charter says that "every person" has an inalienable right to write to the EU in any of the twenty official languages, and get a reply in the same language. It says that a citizen of any EU country can live, work, or run a business in any member nation, and vote or run for election in the country where she lives. For refugees, the charter declares that "the right to asylum shall be guaranteed." Other fundamental rights set forth in the charter come directly from the European social model: there is a basic human right to health care, a right to free education, a right to join unions and go on strike, a right to "limitation of maximum working hours, to daily and weekly rest periods, and an annual period of paid leave," and a right to "parental leave following the birth or adoption of a child." Article 29 even declares, "Everyone has the right of access to a free placement service" to help find a job. For good measure, the charter says that all workers employed in a country, no matter what their nationality, are entitled to all the benefits provided to nationals of that country.

But the expansive menu of rights and privileges guaranteed to every European doesn't stop there. The charter (Article 17) guarantees a right to "environmental protection." It demands (Article 18) that all shall receive "a high level of consumer protection." It assures the elderly (Article 25) the right "to lead a life of dignity and independence and to participate in social and cultural life." Article 7 establishes a sweeping right of privacy, and Article 8 assures the "protection of personal data," which amounts to a legal right to see any dossier maintained on you, government or private, and to have it corrected if it's wrong. Article 21, the right to nondiscrimination, contains what is probably the most sweeping definition of "discrimination" ever put on paper:

> Any discrimination based on grounds such as sex, race, color, ethnic or social origin, genetic features, language, religion or belief, political or any other opinion, membership of a national minority, property, birth, disability, age, or sexual orientation shall be prohibited.

This just about covers the waterfront, doesn't it? But just in case, that powerful phrase "such as" means the charter may also be invoked to ban some other form of discrimination so abstruse that the authors couldn't articulate it.

With the prestigious and powerful European Court of Human Rights backing it, Europe's Charter of Fundamental Rights has had a broad impact on contemporary Europeans. The court has used the antidiscrimination chapter of the charter to force all European nations to allow homosexuals in the military. Citing Article 24 of the charter ("The rights of the child"), the court has banned spanking in all schools—even in the old "public schools," the British term for what an American would call private schools—where a swift swat on the rear end had been the basic mode of discipline for centuries. On the other hand, the court declined to say that required school uniforms violate the charter. While the United States held hundreds of possible terrorists locked up for years without charges and without the right to a lawyer following the 9/11 attacks, the European Court of Human Rights pressured Britain's home secretary to provide legal help and a formal notice of charges to terror suspects in his country.

One particularly rich area for litigation has been sparked by an apparent conflict in the charter between Article 7, guaranteeing a respect for personal privacy, and Article 11, which preserves "freedom . . . to receive and impart information and ideas." Thus the movie star trying to keep her romantic life out of the papers insists on her "right to privacy," and the tabloids insist on their "right to impart information." This conflict sometimes centers on the bizarre habit of European matinee idols to sell the rights to their weddings to a particular picture magazine. An exclusive contract for pictures and interviews at a hot couple's marriage ceremony can easily bring in a million euros. But other magazines, of course, sometimes choose not to honor the exclusive arrangement. When Michael Douglas and Catherine Zeta-Jones sold rights to their wedding (for a reported $1.5 million) to a British fan magazine called *O.K.!* they were outraged to see that a competing magazine called *Hello!* got hold of some photos and printed them without paying a penny to the happy couple. The newlyweds and *O.K.!* went to court, invoking their right to privacy, and won a sizable judgment.

The same kind of dispute broke out when a London tabloid, the *Mirror,* reported that supermodel Naomi Campbell was being treated for drug addiction. Campbell didn't deny the truth of the story but sued for damages anyway, on grounds that it had violated her privacy. The *Mirror* said the report was a perfect example of press freedom (and added that a woman who maintained a battalion of publicity agents and who regularly discussed the intimate details of her life with the fan mags had no legitimate expectation of privacy in any case). Both sides invoked the European Charter on Fundamental Rights. The British judge split the difference, awarding Campbell a judgment, but not even enough damages to pay her legal bills.

To the consternation of some American conservatives, the EU's Charter of Fundamental Rights and the rulings of the European Court of Human Rights have become a point of reference for judges around the world, even in the United States. In cases like *Grutter v. Bollinger,* involving affirmative action for minority applicants to the University of Michigan, and *Lawrence v. Texas,* the decision that voided a Texas law for banning homosexual, but not heterosexual, sex, the U.S. Supreme Court cited the European charter and decisions of the Strasbourg court in support of its rulings. In the Texas case, Justice Anthony Kennedy noted that "the rights of homosexual adults to engage in intimate, consensual conduct" had been upheld by the European court, and should be upheld in the United States as well. Similarly, when the Supreme Court considered the death penalty for mentally retarded criminals, Justice John Paul Stevens noted the European legal position ("overwhelming disapproval") in deciding to ban the practice in the United States as well.

There's nothing particularly new about American jurists turning to European legal principles for guidance. U.S. judges, including conservative judges, have been citing English cases and English common law in their opinions for two centuries. But the reliance on the sweeping European notion of human rights bothers some judges. In the Texas case, the invocation of European ideas of human rights prompted a sharp dissent from justices William Rehnquist, Clarence Thomas, and Antonin Scalia: "The court's discussion of these foreign views . . . is meaningless dicta. Dangerous dicta, however, since this court should not impose foreign moods, fads or fashions on Americans." The tendency to look to Europe for guidance on human rights concerns has also drawn the ire of former federal judge Robert H. Bork. "One would have thought the meaning of our Consitution derived from the understanding of those who wrote, proposed, and ratified it," Bork wrote, "not by foreign courts."

Article 2.2 of the charter incorporates a key element of the contemporary European worldview: "No one shall be condemned to the death penalty, or executed." This principle has become a pan-European crusade of sorts, and Europeans seem to believe that they have a responsibility to abolish capital punishment not just in Europe but all over the world. This is not exactly a timeless European value. The crucifix, the gallows, the firing squad, and the guillotine were essential elements of European law enforcement for millennia, and the elimination of this final sanction is a recent phenomenon. Most European countries still used capital punishment for two or three decades after World War II. France was killing criminals with the guillotine—*the guillotine!*—until the 1980s. Indeed, Robert Badinter, the eloquent, elegant French politician who fought the death penalty in his country and eventually convinced the parliament to do away with it, has said that the very fact that the antique, bloody guillotine was still in use was a useful point in the argument against capital punishment overall. When he was France's minister of justice, Badinter rose in the Parliament and asked his fellow members "to imagine the sound of the blade as it slices a living human being in two." This chilling image was evidently powerful; France joined the rest of Europe in banning executions. Even today, after a particularly heinous mass murder or rape on the continent, opinion polls in some countries show a surge of new support for the death penalty. For the most part, however, the broadly held European view of capital punishment is close to the opinion of M. Badinter: "It is simply barbaric."

The death penalty has become a fairly potent point of division between Europe and the United States, and its abolition is thus another unifying force pushing Europeans toward pancontinental integration. Europeans are downright proud that they have moved beyond capital punishment. The United States may be the world's dominant military, cultural, and financial force, but the United States still executes criminals. That point alone, to tens of millions of Europeans, makes the European Union a better place to live than the American one. "I am regularly asked to speak about this at [European] universities," Badinter told me. "I wish you could see the students, how perplexed they are, how amazed they are, that the U.S. permits this barbarous deed. After all, U.S. pop culture is part of their life. U.S. technology is on their desks. But when it comes to the death penalty, the U.S. is not a leader. Your country stands with China, Iran, Saudi Arabia, and the Democratic Republic of the Congo in number of executions. And the students say, 'What the hell has the U.S. to do with those four dictatorships?'" A Generation E friend of mine in Germany, Hans Robert Eisenhauer, told me that "for us, the death penalty stands even with torture, with slavery. It should by now be ancient history! Why would Americans want still to use?"

On this point, the sense that "we're superior to those bloody Americans" is not restricted to the political left or to a noisy student generation. Right-wing politicians and media across Europe also denounce the electric chair. Most of the criticism in Europe comes from the political left, but this is an issue on which conservatives, too, tend to criticize the

United States. When a six-year-old shot and killed a first-grade class-mate in Michigan, an archconservative British tabloid, the *Sun*, editorialized that the most likely American response would be to build a kiddie-size electric chair. When George W. Bush became president, the *Daily Mail*, the farthest right of the British newspapers, noted acidly in a profile that the new president is "best known for signing 153 death warrants."

In fact, Bush's advocacy for the death penalty while he was governor of Texas is one of the factors that made him a despised figure in Europe, long before the war in Iraq. The president's reputation as "the world's leading executioner"—as Robert Badinter describes him—was the main thing anybody in Europe knew about him when he entered the White House. Just before the George W. Bush inauguration, newspapers all over Europe were full of stories about a convicted rapist and murderer named Johnny Paul Penry. Penry became the 150th person executed since Bush had become governor, and this milestone was treated as major news. Penry, the convict, was portrayed as a victim; he was mentally retarded, the Europeans reported, and many stories said that he still believed in Santa Claus. Britain's second-biggest daily newspaper, the *Mirror*, devoted its first six pages completely to reports on Penry and the preceding 149 prisoners on Texas's death row (headline: "The Texas Massacre"). On page 7, it ran an editorial: "Bush makes no apology for his hideous track record. And disturbingly, he has mass support from Americans, driven by their out-of-control gun culture and blood lust for retribution."

There are political points to be won in Europe by opposing capital punishment in the United States. For this reason, it is against the law in any European country to extradite a prisoner to the United States for a crime that could bring the death penalty. A British official told Washington that not even Osama bin Laden would be extradited, if captured by Europeans, unless the Americans promised not to execute him. European politicians routinely cross the Atlantic to meet the condemned, generally with the media tagging along. When French education minister

Jack Lang was preparing to run for mayor of Paris, he traveled to Texas to talk with convicted murderer Odell Barnes Jr., who was due to be executed in a few weeks. Claudia Roth, a popular Green Party member of Germany's Reichstag, traveled to the Arizona state penitentiary to talk with two convicted murderers, Karl and Walter LaGrand, before their execution. This did not generate precisely the kind of news footage Roth had in mind. Although the LaGrand brothers were born in Germany, they had spent their entire adult lives in the United States. When they met with Roth, they didn't protest their innocence. In fact, they didn't say much of anything, because neither brother was able to speak a word of German. Undeterred, Roth told the German press later that the meeting "made me really proud of my country and our constitution and our European Charter on Human Rights. A state is not strong only because it executes people. It can be strong in showing mercy."

On dozens of occasions, the European Union and the European Parliament have issued formal declarations of protest against scheduled executions in the United States, usually those involving youthful or mentally deficient defendants. U.S. diplomats in Europe say they are deluged with complaints about capital punishment, some from organized political groups and many from citizens who have read about an upcoming execution in the newspaper. In response, the U.S. embassy in Paris hands out an explanation of the issue; it is defensive in tone, and almost sides with the European view. "The death penalty is an emotional and controversial subject," it says. "Public opinion polls have shown that 66 percent of the American public support the death penalty. On the other hand, some major American organizations, such as the American Bar Association and the Texas Catholic Bishops, have called for a moratorium on its use on humanitarian and human rights grounds."

For all the depth of feeling, there is considerable ignorance in Europe about the death penalty in the United States. It seems to be conventional wisdom that thousands of Americans are put to death every year. (The actual number is around eighty.) Very few Europeans seem to understand that capital punishment is largely a matter of state law. When I was dragged into debates on this topic on European TV networks, I always pointed out that thirty-seven states have the death penalty, and another thirteen, plus the District of Columbia, have decided against it. "You see," I would argue, "this is really a case of democracy at work. The people of each state get to decide if they want it to be used where they live." Generally, that line of debate was a flop. When I tried this tack on the BBC, the brilliant Simon Jenkins, a columnist with the *Times* of London, was unimpressed. "Yes, democracy is a wonderful thing," Jenkins said sardonically, "but not when the democratic will is endorsing an act of barbarism."

At the same time, there seems to be ignorance in the United States about the depth of feeling, the sheer revulsion, in Europe regarding capital punishment. Not long after the 9/11 attacks on America, I attended a meeting in London between U.S. Attorney General John Ashcroft and his British counterpart, David Blunkett. Ashcroft explained that he was touring five European countries, hoping to convince the justice ministers that alleged terrorist prisoners could be extradited for trial in the United States. Blunkett explained, diplomatically, that it is contrary to law in any European country to extradite a criminal who might face the death penalty overseas. Ashcroft replied smoothly that he hoped to change the minds of his European counterparts. He would try to persuade them that, when it comes to terrorism, the death penalty is a just punishment. Of course, there was not a chance in the world that any American could persuade Europeans on this point. In fact, Ashcroft failed in his quest; the French justice minister even went to the theatrical extreme of canceling her meeting with him at the last minute to show her disdain. To the Europeans, the amazing thing was that a senior U.S. government official didn't recognize the force of Europe's Charter on Fundamental Rights, and particularly of Article 2.2. Reporting on Ashcroft's visit that evening, BBC anchorman Jeremy Paxman looked at the camera and said, "What planet does the American attorney general live on?"

The basic principle of the European social model—the idea that the state has a responsibility to insulate and protect people from the harsh vicissitudes of modern life—is also reflected in the European approach to drugs, drug dealers, and drug addicts.

A few nations on the continent still follow the traditional law-enforcement pattern favored in the United States—that is, firm prohibitions on growing, selling, or using narcotic drugs and stiff prison terms for those who do. Sweden and Greece hold fairly forcefully to this "just-say-no" approach. Most European nations, though, have shifted to a new mindset. As described by Professor Jonathan Cave, a drug policy expert at Britain's Warwick University, the standard European approach has changed from "use reduction" to "harm reduction." The basic thesis of "harm reduction," Cave writes, is that drug addicts are people who need treatment, not punishment. "People do obtain and use drugs, even if you spend billions trying to stop them. The U.S. war on drugs demonstrates that. Government doesn't want this to happen, but it happens. The goal is to have it happen without the risk of overdose, of HIV, of random crime to support the habit. The government's job is seen as offering support to people who need help."

Some European countries, including Portugal, Spain, Italy, and Luxembourg, have rewritten their laws to decriminalize possession and use of most drugs. Other nations have effectively done the same by eliminating criminal penalties for addicts who are not found to be dealing. For the most part, users of "soft" drugs like marijuana and Ecstasy are simply ignored by the police in European countries; people caught using heroin or cocaine are picked up but delivered to a treatment facility rather than to jail, unless they are found with so much of the drug they are presumed to be dealing in it.

The "harm reduction" approach stems in large part from the same concerns that built Europe's welfare state—the belief that people need to be taken care of by the government and not left alone to bear the consequences of ill fate or their own bad decisions. To this mindset, a drug addict is by definition a sick person, and Europe's social model does not allow the sick to go untreated. But the shift in drug enforcement is not simply a matter of a benevolent state doing what's best for all. There's also a strong dose of pragmatism involved. Since people are going to use drugs anyway, the thinking goes, it is a waste of police time and public money to try to catch them all and jail them. The Eurocrats in Brussels strongly support this approach. "The general trend across Europe," says Georges Estievenart, a Frenchman who runs the EU's Monitoring Center for Drugs and Drug Addiction, "is an approach that focuses on the traffickers and does not pursue the drug user as a criminal. The basic premise is that it is not in the interest of society to put these people in jail, where they don't get treatment but do get fairly easy access to all kinds of drugs. Some people refer to this as the 'pragmatic approach.' It assumes that drug use is a fact of life that society can't stop, so policymakers should try to control the damage."

The pragmatic approach was pioneered in the last century by the Netherlands, where the government permitted development of the famous "hash houses" that draw a steady clientele of locals and tourists. In the dark coffeehouses that line the old canals of Amsterdam, customers are faced with two different menus. First you pick the type of coffee you want—espresso, cappuccino, and so on. Then you pick from an even wider selection of hash varieties—"Nepal," "Kashmir," "Thai," "Kabul"—and the barman rolls a joint. A joint costs about $3. For nonsmokers, there are "space cakes," the Dutch version of that famous hippie dessert, the marijuana-laced brownie. Contrary to Amsterdam's freewheeling reputation, the hash houses tend to be quiet and controlled. At risk of police closure, the shops strictly enforce the mandatory age limits—customers have to be eighteen to buy hash, two years older than the legal drinking age. They refuse requests for a doggy bag to take extra joints home. This decriminalization has worked fairly well in the Netherlands. Drug use in general in the Netherlands appears to be lower than in the prohibitionist United States. Among teenagers Dutch government polls indicate that about 18 percent report using some narcotic drug at least once a month; data for the United States show usage above 25 percent. The Dutch police say that few of the hash-house customers move on to harder drugs.

The pioneer of the harm-reduction approach for harder drugs was Portugal. This small country had always had a drug problem, fueled largely by heroin carried across the Mediterranean by smugglers from north Africa. For decades, Portugal's dank, grimy national prison at Leiria was filled primarily with drug offenders; it was also the scene of a lively market in heroin and cocaine among the inmates. Police spent much of their time pursuing drug dealers and users, often sending the same people back to Leiria time and time again. All this seemed futile and frustrating to an urbane, articulate Lisbon law professor named Vitalino Canas. When he was offered a government job, Canas (the name rhymes with *panache*) jumped at the chance to abandon the prohibitionist policy that Portugal had followed.

As the federal drugs commissioner at the start of the century, Canas convinced Portugal's parliament to decriminalize the use of all drugs, and to guarantee treatment rather than imprisonment for all addicts. For political reasons, Canas regularly reminded his conservative countrymen that the new law would not tolerate or legalize hard drugs. "You have to be very careful about the message you send," Canas told me. "We do not say, we have never said, that it is good to use heroin or cocaine. These drugs are still forbidden. What has changed is the means we use to prevent their use. Under our law, the *traficante* [the dealer] is still a felon and faces a severe prison term. But the person buying heroin is not a criminal. He is a sick person. He needs treatment, and we now know that jail does not work as a clinic." Portugal's drug law is so indulgent toward drug takers that it rejects terms like *addict* or *user*. Rather, the person hooked on hard drugs is referred to as a "consumer."

To decide who is or is not a *traficante*, Portugal, like the other "harm reduction" countries of Europe, has made rules based on quantity. When Portuguese police arrest a person on drug charges now, the crucial point at issue is how much heroin or cocaine is found at the time of the arrest.

If the arrestee has less than ten days' personal supply of each drug, the amount is considered to be for personal use, and the individual is declared to be a "consumer." If there is more than ten days' supply, the suspect can be charged with dealing drugs and is subject to prison.

The distinction between a "consumer" and a "dealer" is not always clear, of course. At a treatment center in Lisbon, I came across a man who might fit in either category—Miguel Soares, a sometime auto mechanic and longtime addict. Miguel was twenty-nine, he told me, and had been using heroin and cocaine for a dozen years. He spent between $20 and $100 per day on his habit. To raise the money, "Sometimes I worked in a garage. Sometimes I stole. Sometimes, I sold drugs, if I had extra. I did whatever I had to do to get the money for my next shot." Although Miguel was exactly the kind of person most affected by Europe's new attitude toward drug users, he had never heard of the new policy until he was picked up by the cops in the spring of 2002 carrying one envelope with several grams of heroin and another with a slightly smaller stash of cocaine. "I thought, Oh, Lord, here we go again," Miguel told me with a grim look. "I figured I was headed straight back to Leiria. I already had two terms in there." In fact, Miguel didn't have enough contraband on his person to qualify as a *traficante*, so he was spared another stretch behind bars. When I met him, he was a free man, dividing his time between part-time work as an auto mechanic and outpatient treatment at Lisbon's biggest drug treatment clinic. "It's a good deal, because what I really want is to give up drugs," he said. "And I could never do that in prison; in there, the dealers were living right next to me."

Shortly after I met Miguel Soares, I ran into the drug commissioner, Vitalino Canas. I told him what had happened with Miguel, and the politician was pleased as punch. "It does not make sense to put a man like that in prison," Canas said. "Prison will not cure his addiction; prison will probably make it worse. And the whole point of government is surely not to make personal problems worse. A government must exist to help people with problems. Isn't that what government is for, in the end? That's the point of our social system."

. . .

In drug policy, the European social model has produced a result that meets the basic goal of the welfare state and saves money at the same time. The fact is, it is cheaper to treat addicts than to jail them. In health care, too, the Europeans provide universal coverage and state-of-the-art treatment for far less money than America spends for a less extensive system. For the most part, though, Europe's cushy welfare state is also costly. Expenses for health care, child care, education, unemployment support, pensions, and so forth comprise by far the largest single chunk of every European nation's budget. Of course, that kind of cradle-to-grave welfare is important to the Europeans, a key element of their definition of what it means to be European. But it takes money. One way the EU nations can find enough public money to fund the social model is by cutting back on another essential form of public spending. But that's another story, which we will take up in the following chapter.

SEVEN

Showdown at Capability Gap

Yiannos Papantoniou was excited. "Today is a great day, an historic day, for the European Union," the Greek minister of defense declared in his nearly perfect English. "One of the main goals of the new Europe, and of the Greek presidency, has now been achieved. With the agreement of all 25 European Union defense ministers, we can today declare that a dream has been fulfilled. We have reached political agreement with NATO and ensured EU autonomy. We have given the green light for the first actual operation of the EuroArmy."

Given his obvious enthusiasm, it is surely excusable that Defense Minister Papantoniou used an unofficial—and indeed, politically incorrect—term on that May afternoon in 2003. Because his nation happened to hold the six-month "presidency"—that is, the rotating chairmanship—of all EU institutions in the first half of that year, it fell to the Greek defense minister to announce a significant development in European military affairs: the initial mission of a new fighting unit that was created to give the European Union some martial clout of its own, outside of NATO and NATO's American commanders. The new air, land, and sea force, under European command, was being dispatched on a peacekeeping mission to Macedonia, replacing a NATO operation there. It was hardly a major military campaign, but it was historic in its own way. For Operation Amber Fox was the first allied military mission in Europe since the end of World War II that did not include Americans.

In essence, the force dispatched to the Macedonian front was a European army, staffed and commanded entirely by EU member nations. And thus the excited Greek defense minister was factually correct when he referred to the "first actual operation of the EuroArmy." As a diplomatic matter, though, Mr. Papantoniou might have spoken more carefully. The fact is, neither the U.S. military nor the NATO brass are pleased with the concept of an autonomous European "army." Accordingly, the official and approved name for the new unit, settled upon after extensive negotiations between Washington and Brussels, is the European Rapid Reaction Force. This mouthful is sometimes referred to by its acronymic form, ERRF. But most people just call it, as Defense Minister Papantoniou did in his burst of enthusiasm, the EuroArmy.

If Americans are unhappy about the EuroArmy—or the ERRF, if you insist—that displeasure is a classic example of the old rule that you should be careful what you wish for. For decades, Americans have been prodding, pushing, and pleading with the nations of Europe to contribute more to their own defense. Particularly since the economic renaissance of the 1950s and '60s made Western Europe rich again, Washington has been complaining that Europe is taking a "free ride" on the NATO gravy train. The Europeans have no good answer to this complaint, because the American side is right. For more than half a century, European nations have relied on American soldiers, American weaponry, and America's awesome military technology as their first line of defense.

This has produced huge savings in European military budgets. Particularly since the end of the cold war, the countries of Europe have reduced defense spending by tens of billions of euros, year after year. This provides the billions of euros required to fund the benevolent but costly welfare state described in the last chapter. That is the basic policy choice of contemporary Europe: scrimp on tanks, missiles, and aircraft carriers in order to spend more on schools, health care, and pensions. The pattern is consistent across the continent. The pan-European decision to value maternity leave over military matters is another powerful unifying element that has helped bring European countries together—and set them apart from the United States. The EuroArmy doesn't break that pattern, because it amounts to self-defense on the cheap.

The ideal of a EuroArmy had been floating around since the dawn of the European Union. But Churchill's initial proposal for a combined French-German force—as further insurance against any future European war—was far too ambitious for the early postwar era. It was the renewed push for "ever greater union" at the end of the twentieth century, and the spread of physical, cultural, and financial connections, that revived the idea of a European military force. In December 2001 the EU heads of state agreed at a summit meeting in Laeken, just outside Brussels, to go ahead with the force. But various disputes and disagreements emerged, and thus it was not until the Macedonia operation in the spring of 2003 that the new military force got its first official mission. It was a small peacekeeping job, with a few thousand troops involved, but it was still a matter of concern to the Pentagon. "Of course we have been urging the Europeans to take a larger role," U.S. Defense Secretary Donald Rumsfeld said in rueful tones. "But we do want our friends to remember the contribution that NATO has made on the continent, and we would not want this new force to undermine in any way our traditional alliance." Rumsfeld's concern was perhaps heightened by the attitude of the Russians, who welcomed the birth of a EuroArmy, for exactly the reasons the Pentagon disliked it. The ERRF, said the Russian envoy to NATO, Aleksandr Vershbow, is "a dagger pointed at NATO's heart."

If so, it was a small dagger, and not very sharp. No matter how far the members of the EU proceed toward defense integration, they are simply not going to pose any significant military challenge to the American behemoth. In sheer woman- and manpower, the continent has a combined military force that is bigger than the Pentagon's. The twenty-five countries together have about 2 million soldiers, sailors, and flyers in uniform; the United States has 1.6 million active duty military personnel.

On every other relevant measure, though—total spending, research and development, and numbers of ships, aircraft, and warheads—the U.S. military leaves all of Europe in the dust. Even before the 9/11 attacks, America's annual military budget was larger than the defense spending of all European Union members combined. (In fact, the U.S. spends more on defense than the EU, Russia, and China combined.) Including the money spent on the Iraq war, the United States spends almost 4 percent of its gross domestic product on defense. The European average is less than 2 percent of GDP. Britain and France generally spend a little more than 2 percent on military matters; Italy, Germany, Spain, and the Scandinavian countries always spend less than the 2 percent level. In total, the United States spends something in the range of $350 billion per year on defense, while the whole of Europe spends less than half as much.

In the aftermath of 9/11, as the United States went to war first in Afghanistan and then in Iraq, George W. Bush increased defense spending by about 15 percent per year. Just the increase in U.S. spending—it came to something over $45 billion annually—was greater than the total annual defense budget of either France or Britain, the two biggest military spenders in Europe. The biggest gap of all is in technology. The Pentagon regularly spends about $28,000 per soldier per year on research and development; that's four or five times the European figure. The hundreds of billions of dollars poured into military research have produced the "smart bombs," the night-vision scopes, the laser-guided missiles, and all the other apparatus right out of *Star Wars* that makes the U.S. military the most formidable force the world has ever seen. No European force comes close.

This so-called capability gap was the reason that Americans kept calling on their NATO allies all those years to put more money into military budgets. This is not to suggest that the Pentagon wants to see European armies with the kind of global sway that America now commands. Rather, the hope was that Europe might take over some of the responsibility for defending its own turf, a responsibility that has been left to NATO (and thus, primarily, to the United States) for more than fifty years. Even if the EU nations were to go on a massive defense spending binge—a hypothetical concept that is not at all likely to occur—the European forces would not begin to compare to America's military profile. There's a fundamental difference in mission.

The United States, with its globe-circling missiles and its bristling naval task groups and its fleet of long-range bombers, with planes in the air every minute of every day, has built a military force that can carry American power anywhere on earth, almost instantly. The European militaries were not designed for that kind of job. In today's Europe, a soldier's place is closer to home. The army is called up to deal with floods and tornadoes, to control riots, to deal with internal violence like the terrorist campaigns of the IRA in Northern Ireland and the Basques in France and Spain. In most European nations, the military plays a large role in the effort to control illegal immigration. When livestock farms in Britain, France, Ireland, and Holland were plagued with a major outbreak of foot-and-mouth disease in early 2001, it was the army in each country that took on the horrendous task of culling the herds, killing the infected animals, and burning their cadavers in mass crematoria.

No European nation could lead an invasion of Afghanistan or Iraq, as the United States has done in the first years of the twenty-first century. European allies assisted the United States in each case, but none of them had the ships, planes, equipment, or communications capability required to mount and direct an overseas war. For that matter, Europeans generally don't have the military strength—or the political will—to fight even on their home continent. European leaders watched and deplored the genocide taking place in several corners of the former Yugoslavia for much of the 1990s. Parliaments passed resolutions of condemnation, and academics signed petitions left and right. But the decisive movement against Slobodan Milosevic and his Serbian army came only when the United States went to war there, dragging the rest of NATO along like a worried puppy on a leash. The treaty that ended the fighting in the European state of Bosnia was signed in Dayton, Ohio.

It was that embarrassment in the Balkan states—together with the shock of 9/11, and the fear that the terrorists might strike next on European soil—that finally convinced the leaders of Europe that they needed an army to represent the interests of the EU. "Europe needs to shoulder its reponsibilities . . . resolutely doing battle against all violence, all terror, and all fanaticism," the heads of state declared at Laeken. To implement this imposing pledge, the nations of Europe have patched together a somewhat unimposing military unit. The European Rapid Reaction Force is not really a EuroArmy at all, but rather a reserve unit that can be called up from various countries when needed. Germany has promised to make about 13,500 soldiers available, Britain 12,500, France 12,000; twelve other countries have also agreed to provide troops when the demand occurs. Even little Luxembourg is taking part, offering to send 500 of its soldiers to ERRF deployments. That is, the EuroArmy will be staffed and supplied out of existing armies; it does not involve any major commitment to more soldiers or more equipment.

In all, the European force will have about 60,000 soldiers on call at any given moment. The member nations will provide up to 300 combat aircraft and 100 warships, most of them destroyers or smaller, for coastal operations. All commanders will be from European military forces; in fact, the absence of American command and control sometimes seems to be the main attraction of this force to the Europeans. "The EU must not leave the impression that Americans are leading" the ERRF, noted Defense Minister Papantoniou on the proud day when he announced the first deployment. In fact, the member countries are so determined to develop an independent force of their own that they've even committed to spend new money—well, some new money—on it. Because no European military has adequate transport planes to deposit the EuroArmy where it needs to be, the EU nations have agreed to buy a fleet of new troop transport aircraft—to be built, of course, by the European airplane maker Airbus. The new plane is called (inevitably) the EuroLift. Until the first models are delivered, Europe's army will borrow transport planes from NATO.

The European Rapid Reaction Force is supposed to be capable of deploying up to 60,000 troops within forty-five days of call-up, and sustain them in a theater of operations "in or around Europe" for up to a year. The quasi-military operations that the ERRF can perform are known as the Petersberg tasks, a name taken from a hotel near Bonn where European defense ministers agreed in 1992 as to the kind of thing their soldiers should be doing. Beyond the catch-all commitment to "provide for the common defense," the operations approved at Petersberg are primarily the stuff that European armies are accustomed to do: humanitarian and rescue tasks, peacekeeping tasks, and crisis management. That first mission in Macedonia was typical; the EuroArmy forces were deployed to replace a NATO peacekeeping force designed to prevent ethnic tensions from breaking out into riots or fighting.

Compared to most of the world's armies, European forces are large and well equipped. The EU member nations have twice as many military personnel as Russia and almost as many as China, and a combined defense budget that dwarfs both of those important powers. Compared to the U.S. defense establishment, however, Europe is a "military pygmy," as the secretary-general of NATO noted acidly in 2002. Beyond the huge disparity in budgets and equipment, there is also the fact that soldiers assigned to the European force have no tradition of fighting for the new, united Europe. On this ground, American foreign policy expert Zbigniew Brzezinski brushed aside the new EuroArmy as a futile effort: "It is simply the case that no European is willing to die for Europe." That may be true, but it misses the point. At the dawn of the twenty-first century, Europeans are not willing to die in warfare, period. Frenchmen are not dying for France, Danes are not dying for Denmark. The whole point of the New Europe in the new century is that soldiers are no longer going to be sent off to die for their country, or for their united continent.

But European soldiers do die in their jobs as peacekeepers and in other Petersberg tasks. Since the fall of the Taliban, far more Europeans have died in Afghanistan than Americans, because the Europeans stayed behind to do the Petersberg work of nation-building there after most American troops were sent home. More than one hundred European soldiers died in the second Iraq war, most of them in the long, difficult mopping-up operation after the main fighting ended. Several hundred peacekeepers from European countries have been killed over the years struggling to maintain order in the Balkans. These men and women did not "die for Europe," but that distinction seems rather trivial when you stand at their graves. The European soldiers are still dead—not because they were fighting for Europe, but because they were willing to put on a uniform and work in dangerous places for European ideals.

Still, the Europeans are not going to spend the money and commit the soldiers necessary to bridge the gap in national defense. There's no will to do so. To the citizens of unified Europe, military power seems an outmoded concept. It's something Europe doesn't need anymore. Following the path blazed by Churchill, Schumann, Monnet, and the like, the European nations have eliminated the threat of war against their EU neighbors. The end of the cold war, in turn, eliminated the threat of a war against the Soviet bloc, since there is no Soviet bloc left to fight. Russia today is seen not as a threat but rather as a potential future member of the EU club. As a result, Europe is at a point in its history where making aggressive war is considered passé, an outdated relic along the lines of burning at the stake or a medieval joust. Of course there will be times and places in the world when invasion and war might be necessary, but the Europeans are willing to leave those situations in the hands of their strong ally, the United States. The American military can lead the charge—and take the casualties—in places like Afghanistan and Iraq. Then the Europeans will come in to patrol the aftermath.

This transatlantic division of military labor has prompted a host of metaphors. American strategic thinkers regularly say that "the United States cooks the dinner, and the Europeans wash the dishes." This description is meant as an insult, and the Europeans feel the insult (although the sting is not bitter enough to make them do anything about it). European policymakers use different terminology to explain the same contrast. They say that "the United States is the war maker, and the Europeans are the peacekeepers." This, too, is meant as an insult, although it is not clear that the Pentagon finds it insulting to be labeled the planet's premier war maker.

These distinctions are reflected in Europe's most powerful military force, which is NATO, the North Atlantic Treaty Organization. As we saw in chapter 2, NATO was one of the two key contributions that the United States made toward the unification of Europe in the first years after World War II. The Marshall Plan paid for rebuilding, to bring European economies back to life; NATO served as a defense umbrella so that democracy and free markets could grow despite the hulking Communist power on the eastern border. NATO's basic role was deterrence, and it worked; the cold war never turned hot. After the collapse of the Soviet union and its bloc of eastern satellites, NATO was in an embarrassing position: it had won the cold war, but lost its mission. Neither the United States nor the Europeans were inclined to shut it down, however. So NATO is still there, a huge military and political bureaucracy in Brussels with its own campus, hierarchy, diplomatic corps, and social scene.

In a classic application of one of bureaucracy's immutable rules, NATO's size increased as its mission shrank. Propelled partly by U.S. political considerations—all those Polish-American voters in Chicago, who wanted to see the old country within NATO—and partly by the same driving impulse toward European unity that made the EU expand eastward, NATO grew from sixteen countries at the end of the Cold War to twenty-six members in 2004. The arrangement is now often called "26 plus 1," because Russia has been designated an official "partner" of NATO, complete with a NATO ambassador who takes part in most meetings and all those glitzy social functions.

Some basic things remain unchanged, however. The United States still pays the bills for NATO—somewhere between 60 and 85 percent of the budget, depending on how you measure—and the United States provides the most advanced equipment. Most important, some fifteen years after the Soviet threat has disappeared, the United States still keeps more than 100,000 active-duty military personnel stationed full-time in Europe. There are some 68,000 American soldiers in Germany, 12,000 in Italy, 10,000 in Britain, and another 15,000 or so scattered around other European bases. Despite the presence of a big multinational staff and a secretary-general from an EU country—in 2004, a Dutchman replaced a Scot in the job—the United States calls the shots. If the United States is against some proposed mission, NATO won't do it. Because of the capability gap, the European members of NATO can't do much of anything without the money, manpower, and firepower that the United States provides.

The huge differential in sheer fighting strength between the United States and any European country has spawned a school of thought in the United States that holds, in essence, that Europe doesn't matter anymore. Since the United States has the military might to go anywhere and do anything all by itself, the thinking goes, it need not pay much attention to the Europeans (or anybody else) with their pipsqueak little armies and aging, low-tech weapons. This thesis assumes that military power is an essential element of being a superpower; since neither the EU nor any other state can match American military power, the theory runs, there can be no other superpower to challenge the United States on the world stage. Zbigniew Brzezinski puts it this way: "The United States is likely to remain the only truly global power for at least another generation. And that in turn means that America in all likelihood will also remain the dominant partner in the transatlantic alliance."

There are several advocates of this "unipolar" view of today's world, but the most prominent, and the most eloquent, is surely Robert Kagan, a Brussels-based American analyst. Kagan turned the America-is-unstoppable theory into a book, *Of Paradise and Power*. The title reflects Kagan's argument that Europe wants to live in a borderless, multinational paradise where disputes are settled by rules and negotiation, rather than fighting; the United States, in this view, is different because it doesn't mind using sheer killing power to resolve problems with its adversaries. Here's the thesis, from the first page of the book:

Europe is turning away from power . . . into a self-contained world of laws and rules and transnational negotiations and cooperation. . . . Meanwhile, the United States remains mired in history, exercising power in an anarchic Hobbesian world where international laws and rules are unreliable, and where true security and the defense and promotion of a liberal order still depend on the possession and use of military might.

More than once in his book, Kagan invokes the metaphor about Americans making dinner and Europeans doing the dishes afterward. But he is best known for coining a different way to say the same thing: "On major strategic and international questions today, Americans are from Mars and Europeans are from Venus." In other words, Kagan says, "on the all-important question of power," Americans and Europeans don't inhabit the same planet, and thus the old transatlantic alliance must crumble because of the difference in military strength. Americans don't need Europe's support or approval for international adventures, Kagan argues: "The United States can go it alone, and it is hardly surprising that the American superpower should wish to preserve its ability to do so. . . . Americans are powerful enough that they need not fear Europeans."

The notion that America is so mighty it doesn't have to pay attention any longer to those pesky Europeans and their covenants and councils and treatises on international law had obvious appeal to a certain segment of U.S. opinion. In fact, Kagan's book spent several weeks on the best-seller list just before the United States invaded Iraq in 2003. The American best-seller list, that is. Not surprisingly, the suggestion that America is strong, Europe is weak, and ne'er the twain shall meet was considerably less popular in Europe.

The Europeans responded to the theory that "America will remain the dominant power" in two ways. First, they argued that the whole thesis of Kagan's book falls apart in the first paragraph. When Kagan writes about "the all-important question of power," the critics said, he is defining *power* much too narrowly. He means only military power. But this is to ignore other forms of power—political power, economic power, cultural power, moral power, and particularly the persuasive power of a driving idea, such as the idea that nations should find methods other than warfare to resolve their differences. "To make military power the litmus test of European integration," writes the German foreign policy specialist Christoph Bertram, "is to repeat Stalin's mistake of judging the Catholic Church by the number of its [military] divisions." Reflecting a common European view, Bertram charges that the Kaganites in the United States are trapped in a "one-track fascination with their own military and technological prowess and the dizziness of grandeur."

Beyond that, according to the response from the European side of the Atlantic, America's military power has hardly made it invulnerable. America's might did not scare off the ragtag terrorists of Al Qaeda who inflicted the most damaging attack ever on American soil—at a time when the United States was clearly the dominant military power on earth. Americans spend nearly $400 billion of their tax dollars on defense every year, but they still have to take their belts and shoes off every time they want to get on an airplane (security measures are far less stringent in European airports). American strength and technology made the initial attack on Iraq in the spring of 2003 proceed swiftly and almost painlessly toward the collapse of Saddam Hussein's government; but all that strength did not deter the diehards and the troublemakers in the cities of Iraq who killed hundreds of American soldiers and left thousands maimed and wounded after the major battles were over. The broad European opposition to America's display of power in Iraq—and the strong antiwar lobbying campaign in the United Nations, led by Europeans—prompted most of the rich countries of the world to refuse to take part in or help pay for the war. Thus America's unchallenged power, in Iraq at least, forced it to pay, almost single-handed, an immensely expensive bill in blood, in dollars, and in international prestige. If that's what being a military superpower buys you, Europe doesn't want it.

The Europeans, in contrast, are banking on the belief that the EU can become a superpower of its own on the world stage without building a military that can match American might. This, after all, was the vision of Jean Monnet, who declared in 1947 that his budding United States of Europe would become "a civilian great power." The nonfighting super-power plans to win its way, not on the battlefied but by corralling more votes than the Americans in the United Nations, the World Trade Organization, the International Monetary Fund, and other international gatherings. The European Union plays both ends against the middle in all these organizations. In debate, it acts as a single unit, frequently with EU officials on hand to do the debating. But when it comes time to vote, the member nations drop the idea of a single unit and jealously guard their right to cast separate votes, country by country. When the EU is united—and it usually is, in international organizations—it has twenty-five votes to cast in opposition to America's one vote. Jean Monnet, the founding father, predicted that the European Union would eventually have unified membership in the UN and other organizations, but the current EU members have no interest in that arrangement. It would reduce their twenty-five votes to one.

Beyond that, the EU generally picks up numerous allies to add to its built-in twenty-four-vote margin in these organizations. It wins these allies not with a stick but a carrot—particularly with a fat purse full of foreign aid contributions all over the world.

In a sense, Europe's commitment to foreign aid—often referred to on the continent as ODA, or "overseas development aid"—is the mirror image of Washington's determination to maintain the strongest military forces on earth. The same global crises that prompt a big jump in Pentagon spending in the United States lead to increased ODA in Europe. In fact, the Europeans refer to foreign aid as "soft security"—that is, another form of national defense. The result is that the European Union countries give more aid to more poor nations than any other donors. For 2003 (when the EU still had only fifteen member nations) aid payments from the EU—both the union itself, and the individual countries—totaled about $36.5 billion; the United States, with roughly the same total wealth, gave only $13.3 billion in development aid, about 36 percent of

Europe's donation. (Japan, the third biggest foreign aid donor, gave about $9.2 billion.)[1] European foreign aid spending has more clout than the American dollar, partly because there's more money coming from Europe, but also because the Europeans spread their donations more widely. The basic tendency—driven, perhaps, by postimperial guilt—is to direct aid money to former colonies. That means the Europeans are funding aid projects all over Africa, in the Caribbean and South America, and in East and South Asia. U.S. foreign aid, in contrast, is fairly sharply concentrated on the Middle East.

The United Nations has set a standard to guide the rich nations in deciding how much of their wealth to give away to the poor. The basic rule is that developed countries should give 0.7 percent of gross domestic product (that is, a country's total annual earnings) each year in foreign aid. Very few of the two dozen wealthiest nations meet this standard. All of those that pass the UN test are European. The OECD's ranking showing the most generous donor nations—in terms of what percentage of their national wealth they give away in foreign aid—looked like this in 2002, which was a typical year in this regard:

Nation	ODA as a percentage of GDP
Denmark	0.96%
Norway	.89
Sweden	.83
Netherlands	.81
Luxembourg	.77
Belgium	.43
Ireland	.40
France	.38
Japan	.23
United States	.13

There's no doubt that all this European giving is prompted by a deep impulse of charity; it would be churlish to suggest that the EU and its member nations are making these donations in order to buy influence around the world. Still, influence often results from a steady program of donations. The recipient nations feel gratitude, and they want to get more aid the next year; thus they tend to pay attention when donor nations start pushing a particular political position.

George W. Bush learned that lesson himself in the spring of 2003, when he and his ally Tony Blair were desperately seeking votes for the United Nations Security Council resolution authorizing a war on Iraq. France and Germany lobbied among the fifteen nations that then held seats on the Security Council for a vote against the war; the United States argued for a vote in favor. This turned out to be an unfair lobbying competition, because a majority of the Security Council members at that point in time (other than the five permanent seats created at the end of World War II, Security Council seats rotate every two years) were regular recipients of EU financial aid. With nine votes needed to pass a resolution, the United States and Britain were never able to attract more than four of the swing nations. The U.S. government raged about the French/German lobbying campaign—somewhat disingenuously, as Washington and London were lobbying just as hard. But the real frustration for the American government was that, for all its military power, it did not have sufficient political power to overcome the European campaign. Europe's political clout proved stronger than American military might.

Of course, neither Europe nor the UN could stop the Americans from deploying their awesome military force. The United States and Britain went to war in Iraq without the backing of the Security Council. But the lack of UN approval was costly nonetheless. Without a formal resolution, many nations that might have been allies in the war declined to support the effort, either with troops or money. After the fall of Baghdad, with American soldiers being killed by Iraqi insurgents at the rate of fifty or more each month, Washington came back to Europe, hat in hand, pleading for help in the task of building a new Iraq. The sense of "we told you so," of sheer satisfaction of seeing the American juggernaut begging for help from those hopelessly weak Europeans, was palpable all across the continent. The Americans could do the war-making, but when it came time for nation-building, they needed European help (or so Europe saw it).

In other areas as well, the European Union often seems to go out of its way to pursue foreign policy goals that run directly counter to American initiatives. The contrast is sharpest in the Middle East, where the EU has emerged as the strongest and most generous backer of the Palestinian state. In the early years of the twenty-first century, when Washington saw Israel as a fellow victim in the war against terror and consequently tilted strongly in its favor, the EU ostentatiously took the other side, criticizing the Israelis and assuring the Palestinians that they had friends in Brussels. When President George W. Bush broke openly with Yasser Arafat and declared that Arafat was "unacceptable" as Palestinian leader, the EU sent a diplomatic mission to Palestine to declare that any leader chosen by the Palestinian people—including Arafat—was "acceptable" to Europe.

When the Bush administration declared North Korea to be part of the global "axis of evil" and cut off U.S. talks and energy funds for Pyongyang, the European Union almost immediately dispatched a high-profile team to visit the rogue nation and talk about EU aid programs that could be made available. When Washington in 2003 called for tougher economic sanctions against Cuba, the EU sent a mission to Havana to offer assurances that Cuban sugar, cigars, and so on could still be traded, and Cuban doctors and lawyers could still be trained, anywhere in Europe. At each annual summit meeting of the G-7 group of rich nations, the Europeans bring up and pass a resolution warning that U.S. budget deficits are dangerous to the global economy. Nobody suggests that this will have any impact on U.S. deficits; it's just a tool to remind the assembled heads of state where the power lies in the G-7 (with four of the seven votes belonging to EU members, and an associate's seat at the table reserved for the president of the EU). And the EU regularly complains about American failure to pay its back allotments of dues to the UN.

If there is a pattern to these transatlantic policy differences, it is that

European foreign policy is built around a principle of multilateralism, around regional and global agreements and associations—that is, it mirrors the experiences of the European Union itself. The EU, after all, is a cooperative community that has been an historic success at its main goals, preventing another war in Europe and giving European nations new stature on the world stage. With that kind of experience, it's hardly surprising that European nations would decide that multilateralism is the right approach to almost any international problem. The former French foreign minister, Dominique Galouzeau de Villepin, maintains that Europeans have an almost sacred mission to spread this communitarian approach to the rest of the world: "We are the guardians of an ideal," de Villepin says, "the guardians of a conscience that puts cooperation ahead of domination. And that must be the future for all the world." The United States, with money and military power that match or exceed all of Europe's, has been much more inclined to act as its own guardian—a tendency that accelerated under the presidency of George W. Bush.

One problem with the American inclination toward independent action is that the rest of the world seems to be leaning Europe's way. All over the planet, nations are eagerly signing up to international agreements, treaties, and conventions, often leaving the United States on the short end of extremely lopsided votes. When the nations of the world gathered in 2001 to implement the Kyoto Protocol on global warming, the final agreement was approved by a vote of 178 to 1. That solitary "no" vote was the United States. The vote on the international treaty banning antipersonnel land mines was 142–0; all European nations were in the majority, while the United States abstained. On the new International Criminal Court, the final vote was 120–7, with 21 abstentions. The United States was one of the "no" voters, along with Cuba, China, Libya, and Iraq; all European nations voted with the majority.

This is not to say that members of the European Union always agree on matters of global policy. Although the EU members formally agreed in 1992 (the Maastricht Treaty) to adhere to a Common Foreign and

Security Policy, the "common" aspect of the CFSP is often nothing more than wishful thinking. The European Union, as we have seen, is a great experiment in pooled sovereignty—but foreign policy is one area where the individual nations have been reluctant to jump into the pool.

Europe's chaotic response to the Iraq war of 2003 showed the world how seriously disunited the European Union can be when it comes to foreign policy. The EU provided the strongest allies of the United States in that war—Britain, Spain, and Italy—but it was also the locus of the most vigorous, and most important, opposition. The widespread disgust with the war turned out to be a unifying force among the European people, as the general population found itself in broad agreement in opposing Washington—and, in some cases, in opposing their own governments. While most EU governments were officially against the war—and refused to provide either money or manpower to assist the Allied forces—the leaders of several important European nations showed at least partial support for George W. Bush. Six weeks before the fighting started—at a time when the streets of European capitals were jammed with antiwar demonstrations—eight European prime ministers signed an open letter that placed them closer to Bush's position than to the demonstrators outside their windows. "The combination of weapons of mass destruction and terrorism is a threat of incalculable consequences. It is one at which all of us should feel concerned," the letter said. The prime ministers didn't explicitly back a war in Iraq; rather, they expressed "our wish to pursue the UN route" rather than a quick invasion. Still the tone was clearly pro-American. At the same time that letter was written, however, most other European prime ministers were strongly against a war. And the European Parliament passed, by a big margin, a resolution denouncing any American attack unless the United Nations approved of a war in advance. In this case, there was in fact a "common foreign policy" among the people of Europe; it was the governments of Europe that couldn't find much in common on a crucial global issue.

This difficulty is evident in the very institutions the EU has built to deal with global affairs. Unwilling to entrust their relations with the world to a single department or official, the EU members originally created, in effect, four distinct foreign offices in Brussels. There was a "high representative" who acted as the union's foreign minister and was supposed to be in charge of the Common Foreign and Security Policy. Then there was a separate commissioner for external relations who oversaw that big foreign aid budget. There is a separate trade commissioner who deals with the WTO and individual nations on import-export issues, and, as we learned in the first chapter of this book, a competition commissioner who represents the EU to foreign companies that operate in Europe. The new EU Constitution in 2004 simplified this system slightly by merging the posts of foreign minister and commissioner for external relations into one cabinet post. While the EU members have largely agreed on a single currency, a single bill of rights, a single central bank, and so on, they still run separate foreign ministries. In any major capital, Embassy Row will include delegations from all twenty-five EU member nations, and from the EU itself. If there really were a common foreign and security policy, those twenty-six embassies could probably be replaced by one.

In the jargon of the political scientists, the kind of power that a nation accrues through military strength is known as "hard power." The influence that comes from economic strength, from cultural and political influence, from leadership in international organizations, is known as "soft power." Along with the rest of the world, the European Union has essentially conceded global dominance in the field of "hard power" to the United States and its unmatchable military forces. But the EU is betting that it can become an actor of equal importance on the world stage—in short, the world's next superpower—through the "soft power" it is consistently enhancing. Indeed, the Europeans argue that hard power is so costly to maintain—and so likely to generate hatred from those who are weaker—that soft power amounts to greater power. The Oxford historian John Pinder makes this point: "Too much American hegemony is dangerous for the Americans as well as for others. The burden is too great for one country to carry alone. Only the EU has the potential to be at least an equal partner with respects to the economy, the environment, and soft security, though not defense."

EIGHT

Generation E

and the Ties That Bind
the New Europe

"It is the crap, it is totally crap, you know, but I love it," Gregor said in his heavily Slavic-tinged English, an exotic variant on the language, all *ee*'s and *z*'s, that might remind an American of Zsa Zsa Gabor. He took a large swallow of a Vodka Bull, leaned onto the bar, and continued: "I mean, this is rubbish—zeess eess roobeesh—but I cannot miss. Every year, I never miss it. That's why we are all here tonight, you know because we all love how strange it is, how crazy. Everybody loves Eurovision. Everybody my age, but not just my age! Everybody loves, because it is totally crap!"

On a Saturday evening in May, as crowds jammed nine and ten people thick around each of the big TV screens in the London club, it was hard to disagree with Gregor. Across the continent, nearly everybody seems to love the annual Eurovision song contest, a pan-European pageant of kitsch, bad taste, and third-rate lounge acts that has been drawing TV viewers by the tens of millions for nearly half a century. Eurovision is to Europe what Oscar night is to the United States, or the Super Bowl—a time when everybody gathers around the TV screen for something that has no importance whatsoever, except for the four hours when everybody is tuned in. Perhaps the closest American equivalent to Eurovision, for pure schlock value, is the Miss America pageant. But the European extravaganza differs from its glitzy American cousins in significant ways. For one thing, the Europeans are more democratic. The winners of Eurovision are chosen not by opening an envelope or consulting a panel of high-minded judges. Instead, the people of Europe get to vote for the winner. On the night of the contest each May, millions and millions of people across the continent phone in their choice for Europe's best pop song. After many hours at Eurovision parties, many of the voters are probably drunk as skunks, which may help explain why the popular favorite is not always determined by the quality of the music. One year, the winner was a German band that displayed minimal musical talent but had the marketing sense to give itself a bizarre name, Orthopedic Stockings. This proved a powerful vote-getter.

Beyond that, Eurovision—unlike the National Football League, say, or Miss America—is a multinational phenomenon. More than two dozen nations from Iceland to Italy (not to mention that well-known European country, Israel) send representatives to compete each year, and the show is televised simultaneously in thirty nations. Amid its sequined slit-thigh skirts and glittering gold lamé suits, therefore, the annual Eurovision Song Contest is playing an historic role. Eurovision has become a celebration of European-ness, a great annual coming-together that strengthens the growing sense among 500 million people that they all belong to a single place on the world map. It is thus one of several forces creating the "common European home" that the founding fathers of united Europe dreamed about in the aftermath of world war. The unification of Europe is not merely a matter of politics and economics. All sorts of borderless links are developing at the dawn of the new century, creating physical, cultural, culinary, legal, technological, and athletic networks that make the continent more connected than it has been in two millennia.

Although Eurovision seems to appeal to all makes and models of Europeans, the annual exercise in televised tastelessness has its strongest following among people like Gregor Sandyk, the twenty-seven-year-old securities trader whom I met on Eurovision night at a popular club in London. Gregor is a Croatian by birth, but there is nothing about his résumé that tells you so. He graduated from a German university and a French business school, then worked at banking jobs in Paris and Rome before taking his current position at an investment house in the City of London. Gregor's coworkers at the office are Brits, Finns, Germans, and Czechs. "There is no need for me to go back to Croatia to go home," Gregor told me. "I am home right here. I am Croatian, yes, but not so much, you know? I will say I am European."

Gregor is a member of "Generation E"—the young adults of Europe, a continent that has been essentially without borders since the time they finished school. While the Eurocrats in Brussels toil away at the job of creating a unified Europe in the markets and the law books, Gregor and his cohort—the age group ranging from about eighteen to forty—are creating a unified European society of their own, in offices and bars, in soccer stadiums, health clubs, and Internet cafés. Sociologists love to study Generation E, because it represents a new breed of European: a person who considers the entire continent—not just one country or city—to be "home."

For the postwar generation of Europeans, the ideal of a continent where a college grad from Dublin would routinely find herself working in Lisbon or Helsinki was a distant dream. Today, Generation E takes it for granted that the ability to live, work, and study anyplace on the continent is a birthright. For a Croatian like Gregor to live and work in London today is no different than a Texan taking a job in Tallahassee. This kind of mobility has been most common among college graduates—still a minority of the European population. But more and more, blue-collar workers are on the move as well, finding new jobs and new friends wherever they land. The night Gregor went to that club to watch Eurovision, he was accompanied by three pals, all certified Generation E types: a banker from Gregor's birthplace, Zagreb, a beautiful blond student from Sweden, and a journalist from Britain. They laughed and cheered and talked the night away in a language that was about 60 percent English, with bits of French and traces of Scandinavian and Slavic slang adding spice to the linguistic stew.

The members of Generation E share a common culture that tends to span the continent. In Tallinn and Seville, in Plymouth, Prague, and Paris, they read the same books, wear the same clothes, watch the same TV shows—including a fairly disgusting sex-and-music variety show that is called, appropriately, *Eurotrash*—and drink the same cocktails. They cheer for the same soccer stars and download the same pop songs to be the ring tones on their mobile phones. (Because the GSM standard makes it a cinch to install a new ring tone, no self-respecting member of Generation E would be caught dead using one of the canned tones that come preinstalled on new phones.) Politically, the generation of Europeans newly arrived at adulthood—the group of young people who think of "Europe" as their native land—tend to be the people most dedicated to the concept of "ever closer union" in Europe. Whenever the various nations hold referenda on joining the union, or joining the single currency, or approving new EU treaties, the members of Generation E vote by significant margins for the pro-Europe side. That's another reason why it's safe to say that the countries which have voted to stay out of the euro will eventually join up; these young Europhiles can be expected to keep voting for the joint currency after their Euroskeptic parents have passed away.

The second-to-last Saturday evening in May each year is an important milestone for Generation E. That's when they get together in homes, bars—and in about twenty major cities, at huge, raucous street parties—to watch, laugh at, and then vote for the contestants in the Eurovision Song Contest. In a sense, this is what Eurovision is all about; the spectacle was the pet project of a French music producer, Marcel Baison, a friend and disciple of Jean Monnet. While Monnet was turning the European Coal and Steel Community into a success, Baison thought he could use the magic of music to build yet another form of European community. In 1956, in Switzerland, Baison staged the first pan-European pop song contest, with seven nations represented. The program was telecast on the European Broadcasting Union's fledgling pancontinental broadcasting network, then known as "Eurovision." The annual contest quickly became the most popular program the Eurovision network broadcast each year, and soon the singing event took over the name.

Eurovision—the contest, not the network—made a quantum leap in public awareness in 1974. That year, an unknown Swedish group won the event with an irresistible pop tune. This previously unsung band was none other than Abba, and their Eurovision entry, "Waterloo," started them on the road to global stardom. Suddenly, Eurovision became important to the music industry, and to the audience. Numerous other pop stars got their starts at Eurovision, including Olivia Newton-John (a ringer from Australia who nonetheless represented Britain in 1974), Celine Dion (a ringer from Canada who nonetheless represented Switzerland in 1988), Nana Mouskouri (a Greek who represented Luxembourg, for some reason, in 1963), Julio Iglesias (a Spaniard who sang for Spain in 1970), and t.A.T.u., the Russian "techno lezpop" duo—two young women given to fondling and kissing each other on stage—who were the pre-event favorites in 2003 but finished a disappointing third.

Eurovision allows each country to enter one singing act, group or solo; each entry is supposed to perform an original song, although many of the numbers are already staples of the nightclub scene in their home countries. The singers are almost always accompanied by hyperenergetic dancing troops in lavish costumes who whirl, leap, tumble, and simulate assorted sexual acts in the background while the music plays. (Turkish singers generally recruit a few belly dancers for backup purposes.) It is de rigueur for Eurovision contestants to wear outlandish outfits in an effort (usually futile) to distinguish themselves from everybody else. Thus the night turns into a bewildering procession of middle-aged men wearing high heels and pink hair, breathy torch singers in white leather boots and tight gowns revealing extensive décolletage, or teenage starlets in tiny vinyl microskirts. In 1997, a British girl band stunned the continent by ripping off their sequined skirts midway through their number—to reveal matching sequined G-strings beneath—and walked away as the winners. Predictably, the tearaway skirt became a routine Eurovision feature, and is seen nowadays about twice in each show.

When all the singing, dancing, and strip-teasing is over, phone banks open in each European capital, and the viewers call in to cast their votes. Then the hosts on the Eurovision stage survey each capital to take a tally; with thirty countries casting votes, this process takes the better part of an hour. As the tally continues, tension rises as a few competitors rise to the top. If the voting is close—and it often is—the winner will not be known until the last breathless report comes in from the last capital city. The proven formula for winning the Eurovision contest is to come up with a song that has a catchy melody and a contagious sing-along chorus, like Abba's "Waterloo," that will captivate a transcontinental audience. Another route to victory is a ridiculous name, either for the band (as witness Orthopedic Stockings) or the song. The list of winning entries in Eurovision includes such deathless compositions as "Boom Bang-a-Bang" (British, 1969), "Boom Boom Boomerang" (Austria, 1977), and "Diggi-Loo, Diggi-Ley" (Sweden, 1984). The winning country each year gets to host the contest the next May; while this can offer valuable national exposure for smaller countries and former Soviet satellites, the honor gets old fairly quickly. When Ireland won five times in six years in the 1990s, the national broadcaster, RTE, complained that hosting the contest over and over had cost it tens of millions of pounds. This prompted a memorable episode of the Irish sitcom *Father Ted* (still available on video), in which two priests enter Eurovision—in clerical robes covered with sequins—and perform a dreadful number called "My Lovely Horse" to make sure that Ireland will finally lose the thing.

In real life, the Irish victory streak came to an end near the end of the last century, with the result that the Eurovision Song Contest has moved widely around Europe in recent years: Manchester, Tallinn, Riga, Istanbul. But Generation E music fans who wanted to be present each year would have found it easy to make the transcontinental trek, because of a huge expansion of the basic transit links connecting the continent. As pan-European consciousness has grown, there has been an outpouring of new roads, rail lines, bridges, and tunnels. This growth in the transportation infrastructure is largely a result of the European Union—and massive EU subsidies for trains, airports, highways, and harbors. As a result, a Europe that is coming together politically and economically is growing closer together physically as well.

There's the huge new Europabrücke—"the Bridge of Europe" in Austria; there are new tunnels to carry truck and train traffic under the Alps and across the Pyrenees. In a belated effort to make transcontinental travel as straightforward as it was in Roman times, the EU is pouring about 100 billion euros into the reconstruction of the ancient Via Egnatia, the long, straight Roman road that connected Italy and Greece to the Balkan states and on to the Middle East (this was the "road to Damascus" where the Apostle Paul had his great revelation). Europe's greatest water highway, the Rhine, has been dredged and cleared and linked by canals to the Rhone, creating so much barge traffic that the Rhine delta at Rotterdam has become the world's busiest freighter port. It is known today, inevitably, as the "Europoort."

A key milestone in this drive for improved connections was the completion of the planet's longest undersea rail line, the Channel Tunnel. The thirty-two-mile, $50 billion "Chunnel" has linked the island of Great Britain to the European mainland for the first time since the ancient land bridge melted at the end of the last ice age some 12,000 years ago. The idea for a connection between France and Britain had floated around for at least two centuries, but one side or other had always quashed it in the past. The project almost came to life in the 1890s, when the same French engineers who built the Suez Canal decided they could build a railroad beneath the seabed between Calais and the white cliffs of Dover. The idea moved ahead rapidly until it ran into a royal obstacle. Queen Victoria was not amused. Her Majesty remarked in 1896 that Britain's greatest defense had always been the island's status as "virgo intacta"; she was not going to let this unsullied virgin be penetrated by some Frenchman's long rail. A century later, though, the drive for a unified Europe overcame this ancient objection. When the Chunnel opened in 1994, the trying seven-hour car-and-ferry journey from London to Paris became a pleasant two-and-a-half-hour train trip. Not surprisingly, the Eurostar trains flashing back and forth between Paris or Brussels and London have become a common meeting place for the members of Generation E. Because the London-Brussels train makes a stop in northern France at the gate of Euro Disneyland, the Chunnel crossing has also become a standard place to see the children of Generation E, particularly on weekends.

To match that east-west link, a pair of massive projects in Scandinavia at the dawn of the new millennium finally made the continent a connected whole from its northern tip to its southern toe. First, a bridge and tunnel joined the main islands of Denmark to the Jutland Peninsula, the long thumb of land jutting northward from the heart of Europe into the Baltic. The main event, on a typically Scandinavian summer's day—cloudy and blustery—came in July of 2000, when Queen Margrethe of Denmark and King Carl Gustaf of Sweden shook hands and exchanged air kisses on a spectacular new bridge over the Øresund Sound between Copenhagen and Malmö, Sweden. The 4-billion-euro "Øresund Fixed Link"—a bridge, a tunnel, and an artificial island to connect them—spanned ten miles, providing both a highway and a railroad line across the sea and essentially shutting down the ferry services that had plied that ice-blue strait for centuries. As a result, a car, truck, or train can travel in a roughly straight line from the Arctic coast of northern Norway to the Mediterranean shores of Spain.

The Scandinavians put up most of the money for the Øresund project—with Brussels throwing in a few hundred million euros for good measure—but they did not think of it so much as an inter-Scandinavian connection. Of course, a lot of Swedes come across the bridge now to take advantage of the lower liquor taxes in Denmark; for that reason, the locals tend to call their sleek new link not the "Øresund" but rather the "Olesund," the "ale bridge." But the point of Øresund was something bigger. "We would not have spent billions on a link between Sweden and Denmark," the mayor of Copenhagen, Jens Kramer Mikkelsen, said rather bluntly. "We get along well with the Swedes, but we did not need this just to get to Malmö a little quicker. The bridge came about when we realized that we are no longer just Danes and Swedes. We are Europeans, and Scandinavia needs connections to the European mainland. We needed to have that mental bridge before we could build the concrete one."

No matter where Generation E travels, it likes to travel fast. Europe in the twenty-first century has the world's fastest passenger planes, trains, boats (a fleet of hydrofoil ferries that zip across the sounds and straits at speeds above 50 mph), and highways. Europeans invented the automobile and the limited-access expressway—General Dwight D. Eisenhower was so impressed with the German autobahn during World War II that he brought the idea home with him and created the Interstate Highway System—and the EU has maintained the tradition by funding the fastest network of highways on earth. The speed limit on the various *autostrade, autovia,* and dual carriageways that link Europe's major cities is 130 kilometers per hour (that is, 81 mph) or higher. Racing to a meeting in southern Germany one spring morning, I was tooling down the smooth, fluid autobahn at 120 miles per hour. Yet I lost count of the number of young European drivers who came up from behind and passed me. There was nothing illegal about it, either; the speed limit on German expressways is whatever you can safely maintain.

But the grandest way to get around the united Europe is the rail network, with the fastest trains on earth. In 1981, the French national railway designed a new locomotive specifically to beat the 220-kilometer-per-hour speed of the Japanese Shinkansen, or bullet train. After two decades of improvements, the sleek, missile-nosed TGV—that's the Train à Grande Vitesse, or "Train of Great Velocity"—races today from London to the Alps, from the North Sea to the Mediterranean, at some 300 kilometers per hour, or 186 mph. (For comparison, the fastest American train, Amtrak's Acela, hits 150 mph at points on its run from Washington to Boston.) Aboard the TGV, though, you never know that you're traveling that fast. You zoom smoothly along in quiet comfort, glance at the headlines in *Le Monde,* sip a perky young Beaujolais, and watch the medieval villages and the handsome rectangular church steeples of rural France race by outside the window. *C'est magnifique!* The one little flaw in this magnificent mode of travel, though, comes from another aspect of pan-European connectivity. Unless you are careful enough to seek out the car with the understated sign reading "Pas de Telephone, S'il Vous Plaît," your silent windowside reveries are interrupted every thirty seconds or so by the dreadful bane of European classrooms, theaters, planes, and trains: the biddly-biddly-beep of somebody's cell phone.

American rail fans are always told that the United States is too wide and too sparsely populated to support a serious passenger rail operation. Somehow, these problems haven't stopped the Europeans. The distance from Moscow to Madrid, something over 2,100 miles, is roughly equal to a trip from Denver to New York. But there are crack trains crossing that route every day, and passengers to ride them. Tens of thousands of tiny towns in sparsely populated areas of Europe are served by train, which helps explain the popularity of the European hobby of "rambling," or cross-country trekking. You can ride a train in the morning to Little Whinging, ramble across the pristine countryside to the station at East Twee, and board a train there to get home. Another admirable feature of European trains is that most routes have names: the Royal Scot, the Eurostar, Artesia, Le Train Bleu, and so on. The best named-route in all of Europe, for my money, is one that links the two major seats of the European Union, Brussels and Strasbourg. Since the EU is the only reason to connect those two cities, and since Eurocrats and European Parliament members are the main passengers on the route, somebody with a nice sense of history named this comfortable train the Jean Monnet.

Another transcontinental connection beloved by Generation E travelers is the plethora of budget airlines. Europe has some of the most expensive airline tickets on earth, on the great flag carriers like British Airways, Air France, and Alitalia. But the continent is also home to most of the world's cheap airlines—and here we mean dirt cheap, with prices along the lines of 10 to 30 euros (that is, $11 to $33) for round-trip international connections, if you book early enough. These airlines have deliberately friendly, nonbusinesslike names along the lines of Go, Buzz, Debonair, and (my favorite) Be My Baby. The Henry Ford of this kind of travel is a classic Generation E figure, Stelios Haji-Ioannou, a Cypriot who studied in France and then rented an office in the London suburbs to house the company he created, a budget airline called easyJet. Stelios—he's always referred to by his first name—created the business model that all the other no-frills airlines try to follow. The basic rule is that prices are low, and so is service. There are no tickets, no refunds, no assigned seats, no meals, and nobody to help if your plane happens to be late or gets diverted to the wrong city. You bought a no-frills ticket, so it's your job to cope with any problems that develop. The pricing plan is simplicity itself: the earlier you book, the cheaper your seat. To get that 10-euro round trip from London to Brussels, you have to reserve, and pay, a month or more ahead of time. If you buy a seat on Buzz or easyJet an hour before takeoff, you'll pay just about as much as you'd pay on Lufthansa or KLM. Younger Europeans have become past masters at dealing with these cheap but difficult airlines, and that's one reason why Generation E is constantly in transit around the continent. Since every major European airport has a big train station in the basement of the terminal, Euro-travelers can jump off the plane and straight onto the TGV train to complete the journey.

European travelers don't even have to slow down anymore when they cross from one country to the next; indeed, passport-free travel was considered a key element of European unification from the days of the founding fathers. One of Churchill's contemporaries, the postwar British foreign minister Ernest Bevin, observed that a key reason for bringing Europe together "really was to grapple with the whole problem of passports and visas." Bevin said he wanted to "go down to Victoria Station, get a railway ticket, and go where the hell I like without a passport or anything else." Today, the European Union officially describes itself as "an area without internal frontiers." In a treaty signed at Schengen, Luxembourg, in 1985, the member states agreed to eliminate border controls between EU countries—and to strengthen the borders at the union's external boundaries, to control the flood of immigrants trying to get to rich European countries. Today, nearly all EU members have signed up to the Schengen agreement. Britain—where the anti-immigration lobby remains strong—and the Republic of Ireland, which had to stay out of the Shengen deal in order to keep its traditional open border with the British province of Northern Ireland, are the main abstainers.

Anybody traveling around Europe these days will see that Schengen works. In a car, you often don't know that you've crossed a border until you see the language on the highway signs begin to change. On the train, there's no longer an immigration guard to check your passport, no matter how many countries your trip will go through. This borderless travel has been one of the most popular innovations of the united Europe, but it is not at all popular with travelers like me, who used to cherish all those exotic visas stamped in the passport. For citizens of any EU country, there are no limitations on working or studying in any other member nation, and that's a key reason why Generation E has been so mobile. Paradoxically, this elimination of internal border controls has required the extension of border policing for nations at the fringe of the EU. Poland, which has always maintained open borders with its giant neighbor Russia, suddenly had to set up a whole new immigration control apparatus there. Otherwise, anybody crossing into Poland from the East would be free to travel anywhere else (except Britain and Ireland) in the EU without a glance from a border guard.

With all the new bridges, concrete and otherwise, that are sprouting across Europe, it's not surprising that Europe is also developing cultural norms that transcend the old borders, customs, and culinary traditions. Yes, the Finns still love a good reindeer steak, the French have a thousand different cheeses, and the Greeks like to put olive oil on everything. And yet, as the continent unifies politically, economically, and culturally, there is a common European diet emerging—particularly among the younger Europeans, Generation E and their children. From the top of Norway to the toe of the Italian boot, you find a standard breakfast: a cuplet of severely strong coffee together with the kind of sweet roll that Americans, for some reason, call "Danish pastry." You can get a "Danish" in

Denmark, but no Dane ever calls it a Danish pastry. In fact, no Europeans use that term, except for TV comedians making fun of Americans. In Denmark, and in most of Europe, that breakfast pastry is generally called *Wienerbrod,* or "Vienna bread."

The favorite quick lunch for young Europeans almost everywhere is a crunchy baguette sliced lengthwise and turned into a sandwich about the length of a forearm. The continent's standard snack is *frites,* the food that Americans call "french fries"—another culinary term that leaves Europe mystified. "I don't know where you get that 'french fry,'" complained Jacques Urtel, the chief potato fryer at a sidewalk *friterie* on the ancient market square in the beautiful town of Bruges, Belgium. "Everybody knows that *frites* are all over Europe." The French are particularly annoyed with the term "french fries," or least with the product sold under that name in the United States. When Americans turned against France during the second war in Iraq, restaurants all over the country—including the House of Representatives dining room in Washington—sought to show their displeasure with Paris by renaming "french fries" to "liberty fries," or some such. If this change of nomenclature was intended to punish the French, it probably didn't work. To the gourmets of France, it is a greater insult to see their country's name attached to the large, puffy, greasy potatoes sold as *frites* in America.

Despite Europe's world-renowned vineyards, the real national drink of Europe—and particularly for Generation E—is beer. Europeans consume vast quantities of black beer, white beer, red beer, gold beer, cherry-, lemon-, and strawberry-flavored beer, beer for breakfast, beer at bedtime, beer even at McDonald's. (A beer with your Big Mac costs about .90 euro, roughly $1.15.) When European soccer teams played in the World Cup in Japan and Korea in 2002, parliaments all over the continent had to rewrite their liquor laws to allow bars to serve beer at the crack of dawn. A midafternoon kickoff in Tokyo meant the game began at seven-thirty in the morning in Paris or Berlin. Since much of Europe equates a game of soccer with the consumption of beer, the fans demanded that the law be changed so that the taps could be opened.

The various parliaments might not have made that change for just any sport, but soccer is not so much a sport today as it is a passion that spans all cultural and political borders—and thus serves as another force unifying Europe. There are, of course, national sports across the continent. The Norwegians idolize cross-country skier Bjørn Daehlie; the French love bike racer Laurent Jalabert; the Dutch are wild about speed skater Rintje Ritsma. But these local enthusiasms pale compared to the transcontinental obsession with soccer—or "football," as it is known in most of Europe. In America, where the game has never really caught on, the notion of soccer in Europe brings to mind drunken hooligans battling in the stands. That happens. But mostly, European soccer is a pastime that draws tens of millions of fans every weekend and reaches across all national borders. On any given Sunday or Monday, virtually every European newspaper will have page after page of soccer results, reporting on games from every country on the continent.

In a tiny farm village in Alsace, on the border where France and Germany meet, I met a cable TV salesman, Jacques Laurent, a thirty-three-year-old Generation E type—born in France, works for a German company, and routinely visits ten other countries on the job. When our conversation turned to sports, M. Laurent gleefully compared European soccer to American football and baseball. He gave no quarter. "Baseball is a good game," he said, "but in the championships, where do you get the right to say it is the 'World Series'? You have just one country playing, or maybe two. I think they let the Canadians get in now and then. In Europe, every nation plays football, every nation plays every other nation, and every fan knows the teams and players from anywhere in Europe. We have the European Cup, and the UEFA [that is, the Union des Associations Européennes de Football] Cup, and the premier league. The teams play in every country. It is not just German teams against Germans, the way you Americans do it.

"Football brings millions and millions of us together," Laurent went on. "I myself have traveled to, let's see, nine countries at least, to see games. Football is Europe, don't you see? If I meet somebody from

England, or Norway, or Spain, I just say, 'David Beckham,' and we immediately have something we share."

David Beckham, the soccer superstar who plays for Spain's Real
Madrid, is a Generation E idol, a common property who tends to make
Europe more like a single nation than a divided continent. Beckham has
been called Europe's version of Michael Jordan, and the comparison is
apt. Both men are surpassingly good at putting a ball into a net, both
have earned hundreds of millions—of dollars, pounds, or euros—for
doing it, and both have built global followings. In fact, though, Beckham,
as the highest-paid and highest-ranked star of Europe's biggest sport, has
a kind of stature and celebrity that exceeds anything Michael Jordan
achieved during his tenure as America's ranking basketball hero. There
are tens of thousands of young women, from Spain to Japan, who like to
cut their hair in whatever style David Beckham is using at the moment—
a trend that made for some strange scenes on the streets of Madrid and
Tokyo in 2002–3, when Beckham sported a Mohawk. When Beckham
suffered a minor foot injury shortly before the 2002 World Cup championships, reporters overheard the queen of England and the president of
France debating the proper treatment of his fractured metatarsal. (Her
Majesty's prescription: massage therapy.)

The Beckham home life is also a pan-European concern. The soccer
star himself is a quiet, understated individual who lets his trademark free
kicks and crosses do all the talking. This makes him just about the polar
opposite of his wife, Victoria Adams Beckham, the former Spice Girl
who was assigned the nickname "Posh Spice" during her career with that
British pop group. Since her $2 million wedding to the soccer star in
1999—with bride and groom seated on matching gold-and-chromium
thrones, a classic Posh Spice touch—Victoria has done her best to live up
to that sobriquet. On the eve of the English team's departure for the
World Cup in 2002, Mrs. Beckham hosted a going-away party at the
couple's home—a sprawling rural mansion popularly known as "Beck-
ingham Palace." It was a classic demonstration of the Posh style, with
60,000 orchids, a seven-acre tent, two dozen geishas to greet guests,

$125,000 worth of champagne, and a dress code set forth on the hand-written invitation: "white tie and diamonds." Amazingly, all these details of this private party leaked to the breathless tabloids. But then, the European media manage to capture every smidgen of the Beckhams' private life. Everyone knows, for example, that the couple's first baby was named "Brooklyn" because that's where the boy was conceived. This news prompted wags to hope out loud that the next Beckham baby would be the result of a wild night of love in the English town of Peckham. (As it happened the new Beckham baby was named "Romeo," with no suggestion as to where conception may have occurred.)

If a young European is going to knock back a beer, turn on the game, and start talking about the Beckhams with her Generation E pals, it is most likely that she'll be doing so in Europe's common language: English. Of course, the Europeans cherish their many languages and dialects. Indeed, the European Convention on Human Rights says that all people have a fundamental right to learn and use the traditional language of their region, no matter how few speakers might be left—a new "right" that has forced governments to open schools teaching in Welsh, Catalan, Basque, and a dozen other regional languages that may have only a few hundred thousand speakers. The European Union has a regulation guaranteeing that representatives of any member nation can use their national language in any EU forum—which means the translators on hand at committee sessions sometimes outnumber the speakers. The French, of course, are famously combative about keeping French in and English out of their citizens' discourse—even though *le ski boot, le laptop,* and even *le French fry* are now standard usage among the younger generation. Efforts like that are doomed to fail; when Generation E gets together these days, people tend to leave all those traditions behind and converse in the one language that every young European shares, which is English.

Every European country requires students to take years of English in school; other languages may be offered, but English is mandatory. As the standard second language, English tends to be the chosen tongue when, say, Greeks, Swedes, and Spaniards get together. This is true even in the august offices of the European Union itself. At the European Central Bank, in Frankfurt, Germany, the official language for all business is English. Even at the European Parliament, with elected members from all twenty-five member countries, English rules. A staff member, Thomas Lynn, did a study of the language used in hallway conversations. The conclusion: about 80 percent of all conversations are in English now. Companies operating across borders in Europe routinely require their employees to converse in English. On MTV Europe, about 80 percent of the DJs use English; the songs are primarily in English—or as close to English as contemporary rap lyrics ever come. Even *Le Monde,* that venerable organ of the chauvinistic French intelligentsia, now prints a daily section in English, to make the paper accessible to traveling Europeans.

English is the language of European baseball caps, backpacks, T-shirts, and tattoos. English is the language of almost every new song performed at Eurovision. English is even the common language of European anti-American rallies. The German, Swedish, and French demonstrators paint their big banners—"No More McDonald's"; "Bush Is the Real Terrorist"—in English, partly for the benefit of American TV viewers, but mainly because it is the language that all of Europe will understand. And of course, English is the common language of the text message—or, more precisely, the txt msg—the abbreviated lingo that a hundred million young Europeans use every day to communicate by mobile phone (because the GSM system makes it possible to send a txt msg to any user on any network in any GSM country). A message like "CNT W8 2C U 2NT. F I M L8, U GO B4"—meaning, essentially, "I can't wait to see you tonight. If I'm late, go ahead before me" is lingua franca now for Generation E members, no matter what their native tongue. Deathless lines from English literature have been turned into txt msg form: "2B R NT 2B?"

Europe's common language has become so common it appears in unexpected places. The advertising slogan of the postal service in Belgium—

a nation of French, Flemish, and German speakers—is the English phrase "Belgian stamps are cool." On the steep mountain pass that links German-speaking Austria with Slavic-speaking Slovenia, there's a billboard that declares, in huge letters, "Hit my airbase!" This turns out to be a popular sales campaign for an Austrian cigarette brand called Memphis Blue Lights. Maria Ortega, a Generation E ski instructor—she's a Spaniard who works in France in the winter and Switzerland in the summer—told me, at a French resort high in the Pyrenees, that she is a native Spanish speaker and a fluent French speaker, but prefers to deal in English. "The thing about English is, you can use it anywhere in Europe," she said in accented but excellent English. "I guess you can use it in America, too, but I never go there. Up here in the mountains, when I meet someone, I try Spanish. Then I try French. And if it's not working, I say, 'Hello.' That's the signal, and we communicate no matter what country we come from."

While the New Europe, and particularly the younger generation of Europeans, has drawn closer together because of this broadly shared pop culture, twenty-first-century Europe has lost—or at least, almost lost—one of its most powerful connections, which virtually defined the continent and its inhabitants for much of modern history. For nearly 1,500 years, Europe was more or less synonymous with Christendom. From the fourth century AD, when the Roman Empire became a Christian empire, through the Holy Roman Empire, the Middle Ages, the Reformation, the Renaissance, the Industrial Revolution, and even through the wars of the twentieth century, Europe was a devoutly Christian place, and the global center of the Christian faith. The power of religious conviction spawned bloody battles, inspired timeless works of art, and spurred thousands of people to spend decades or centuries erecting the awesome cathedrals that mark all great European cities. Christmas, Easter, and the other great ceremonial days of the Christian calendar defined the European year. Until well into the last century, the majority of educated Europeans got their education, at least in part, in Christian schools. Europe's great art and architecture, music and literature, were all deeply touched by the pervasive influence of the church. The faith created bonds that reached across all borders.

But today, Western Europe—the home of the world's biggest religious denomination, the Roman Catholic church, and the birthplace of most major Protestant faiths—has turned its back on religion. The Dutch sociologist Nan Kirk de Graaf, who studies faith and belief around the world, reports that twenty-first-century Europe has "one of the least religious populations in the world." A continent that is full of ancient churches and religious shrines is increasingly empty of practicing religion. In Britain, France, Germany, Holland, and Belgium, fewer than 10 percent of the population attend church as often as once a month. Only 12 percent of Britons describe themselves as "active" members of the Anglican Church. In Scandinavia, the handsome high-steepled churches that mark every city and village attract less than 3 percent of the people, and governments no longer subsidize the disestablished Lutheran Church. In Amsterdam, the Dutch Reformed hierarchy is converting cathedrals into luxury apartments to pay its bills. In the former Soviet satellites east of the iron curtain, nobody has seen a need to restore many of the ancient churches that the Red Army turned into barracks or warehouses.

I have attended church on Sunday morning in dozens of European cities and villages. Sitting in those marvelous old cathedrals, listening to the mighty organs echo in the vaulted ceilings, two things always struck me: how beautiful those structures were, and how empty.

Beneath the towering steeple of the 700-year-old St. Jacob's Church in the heart of Stockholm, I counted 29 people at the only Sunday service—in a stupendous church that would comfortably fit 900. The pastor, David Olson, was hardened to this. "That's about a normal turnout now," he told me with a shrug after the service. "Showing up at church on Sunday morning; that's not the Swedish way anymore. It's a secular society. People don't even know how to go to church. They call me up and say, 'Do I need to reserve a seat for Sunday morning?'"

On a beautiful spring Sunday during Lent, I wended my way to Canterbury, England, and the majestic old cathedral that used to draw multitudes of pilgrims who came, as Geoffrey Chaucer put it in the first great book in the English language, "the holy blisful martir for to seke." But the multitudes are no longer present. At morning prayer the day I was there, Canterbury Cathedral—the mother church of the worldwide Anglican/Episcopalian faith—hosted a grand total of 13 worshippers. At a midday communion service, the tally of churchgoers reached 300—but only if you counted the choirboys in their white ruffled collars and a phalanx of tourists with video cameras. That still left 80 percent of the seats unused. Among those in my pew was Yves Evereux, a high-school student from Normandy who came to Canterbury on a class field trip. "For us, this is just the history lesson," Yves told me (in excellent English) after he asked me to take his picture at the cathedral's marvelous vaulted entrance. "I don't go to church, not ever. My parents not either." The most exciting thing about the cathedral, Yves said, was the murder that took place here in 1170, when Saint Thomas à Becket—Chaucer's "blisful martir"—fell victim to a long-running battle between clergy and monarchy.

European clergy have different attitudes toward this turning away from the church. Some say it is an inevitable consequence of the modern era. "It's a secular age," Canon Michael Chandler, the vice dean of Canterbury Cathedral, told me on that Lenten morning. "We're breeding a whole generation without much spiritual perception. We can, and do, try to fight it, but this is the age we live in." Churches are trying to accommodate this trend by tolerating greater skepticism among believers and clergy alike. Until 1980, the Church of England required new priests to swear that they "unfeignedly believe all the canonical scriptures of the Old and New Testament." Today, potential clerics need swear only that they "accept the holy scriptures as revealing all things necessary for eternal salvation through faith."

On the other hand, there are religious leaders who say that the decline in organized religion is a demographic blip that will quickly be reversed.

The argument here is that the big problem facing institutional religion in Europe is not the religious part of the equation, but the institutional aspect. That is, more and more Europeans tend to act out what faith they have outside the official structure. They pray at home—or in the car during the morning commute. They flock to carol services at Christmas and buy CDs of religious music, which perhaps explains why records of Gregorian chant have been best-sellers in several European countries in recent years. Europeans still travel to places like Vatican City or Lourdes for personal moments of religious rapture. That flicker of individualized faith is one of the great hopes of European church leaders. Another is that non-Christian religions seem to be healthy. Hindu and Muslim denominations, brought to the continent by a wave of mass immigration, are expanding rapidly. In the same cities where churches stand empty, Islamic immigrants are building immense new mosques. The continent's Jewish population is holding steady, although the United States has more Jews than all of Europe combined.

But the striking fact remains that "Christian Europe" is hardly Christian anymore, except as a collection of inspiring Gothic reminders of Christianity's past. "For the first time in 1500 years," wrote historian Norman Davies in the late 1990s, "Christianity was becoming a minority religion" in Europe. The European Union in particular is a pervasively secular institution. When Giscard d'Estaing's Constitutional Convention produced its proposed constitution to govern the expanded, twenty-five-nation union, the draft text made no mention of Christianity or God. The Vatican and other Christian leaders complained loudly about this omission. But the members of the drafting committee argued that Europe's constitution should deal with government, not faith—this on a continent where nearly every nation has had an official, government-subsidized Christian denomination.

It may be a sign of the demise of religious practice that the institution of marriage is also in decline among Generation E members, particularly in Western Europe. Europeans still form monogamous unions, raise children, attend parent-teacher night at school, and buy out the toy stores in the weeks before Christmas. But they do all this without bothering to get married. The result is that the wealthy nations of Europe—particularly the northern countries—have the world's highest rates of children born out of wedlock. Americans who are disturbed that some 30 percent of babies in the United States are born to single mothers should perhaps be relieved they don't live in Norway (49 percent of all births to unwed parents), Sweden (48 percent), France (41 percent), Britain (38 percent), or Ireland (31 percent). On the other hand, most of the "out-of-wedlock" children in Europe are actually living with both parents—a significant difference from the United States, where the typical single mom doesn't have the father around the house. It's just that European cohabitors—they call themselves "partners" or "companions" or sometimes "spouses"—don't ever go to church, not even to be married. A Norwegian named Haakon lived happily with his partner and their child for years without being married. Eventually, Lutheran leaders convinced Haakon that he should, indeed, find the time for a formal marriage ceremony—since he is, after all, Norway's crown prince. In Ireland, Prime Minister Bertie Ahern raised a few eyebrows when his unmarried companion moved in with him—but not many, evidently, because Ahern was easily reelected at a time when the whole nation knew that he was "living in sin," as the church used to say. Perhaps because they are eager to encourage marriage in any form, European countries have been significantly more open than American jurisdictions to same-sex unions. Belgium and the Netherlands both offer full legal recognition of gay marriages, and most other European countries have authorized civil ceremonies that give gay couples all the legal benefits that their heterosexual neighbors are entitled to.

Does it make any difference in daily life whether Europeans still believe in God, or go to church? It is hard to argue that twenty-first-century Europe is a less moral or caring society than the church-going United States. Yes, Americans put up huge billboards reading "Love Thy Neighbor," but they murder and rape their neighbors at rates that would shock any European nation. Corruption in business and government seems equally prevalent on both sides of the Atlantic. Norwegians don't go to church much, but they give away ten times as much per capita as Americans do in aid to poor countries. Indeed, every West European government devotes a considerably higher share of its budget to foreign aid than the United States does.

On the other hand, the weakness of Christian belief makes it harder to transmit Europe's cultural tradition. When Generation E tours the great art galleries, it is confused by the most basic iconography of the art on display. The National Gallery in London reports that visitors keep asking what the label "INRI" stands for in the great crucifixion paintings.[1] People don't recognize the saint who is depicted with birds and forest animals.[2] Even in Scotland, schoolchildren don't know anymore that the saint who is always depicted with an arrow through his hand is Saint Giles, a Scot who was wounded, the chronicles relate, when he stepped between a hunter and a deer in order to spare the animal's life.

Perhaps the most significant implication of the secularization of Europe is that it deepens the divide between Europeans and Americans. Depending on how the question is asked, up to 95 percent of Americans say they believe in God; in most of Europe, the figure is closer to 50 percent. The public religiosity that is part and parcel of American life is rarely seen on the continent; the only televangelists on European screens are piped in via cable from Newport News and Houston. Europeans tend to be surprised, or amused, when U.S. politicians end a speech with the words "God bless America." "When they hear that, the intellectuals break out in a little smug smile," reported Jonathan Freedland, a columnist with London's *Guardian* newspaper. "It's almost impossible to imagine a prime minister over here saying 'God bless Britain' or 'God bless Sweden.'" When George W. Bush cited "holy scripture" and argued that going to war in Iraq was a straightforward matter of "good against evil," demonstrators by the million took to the streets of Europe. "Don't send us to fight religious wars," read a banner I saw at a demo in Salzburg. At a time when many European leaders are vigorously promoting the notion that the united Europe should stand as a counterweight to American influence in the world, the different status of religious belief serves to heighten the notion that there is a basic difference of worldview on the opposite sides of the Atlantic.

Another fundamental difference between the American worldview and the outlook of today's Europeans is their attitudes toward technology. Europeans are rich enough to have access to all the high-tech equipment and inventions of modern life, and they use the stuff. But Europeans are often afraid of advances in science and engineering, and that fear has draped a blanket of worry, of insecurity, over some aspects of contemporary life that Americans take for granted.

Well-educated, well-read Europeans will tell you, in perfect seriousness, that a bowl of cornflakes can kill you—not to mention a ham sandwich or a T-bone steak. Getting vaccinated can kill you. Flying economy class can kill you, and business class isn't much better. The rubber duckie in your bathtub can kill you (and your children). And even though they use their cell phones far more than Americans do, the members of Generation E do so with a nagging sense that a cell phone might kill you, too. In fact, the woeful catalog of warnings about this food or that technological device is such a standard part of modern European life that the continent seems to veer almost every month from one health panic to the next. The fact that there's often no scientific basis for these fears doesn't stanch the flood.

A good example of how this works is the scare surrounding the measles-mumps-rubella vaccine, a standard preventative shot given to babies in virtually every developed country. In 2001, a single British doctor suggested, in a TV interview, that there might be some link between the MMR vaccine and autism. Both the British and the EU departments of public health quickly issued clarifying reports pointing out that there was no basis for this alarming statement. No study had ever found such a link, and there was no scientific rationale as to why there should be one. Babies in the United States, Asia, Africa, and so on continued to get the shot as advised. Tony Blair—the father of a child born in 2001—was seen on TV screens across Europe advising parents that MMR was both safe and essential for infant health. Nonetheless, many European parents—particularly Britons—decided not to "take the risk" of having their children vaccinated. The result, sadly predictable, was that rates of measles, mumps, and rubella went up dramatically among the eighteen-month-old children of Generation E. (There was no decrease in the rate of autism, further proof that the supposed connection to the vaccination never existed.) By the summer of 2003, a British study found that measles—a disease that had been virtually eradicated from western Europe a decade earlier—was once again a common threat for British toddlers. The moral is ominous: in contemporary Europe, the completely unfounded fear of a new health threat can be strong enough to overcome parental worries about a traditional baby killer.

The strongest and most consequential scares sweeping modern Europe involve food—especially any food product produced with new technologies. Most intense has been the reaction against genetically modified crops, known in Europe by the shorthand term GMO, for genetically modified organism. Some 300 million Americans and Canadians consume genetic hybrids of corn, soybeans, and other foods every day, with no evidence of a health risk. A U.S. National Academy of Sciences study concluded that new varieties are no different from traditional hybrids. Britain's Royal Academy reached essentially the same conclusion. And yet GMOs are restricted across Europe; the media treat the crops as if they were lethal. When it was reported that minute quantities—well below 1 percent—of GMO seeds had inadvertently been mixed into bags of Canadian seed sold to European farmers, newspapers across the continent warned of "contamination" and "poisoning." Frightened consumers returned boxes of cornflakes to grocery stores, demanding refunds.

In Norwich, England, a group of Greenpeace demonstrators broke down a wall and fence to storm a farm. They wrecked tens of thousands of pounds worth of tractors and harvesters, and trampled acres of grain just before it was ready to harvest. When the farmer took these vandals to court, a jury found for the protestors. The farmer had been growing an experimental crop of genetically modified corn, and that was considered a greater crime in Norwich than the destruction of the man's property.

Similar scares surround beef and pork fed with growth hormones; steaks and hams from such animals are consumed daily around the world, but not in Europe. Rubber toys containing softeners called phthalates have been the subject of health scares. In 2002–3, the British newspapers identified a major new health threat they called "economy-class syndrome"—the fear that long hours spent in a cramped airplane seat will lead to "deep vein thrombosis," causing blood clots to travel to the lungs. There have been a minute number of reported cases of this syndrome (one of them involving a passenger in business class). Still, all the major European airlines felt the need to issue written warnings to all passengers; many people have changed their travel routines so as to break up long flights into a series of smaller segments. Even Europeans' beloved cell phones contribute to general dread of technology. In 2000, a consumer group warned that transmission signals from these phones might cause brain damage; its report suggested the use of earphones, to reduce the risk that supposedly results from holding a phone next to the brain. Just as European worriers were getting accustomed to that, another blue-ribbon panel suggested a year later that earphones might increase the risk. The British government issued a study showing no linkage at all between cell phones and brain damage, but the worries are still prevalent.

The pervasive technophobia that throbs like background music beneath the rhythms of daily European life came as a surprise to me. Europe, after all, gave the world the Industrial Revolution, quantum physics, and modern genetics. Europe is the proud home of the Nobel Prizes, the world's most prestigious awards for scientific innovation. Why should Europeans, of all people, be scared of technology? I got the chance once to ask that question of Tony Blair, the British prime minister. He had obviously spent time pondering the same paradox, and he had a ready explanation. "There's been a loss of faith in science, without any doubt, in Europe," Blair said. "There is a sense, you know, that scientific advances are harmful as often as they are helpful. There's a distrust of scientists, and a distrust of government when it relies on science. This feeling is real and it is strong—and you can trace it straight back to the horrible experience we all had with BSE."

Blair was referring to the outbreak—first in Britain and later in France, Germany, Italy, and Scandinavia—of bovine spongiform encephalopathy, a disease sometimes known by its abbreviation BSE, but more commonly as "mad cow disease." When the epidemic was first detected on British beef farms, government officials went out of their way to assure the public that there was no danger to consumers of beef. (One British health minister actually led his four-year-old daughter to the television cameras and fed her a hamburger made with British beef—a stunt that revolted the public and effectively ended the minister's political career.) In fact, humans could contract a form of the disease, and several dozen people died. By this time, government officials across the continent had reversed their tune and ordered the slaughter of millions of head of cattle. The public, looking on, concluded that there really was a health problem, and that government types were not to be trusted when they tried to suggest otherwise. "When there's some kind of scare now," Blair explained, "people are just not very willing to listen to experts who say 'There's nothing to worry about.'"

Mart Saarma, a biologist at the Helsinki Institute of Technology, has studied European health scares, looking for a common thread. He concluded that it is not any inherent danger in innovation that sparks European fears; "if these stories were true, we should all be dead by now," he says. Rather, the root of the fear is in the European psyche. "It is a matter of emotion. Americans seem to be pragmatic about new ideas and inventions. Europeans tend to be pessimistic. That leads to this concept of being always on the safe side—being against anything new until it is absolutely proven." Saarma says that Europe's constant wariness reflects the feeling of anomie, of systemic breakdown, that is central to a lot of contemporary European philosophy. The choirmaster for this particular European chorus is surely Günter Grass, the German novelist who has championed the emergence of a peaceful union across the European continent. "The proper response to the lusty appeals of progress is melancholy," according to Grass. "In contrast to the American conception of happiness embodied in the say-cheese smile," he goes on, "the European is more comfortable with the knowledge that engenders disgust."

Whatever their cause, the recurrent health scares and the distrust of technology have become another aspect of European life that tends to build a sense of common belief, common lifestyle, among the citizens of the EU. Grabbing the chance, the Eurocrats in Brussels have on occasion taken advantage of these fears to serve their own political purposes. As we will see in chapter 9 of this book, Brussels has played on the fear of genetically modified crops and livestock growth hormones to keep American-grown commodities out of Europe's markets. This gives European farmers and food processors some protection against overseas competitors; meanwhile, it plays perfectly to the anti-Americanism that is never far from the surface among Europe's intellectuals.

In all these varied ways, the people of the New Europe—and particularly the members of Generation E—are moving toward a common European culture. Despite the continent's potpourri of languages, customs, cuisines, and a long history of cross-border animosities, they're doing a pretty good job of it on their own. Nonetheless, the leaders of the EU are constantly looking for ways to help forge a unified continent. The Eurocrats in Brussels turn out a bewildering array of books, brochures, pocket cards, posters, pamphlets, TV ads, and educational materials at every grade level to remind the people of Europe about their new supranational government and the union it serves. One of the major efforts at building unity occurs each May 9, the day the EU wants to be celebrated as the Fourth of July of the United States of Europe. "Europe Day" is not as important yet for most Europeans as, say, Eurovision. But in several countries, the celebration has caught the public's fancy. I was in Belgium in early May one year and saw a poster advertising the national *Europatag* celebration: there would be picnics and concerts, essay contests and costume parties (dress up like your favorite EU country). But the biggest event scheduled was a free guided tour of the EU headquarters, in Brussels' Quartier Européen. I laughed out loud. A tour of an office building! That will really draw the crowds! In fact, this was no laughing matter to the Belgians. On the morning of May 9 literally thousands of people formed a long line outside the headquarters building, waiting for the tour.

Not every European nation responds quite so enthusiastically to Europe Day pageantry, but a few things are supposed to be observed at every May 9 celebration. The twelve-star EU flag must be abundantly evident, of course, and a map showing the twenty-five member countries and the applicant nations hoping to be admitted. There should be demonstrations of regional arts and cuisine from all the corners of Europe—tacos, pizzas, sauerkraut, *Wienerbrod,* and on and on. Finally, all Europe Day events are supposed to end with a rousing rendition of the EU anthem, the "Ode to Joy" from the fourth movement of Beethoven's Ninth Symphony. And therein lies a major problem. Nearly every European knows that classic melody, but nobody has yet agreed on what the words should be for Europe's national anthem.

There is a strong movement—centered in Germany, naturally enough—to keep the text that Beethoven had in mind when he wrote that great choral movement. That, of course, was the German poet Friedrich von Schiller's "Ode to Joy." Indeed, some verses of his 1786 poem do seem to suggest, in a vague way, the political, economic, and cultural union that the EU stands for:

Deine Zauber binden wieder,
Was die Mode streng geteilt;
Alle Menschen werden Brüder,
Wo dein sanfter Flügel weilt.

With your magic, reunite us
Whom the times did once divide.

Then we all shall stand as brothers
Where your gentle wings spread wide.

But there are also forceful advocates for a new lyric that will celebrate the new Europe born out of the horror of last century's wars. The Europe-wide association of Chambers of Commerce (an organization known, inevitably, as "Eurochambers") has launched a transcontinental contest to write new, EU-specific lyrics for the EU anthem. The basic concept is a common verse in (what else?) English, and then nineteen more verses, one in each of the nineteen other official languages of the union. Hundreds of entries have been received, although the early favorite seems to be this one, submitted by a German songwriter, Karl Wolfgang Barthel:

People, gather close together
On this ancient continent.
We are all now Europeans
No war keeps us separate.

It's fairly easy to suggest what themes ought to be represented in an anthem to the New Europe. The verse would have to include a reference to the dogged pursuit of peace, the primary motivation that prompted founding fathers like Churchill, Monnet, and Schuman to start dreaming of a United States of Europe in the first place. An anthem to the cause of European unity might also set forth some of the things that today's unified Europe has in common—the food, the fears, the faith (or lack of same), the sports and music, the vast transit infrastructure, the shared language, and maybe even Eurovision. And perhaps the anthem should also pay heed to another basic impulse that has always been central to the drive for "ever closer union"—the concept of the United States of Europe as a force in the world equal to the United States of America.

NINE

Waking Up to the Revolution

This book began with a warning that Americans have been ignoring a revolution. A geopolitical earthquake is taking place in Europe that will have a profound effect on the world of the twenty-first century, and America's place in it—but so far most Americans have chosen to overlook the tremors. The construction of the New Europe, with more than two dozen nations ceding much of their sovereign authority to a common central government, has created a new species of united state: a largely borderless federal union that is not exactly a single country, but is much more than just another international organization or trading bloc. The European Union was originally designed to be an alternative to warfare, and it has achieved that noble goal with stunning success. In its first six decades, the EU has proven to be an effective instrument of peace on a continent that was lethally divided for much of the last century. This has saved the people of Europe from the horror of war. It has also saved the finance ministries of Europe from the need to finance national defense. Europeans don't have to spend anywhere near as much tax money on military matters as Americans do—in part because Europe has managed to get the United States to pay most of the expenses of the common defense shield, NATO. The huge saving on military expenditures makes it possible for the EU nations to fund the world's most generous network of health, education, and welfare benefits, and to offer the comforts of this welfare state to every inhabitant of the union. The Europeans would rather have their munificent social model than a mighty military force, and U.S. defense policy frees them to make that choice.

Along with peace, European integration has brought power. The elimination of trade barriers, the adoption of a common regulatory apparatus, and the advent of the euro, the world's strongest currency for much of its life, have made the European Union a financial and commercial superpower. The EU has more people, more wealth, and more trade than the United States—and more influence in almost every international body. Europeans have constructed a multibillion-euro transit infrastructure that makes the continent more connected than it has been since Caesar's legions marched along those famous Roman roads from Britannia to Germania. The citizens of this New Europe have also built a common Euroculture that is particularly strong among the members of Generation E, the young people who will run the EU and its member states for the first half of this century. Although it's not much fun to watch from the western side of the Atlantic, a key element of this pancontinental culture has been a powerful mood of anti-Americanism (or at least, anti-Bushism) that inspires a fairly constant barrage of America-bashing on the page, the stage, and the screen. For many Europeans today, the familiar concept of "the West," the transatlantic alliance with shared values and common enemies, is a relic of the last century. In the new century, the united Europe is determined to challenge American claims to global supremacy and gain equal standing with the United States on the world stage.

Most Americans have indeed slept through this European revolution. But more and more, we are being subjected to rude awakenings at the hands of a unified Europe. As we've seen in these pages, Jack Welch lost the biggest business deal of his brilliant career because he didn't understand the European Union until it was too late. Corporate giants including Boeing, Coca-Cola, MCI, Microsoft, Monsanto, and Motorola have been humbled by EU competitors or regulators. President George W. Bush compiled a mixed record vis-à-vis the New Europe. In the case of

Afghanistan, Bush adroitly recognized the Europeans' ambition to be global players; he recruited the EU to provide major help in the war against the Taliban. As a result, Europeans have borne more than half the casualties, and half the cost, of that effort. But in the war to overthrow Saddam Hussein, Bush failed to give the Europeans the kind of attention and respect they have come to expect. Europe, in turn, used its worldwide political clout to defeat the American position at the United Nations. The result was painful: the United States took more than 90 percent of the human losses of the Iraq coalition, paid about 95 percent of the costs, and suffered grievously on the battleground of global opinion.

During its first term, the Bush administration badly soured relations with Europe by adopting a policy of "divide and conquer" toward the member states of the European Union. When Defense Secretary Donald Rumsfeld declared in 2003 that "there is Old Europe and New Europe," he was enunciating a wistful hope in the administration that Washington could deal with its perceived friends on the continent and ignore its adversaries. This policy turned out to be a spectacular failure. Even the former Soviet colonies, which Rumsfeld defined as particular "friends" of the U.S., declined the honor. "There is only one Europe," Polish Foreign Minister Adam Rotfeld snapped when Condoleeza Rice came to visit him, "and we are part of this Europe." In his second term, prodded by Britain's Tony Blair, George W. Bush reversed the divide-and-conquer policy. Bush himself became the first president of the U.S.A. to make a formal visit to the president of the U.S.E. at EU headquarters in Brussels; there he expressed America's respect for "this strong, united Europe that we are eager to work with." And Rumsfeld made it clear, in his engaging way, that the "Old Europe, New Europe" approach was officially defunct. Addressing an EU gathering in Munich in 2005, Rumsfeld said "the secretary of defense who made that comment was the Old Rumsfeld."

By expressing his determination to "work with" the EU, the second-term Bush was returning to the traditional U.S. stance toward a united Europe. As we saw in chapter 2, the United States of America played an important role in the creation of the United States of Europe (although today's Europeans don't like to remember it). The United States offered enthusiastic encouragement—not to mention billions of Marshall Plan dollars—when the European Movement was just starting to emerge from the postwar ruin. Successive American presidents have applauded (publicly, at least) as the European Union grew rapidly both in depth and breadth. But the European response to this consistent record of support can sometimes be—as King Lear said of his ungrateful children—"sharper than a serpent's tooth." The economist Irwin M. Stelzer made the point nicely:

> When our foreign policy establishments encouraged the Europeans to integrate their economies, we surely did not anticipate that one result would be a large economy intent on challenging the United States for world economic leadership and challenging the dollar as the world's reserve currency.
>
> When we encouraged the Europeans to do more for their own defense, we hardly intended for them to form a defense force independent of NATO.
>
> And when we encouraged the Europeans to set up one telephone number that we could call, we did not intend it to be answered by a French policy-maker whose most frequent response would be "*non*."
>
> Having worked for decades to encourage a united Europe, America appears to face an emerging continental superstate defiantly determined to cut it down to size. Certainly, to anyone following Europe's media, or listening to the speeches of its leaders, there can be no mistaking the seriousness of that determination.

The path toward European unification has not run consistently smooth or straight. Ever since those halcyon days when the initial six members started their common market in coal and steel, the Europeans have found a great deal to argue about. Many of these disagreements have been exacerbated by the growth of the union from six neighboring states in Western Europe to a continent-wide federation of east and west, north and south, rich and poor, industrial and agricultural. For all the momentum toward economic union, the EU's members have made little progress in half a century toward one of Jean Monnet's initial projects, a common financial market. Arguments have raged, and still rage, over burning issues ranging from agricultural subsidies to labor laws to the intricate grocery-store rules that got England's Metric Martyr in so much trouble. Even the basic structure of the EU itself—should it be a federal union with a powerful central government, or should it be a voluntary association of powerful states?—remains unsettled, despite decades of interplay between Brussels and the various national capitals. The member nations haven't yet found a way to agree on a united stance toward the millions of migrants trying to get inside the wealthy EU and land jobs. As a demographic matter, it is clear that the nations of Europe, with fewer and fewer marriages and falling birth rates, badly need the influx of new blood and new workers that the immigrants would provide; as a political matter, though, many EU nations simply refuse to accept this reality. Some EU members have held out against joining the common currency (although the euro has been so popular and so successful that sticking with the pound or the kroner looks more like a delaying tactic than a long-term policy choice). The effort to write a constitution for the supranational government of a twenty-five-nation union was stalled by furious arguments—familiar to anyone who has studied the disputes that wracked America's Constitutional Convention in 1789—over how to allocate power among the big and the small member states.

It's tempting for Americans to tell themselves that the unified Europe is doomed to fall apart under the pressure of these seemingly endless disputes. For more than fifty years, though, the New Europe has been running up against these obstacles—and finding ways to get around them. The essential forces driving the revolution in Europe—the deep yearning for peace on a continent that has known too much war, and the intense desire to stand tall again as a driving force in global political and economic affairs—have not diminished since those goals were first embraced by the likes of Churchill, Schuman, and Monnet. There is a basic momentum to European unification that will not be thwarted.

This geopolitical earthquake is sending its shock waves across the Atlantic Ocean. More and more, American farmers, manufacturers, lawyers, software writers, brokers, and accountants are dancing to Europe's tune. Because of the sheer size of its market, and because the Eurocrats are more philosophically inclined to regulate than their counterparts in Washington or Tokyo, the EU has become the de facto global policeman for a vast panoply of agricultural, industrial, and financial products. In the twenty-first century, the rules that run the global economy are largely Brussels' rules. "Twenty years ago, if you designed something to U.S. standards, you could pretty well sell it all over the world," notes Maja Wessels, of United Technologies, an industrial giant. "Now, the shoe's on the other foot." Ms. Wessels was commenting after her employer, an American company headquartered in Hartford, Connecticut, learned that most of the machines made by United Technologies' air-conditioning subsidiary, Carrier, could not be sold in Europe. The EU in 2002 established new recycling regulations for air-conditioning and refrigeration equipment; these rules effectively prohibit the use of various chemicals that had been routinely used in Carrier air conditioners (and were acceptable to the U.S. government). Since Carrier couldn't possibly give up its European business, and couldn't economically build machines for a series of different regulatory regimes, the firm bowed to Brussels and redesigned all its equipment to meet the tougher European standard.

The same holds true for countless other American-made products, from bourbon to barbells to Barbie Dolls; the EU rules on labeling, content, manufacture, design, and safety have become the rules that manufacturers must follow all over the world. American cosmetics makers changed their formula for aftershave lotion because Brussels passed a rule banning ethanol, an ingredient that was just fine with the U.S. government. McDonald's changed the rubber toys placed in its Happy Meals all over the world because Brussels passed a rule banning a softening chemical that McDonald's had used for years with no complaints from regulators in Washington, D.C. The EU makes rules that govern Amazon.com's sales techniques, and the bumpers that General Motors puts on its Corvettes, and the kind of wheat that General Mills can put in its Wheaties. These American companies have no choice but to comply because they need access to the lucrative European market.

If you look at the small print on the labels of packaged goods in an American supermarket, a lot of the stuff you're reading was put there to satisfy regulators in Brussels. For decades, Americans have steadfastly resisted various academic and governmental efforts to convince them to adopt the "Systeme Internationale d'Unites"—that is, the metric system of measurement. No matter how efficient and logical metrics might be, we still prefer our inches and feet, ounces and pounds, yards and miles. But American food and drink labels today are going metric. You can't buy a "fifth" (that is, a fifth of a gallon) of American whiskey any more; all liquors are sold by the centiliter today, because that's how the European market demands it. Instead of a "fifth," the standard bottle now is 70 or 75 centiliters, which turns out to be a few sips short of a fifth of a gallon. It is because of the European regulatory influence that Americans routinely buy 2-liter bottles of Coca-Cola and 354 ml containers of Log Cabin syrup and 1.13 kg jars of Skippy peanut butter.

The European Union also dictates to businesses around the world on issues of personal privacy. As we saw in chapter 6 of this book, the European Charter on Human Rights provides an explicit guarantee of the privacy of personal information, and Brussels has imposed this guarantee on any company doing business in Europe. The EU has become "privacy cop to the world," issuing strict restrictions on the personal information that companies and governments can maintain and exchange about customers, employees, suppliers, and so on. The EU rules essentially prohibit many practices that are considered the basic stuff of business in the United States. They make it hard—in fact, nearly impossible—for companies to collect or trade basic data about customers, including name, address, phone number, buying history, and credit history. General Motors Corp. ran afoul of the EU's privacy police in 2002 when it tried to update its online employee address book. The idea, GM said, was to help its far-flung employees keep in touch with each other and with the company. The problem was that if such an internal telephone book were to be sent to GE's headquarters in the United States, it would break European law. Brussels has designated the United States as a nation with "inadequate" privacy laws, and thus it is illegal for European countries or governments to send personal information on anybody to a recipient in the United States. And the stern European rules even apply to industries like insurance, banking, and telecommunications, where keeping huge files of personal information has been standard operating procedure in the past. Today, in the EU, it is basically illegal to compile, keep, or pass on personal information about anybody without written consent from each individual whose records are on file. Every company, European or foreign, that has a record on any European customer must give those customers a periodic warning that information is being held, and the right to check the corporate records to make sure the personal data is accurate.

The EU has toughened the protection of personal privacy at the same time the United States has been moving the other way. Since the attacks of 9/11, the U.S. government has greatly increased its record-keeping about all of its citizens, and loosened the safeguards regarding the use and exchange of such information. Under the USA Patriot Act, federal and local governments are empowered to keep track of private data on anybody, generally without any warrant or judicial approval, and to demand such information from companies, doctors, libraries, and so forth. Almost all that record-keeping would be a violation of law in the European Union. This creates dilemmas for many companies, which are prohibited from sharing information about you and me under European law, but required to do so in America. Washington has demanded, for example, that any airline operating in the United States must provide itineraries, baggage information, and credit records for any passenger the government might be interested in; European law, in contrast, makes it illegal to turn over such information. For any airline operating across the Atlantic, this posed an impossible conflict, until the EU convinced Washington to ease its rules.

One result has been a boom in a new line of employment—the corporate privacy officer. Hundreds of American firms have created the new post of

CPO—chief privacy officer—or "director of corporate privacy" primarily to deal with European requirements. Under the threat of severe penalties in the world's biggest market, some 400 major U.S. companies have signed privacy agreements with the EU, guaranteeing that they will abide by the European rules no matter what might be authorized under the looser regulations at home. Since corporations everywhere have little choice but to follow the EU regulations, many other countries—including Canada, Australia, much of South America, and the democracies of East Asia—have adopted the Brussels privacy regime as their national standard. "In privacy law, we went to sleep and the Europeans moved ahead," noted Alan F. Westin, an expert in the field at Columbia law school. "The Europeans now set the rules that our companies have to follow."

Business executives who have dealt with Eurocrats on consumer, safety, privacy, and labeling issues are fully aware that the EU's commercial clout makes Brussels the world's regulatory superpower. It is highly unlikely that Jack Welch's successor at General Electric, Jeffrey Immelt, would underestimate the power and determination of the Europeans the way Welch did. Immelt spent years as the head of GE's medical equipment division, which produces its machinery mainly in the United States but sells all over the world. Immelt's division had a long struggle with the EU over the permissible amount of radiation that a patient could receive from General Electric X-ray machines. In the end, Immelt incorporated Brussels' dosage regulation—considerably tougher than the American standard—into all GE machines, including those sold in the United States. Ford Motor Co. chairman William Clay Ford Jr., who was worked with the Europeans on safety and fuel-economy issues, says that European market power is simply a basic fact of life for American companies today. "Of course you have to deal with Brussels," he says. "It's part of business now."

You can see numeric proof of the EU's global regulatory clout in the fast-growing roster of lobbyists filling the new office buildings surrounding Brussels' Quartier Européen. In the early 1990s, the club of corporate lobbyists dealing with Europe's regulators was so small that they could all fit in a single room for their luncheons. Today, well over 10,000 lobbyists are working the EU corridors in Brussels—perhaps a third of them representing U.S. companies—and every major U.S. law firm either has a Brussels office or is planning to open one. Among the U.S. firms that recognized the value of a corporate presence among the Eurocrats was Jack Welch's GE, which opened a new European headquarters in Brussels shortly after the antitrust czar Mario Monti doomed Welch's final corporate project. By sheer coincidence, GE chose one of its chief Italian executives, a man who happens to be a friend of Mario Monti, to head the new lobbying operation.

It is not just corporate types in pin-striped suits, though, who are waking up to the revolution on the European continent. All over the American heartland, farmers in mud-streaked jeans and baseball caps understand the European Union's position as a "counterweight" to American economic power. Amid the amber waves of grain that stretch endlessly across the rolling hills of Sherman County, Kansas—the very heartland of America, some 6,000 miles from the busy streets of Brussels—farmers like Ken Palmgren learned long ago to pay attention to the rules the Eurocrats make governing agricultural trade. "Fact of the matter is, you gotta know what Brussels is saying if you want to sell your crop," says Palmgren, who farms some 5,200 acres of the world's most productive soil, producing primarily wheat, corn, and soybeans. "Farming is a global business. An American farmer is shipping crop all over the world; if you don't follow the EU rules, you lose some of the best markets we've got."

For Ken Palmgren and millions of other American farmers across the great plains, the chief concern coming out of Brussels is the EU's position on genetically modified crops. As we saw in the previous chapter, the Europeans view these "Frankenfoods" as if they contained anthrax or cyanide. Relatively few American farmers share this alarmist view, and yet large numbers of them refuse to go anywhere near the new generation of genetic hybrids. "The salesmen [from the seed companies] come around here all the time, and they have some good points. There are a lot of advantages for the farmer in the genetics," Palmgren says. "You can raise a crop with less water. You can use a lot less chemicals, for fertilizer or weed control." But a farmer who is attracted by those lures pays a key price on the global market. Because the EU requires clear labeling of any food product that contains 1 percent or more of genetically modified foods, a farmer who gives in to the temptation of GMO seeds is cutting himself out of the world's richest single market. Beyond that, many third-world countries—places that desperately need food, genetically modified or not—have adopted the European restrictions. "You may be way out here in the hills of west Kansas," Palmgren says. "But you've gotta keep an eye on your markets. That gives Europe its power. Frankly, those guys in Brussels have a lot of control over what me and my neighbors are planting out here."

Those guys in Brussels also have control over American tax laws, to the consternation of the U.S. Congress and American industry. In the late 1990s, the Eurocrats decided to stage a demonstration of the muscle that comes with being the world's largest trading bloc. Brussels targeted an American statute called the Foreign Sales Corporations and Extra-Territorial Income Exclusion Act. This venerable law provided a tax break to American firms that sell goods overseas—in effect, an export subsidy that allows American companies to cut prices in order to win business in foreign markets. The tax benefits were huge; between 1994 and 2000, the General Accounting Office calculated, the statute meant $1.2 billion in savings for Boeing, $1 billion for General Electric, $773 million for Intel, $351 million for Motorola, and hundreds of millions more for hundreds of other U.S. exporters. For years the Japanese, the Chinese, the Argentines, and most European governments had been writing diplomatic missives to the U.S. trade representative complaining that the subsidies were unfair under global trading rules. For years, Washington has been ignoring these polite appeals, on the eminently sensible theory that American tax policy should be made in Washington, not in Tokyo or Brussels.

By 1997, though, Brussels felt strong enough to mount a frontal assault on Washington's position. The EU trade commissioner filed a formal complaint with the World Trade Organization (WTO), arguing that the Foreign Sales Corporations Act was a violation of international trade rules that say governments can't subsidize exporters. The EU then mounted an intense lobbying campaign at the WTO—where EU member nations comprise the largest single bloc of big trading nations—to see that its complaint was acted on. Five years later—lightning speed by the standards of the World Trade Organization—the WTO told the United States that the subsidies were illegal. If Washington didn't change its tax law, the EU was empowered to impose billions of euros worth of punitive tariffs—penalties that would essentially close Europe's huge market to a vast range of American products. The U.S. government responded by reiterating its basic position: American tax law should be made by Americans. Just because the World Trade Organization had authorized Europe to impose those tariffs, the EU wasn't required to do so. Surely there's a diplomatic solution, the Bush administration declared hopefully. Surely Europe wouldn't want to use its victory at the WTO to punish its trusted ally across the Atlantic.

Europe would, and did. On March 1, 2004, the EU announced the first phase of a new tariff schedule aimed at a broad range of American products, from Carolina textiles to Wisconsin paper to West Virginia steel to Florida citrus fruit—a list clearly targeted at states George W. Bush needed to win in the 2004 election. Initially, the tariffs were mild, but they were set to increase by tens of millions of dollars each month until Congress changed the U.S. tax code. Pascal Lamy, the EU Trade Commissioner, was blunt: "The name of the game is repeal of the U.S. law." Not surprisingly, members of Congress were outraged. "My gut feeling about this is that we fought a revolution 230 years ago to stop Europeans from telling us how we have to tax in this country," said the Speaker of the House, Republican Representative Dennis Hastert of Illinois. But Europe held the trump cards. At a time when the United States was already facing an immense balance-of-trade deficit, American industry desperately needed access to the EU, its richest export market. "It puts the hair up on the back of my neck that we have to consider this at all," Hastert said. "But the fact is, we have to do it. The EU and the WTO have a sort of sword to our head. We don't like it, but we have to do what the Europeans are telling us to do."

. . .

Another element of the New Europe's global power is the euro, the common currency that has been a skyrocketing success in the financial markets since it hit the streets of Europe on New Year's Day of 2002. When the new European money first appeared, most American financial advisers urged their clients to bet against the EU and its currency; the consensus view was that investors should cling to their dollars and watch the new euro fall off a cliff. Of course, any investor who followed that advice lost a lot of money. As it turned out, it was the dollar that plummeted in value in the years following the euro's arrival, while the euro became the darling of currency speculators everywhere. As America's "twin deficits"—that is, the government's budget deficit, reaching nearly 5 percent of GDP, and the nation's balance-of-trade deficit, which was nearly as large as the government shortfall—rose larger and larger, the EU went the opposite direction. The nations of Europe maintained a fairly steady balance-of-trade surplus—that is, they sold more goods and services overseas than they bought—and the Stability and Growth Pact held government deficits to a fairly low level. For investors around the world, it was a fairly easy decision to stock up on the currency of a nation in surplus, and unload American money. In March 2002, when the last of the traditional European currencies was withdrawn from circulation, 1 euro was worth 86 American cents. Two years later, a euro was valued at $1.30—a 50 percent gain against the dollar—and looked likely to grow stronger as long as the American deficits persisted.

Except for a small platoon of professional currency traders who spend their days in front of computer terminals tracking the minute ups and downs of the dollar, the euro, the pound, the yen, and the yuan, this aspect of the revolution in Europe has so far had little impact on Americans. But it could have a huge, and heavily damaging, impact, if the trends in currency values continue along the tracks they've followed since Europe's new currency came into existence. If traders, consumers, and finance ministries around the world come to the conclusion that the rising euro is a more reliable currency than the falling dollar, it could spell the end of the dollar's long reign as the world's preferred reserve currency. That could cost Americans a lot of dollars.

As long as nations have used money (rather than straight barter) as a means of trading with each other, there has always been a currency (or sometimes two currencies) that people adopt as the money they want to hold in reserve, as a fallback in case their own currency loses its value. Since the Bretton Woods agreement in 1944, the reserve currency preferred almost everywhere on earth has been the U.S. dollar. Basically, the "reserve currency" is the money that any seller will accept from any buyer. In Kathmandu, Cairo, or Cartagena, a hotel manager or shopkeeper may be unwilling to take payment in, say, Thai bhat or Kenyan shillings; but the same manager will happily do business in dollars. International oil transactions have long been priced in dollars, even if the seller's home currency is the dinar and the buyer's is the rupee. The dollar is so ubiquitous and so popular that even currency exchange tends to involve dollars most of the time; a Mexican heading off to a vacation at a beach resort in Malaysia will usually find it easier and cheaper to turn his pesos into dollars, and then use the dollars to buy Malaysian ringits, than to make a direct conversion from Mexican money into Malaysian.

The international stature of the dollar is a huge boon to American citizens and businesses. The former French president Charles de Gaulle complained that the dollar's global position "confers an enormous privilege" on the United States and its citizens. Because the rest of the world has been eager to obtain our money, Americans often don't have to bother with the time and expense of currency exchange. If a Canadian traveler finds herself in Nairobi, she will have to buy Kenyan money to pay for room, meals, shopping, and so on. An American can generally skip that step, because any business in Kenya will happily take the money that the American already has in her pocket. That's one value of the dollar. But the dollar's global allure is far more important as a crutch to prop up America's incorrigible habit of deficit spending.

America is such a rich country that it can buy foreign goods and services—not just meals and hotel rooms, but cars, clothes, airplanes, food, industrial machinery, and oil—in huge proportions. All those American jobs that are being "outsourced" to India and other developing nations increase the outflow of American dollars to foreign countries. Americans sell goods and services—including Ken Palmgren's corn and wheat—overseas as well. But we don't export enough to pay for all the goods we buy. Every month, the United States spends about $50 billion more on foreign goods than it earns in foreign sales. That monthly $50 billion—reaching a total that will top $700 billion in 2005—is the balance-of-trade deficit. Most nations could not continue to run a deficit like that for very long; their currency would crash, their loans would be called, and the nation would face bankruptcy. A visit to Argentina, a formerly wealthy country where millions now dig through garbage cans every day looking for something to eat, will make it plain how painful that can be.

But the United States can sustain this steady outflow of money because the rest of the world has been willing to send back the dollars we use to buy foreign goods. This return flow comes in the form of investment—foreign investors buying American stocks or, more commonly, lending us money by buying corporate or government bonds. When the U.S. Treasury spends more than it receives in taxes—early in the twenty-first century, the U.S. government was spending nearly half a trillion dollars more each year than it took in—it makes up the difference by floating Treasury bonds. A bond is a loan from the bond buyer to the United States; the Treasury agrees to pay back the value of the bond, plus interest, in twenty years or so. Every year, a major share of Treasury bonds is purchased by foreign investors, and this, in effect, brings home many of the dollars that went overseas in trade. Those foreign investors putting their funds into Treasury bonds are lending Americans the money we use to buy more imports.

For years, the United States has gotten away with this recurring cycle of spending and borrowing largely because investors around the world have had no better place to put their money. The huge American economy and the always-reliable U.S. Treasury made the United States the world's safest haven for investors. Central banks around the world, in fact, have had rules requiring that they lend their excess money to the

United States. When the People's Bank of China, for example, receives tax revenues each spring, it quickly invests the money in Treasury bonds, knowing that it can depend on the U.S. government to repay the loan without quibble. For most of the past half century, there's been no investment vehicle as trustworthy as the almighty dollar.

The threat facing the United States is that the euro, a strong currency backed up by some of the world's strongest economies, is beginning to look like a reliable alternative to the dollar. Barely three years after its arrival on the world financial scene, in fact, the euro had virtually achieved equity with the dollar as a vehicle for international investment. According to the Bank for International Settlements, the world's watchdog of global credit transactions, the value of euro-denominated bonds (both corporate and governmental) rose from zero in 1998 (when there was no euro) to some $4 trillion in 2004—virtually equal to the amount of money invested in dollar-denominated bonds in 2004. The members of OPEC, the cartel of oil-exporting countries, are already moving toward selling their product in euros. (Before he was overthrown, Saddam Hussein did offer to price Iraqi oil exports in euros, but this was more a political snub than an economic decision.)

The explosive increase in euro-based international transactions suggests the worrisome possibility that foreign investors may have found a place other than the United States where they can safely store their money. By 2005, private investors and central banks around the world were making major shifts in traditional investment patterns, putting significant portions of their reserves into euro bonds rather than dollar bonds. Central bank chiefs in Russia, Japan, South Korea, and several other countries announced that they would buy fewer U.S. treasury bonds in the future, and more euro-denominated securities. Indeed, a survey of central banks in early 2005 showed that two-thirds of the world's sixty-five richest nations were planning to shift investment out of dollars and into euros. If this trend continues—and most economists say that it will—it will be much harder for America to continue its import-and-borrow pattern of consumption. And if euro bonds are seen to be as reliable, as normal, as dollar bonds, foreign investors may decide to lend their money to the euro countries rather than the United States. The U.S. Treasury would then have to raise the interest rate it pays on bonds, to attract foreign loans. At a time when America's twin deficits are skyrocketing, in short, America could be forced to pay much more to borrow the money required to finance those deficits. To put it simply, the success of Europe's common currency could bring America's financial house of cards tumbling down. The dollar could lose much more value on international markets; foreign investors could pull out of American markets, sending stock market indexes steeply downward; the U.S. government could be forced to raise taxes to make up for the bonds it can no longer sell around the world. If all that happened, Americans would wake up to the revolution in Europe in the most painful way.

But the emergence and growth of the United States of Europe as a countervailing power doesn't have to be a nightmare for Americans. In countless ways, the united Europe is a downright boon to the United States. On the most basic level, the world's largest trading market is a market that is wide open to American business. This is instantly obvious if you travel through the counties of Ireland west and south of Dublin, where the misty green hills are now dotted with the factories and warehouses and office buildings of American companies making cars, computers, chemicals, cosmetics, and a thousand other products. These American goods can be shipped anywhere in the EU without a penny of tariff or import duty, and earn profits in the world's strongest currency for American investors. What could be wrong with that? As we have just seen, Americans selling goods and services in Europe have to comply with all the rules and requirements that the EU has imposed; but since Europe's regulations are spreading around the world, American companies have to comply with them in any event.

Beyond the opportunity for profit, Americans can only benefit if an ambitious united Europe begins to take on some of the burdens that necessarily fall to a superpower. If Europeans want to take part—and they do—in such dangerous, difficult, and often thankless tasks as fighting AIDS in

Africa or finding food for starving South Asians or trying to preserve the purity of our planet's air and water, Americans should be delighted to have the helping hand. The EU and its member states send ten times as many soldiers as the United States to peacekeeping missions in Africa, Central Asia, even Central America. This is a clear boon to the U.S. Armed Forces, which generally avoid that kind of mission. When the EU's diplomats seek to manage a seemingly impossible global project like a peaceful solution to the Middle East or a painless reunification of the Korean peninsula, Americans should gladly step aside and welcome the assistance. If the European Union finds a way to create a seamless pancontinental mobile telephone network, or a health-care system that provides prompt and effective treatment for everyone at affordable cost, or a no-frills airline industry that makes it cheaper to fly than to drive, Americans should be happy to learn from the example of the united states across the sea.

To secure these benefits, though, Americans will have to wake up to the revolution. We need to recognize and accept the plain fact that the planet has a second superpower now, and that its global influence will continue to increase as the world moves toward a bipolar balance of economic, political, and diplomatic authority. To put it simply, the United States of America has to show respect for the United States of Europe. Indeed, that kind of respect was one of the main goals the Europeans were looking for when they set out to create a united continent amid the misery and wreckage of World War II. As with so much else about the new, united Europe, this basic truth was first articulated by Winston Churchill. In the famous speech in Zurich that launched Europe's revolution in 1946, the great man made the point in his characteristic rolling cadence: "We must build a kind of United States of Europe. . . . Why should there not be a European group which could give a sense of enlarged patriotism and common citizenship to the distracted peoples of this turbulent and mighty continent? And why should it not take its right place with other great groupings in shaping the destinies of mankind? Mighty America must be the friend and sponsor of the New Europe, and must champion its right to live and shine."

The States of Europe

For the hard-core geographers, the continent of Europe is not actually a continent at all, but rather a subcontinent, a relatively small appendage of the great Eurasian land mass that stretches across half the planet from the Pacific to the Atlantic. But Europe—extending, in the traditional definition, from Ireland's intensely green Connemara coast to the stark rocky slopes of Russia's Ural Mountains—has earned the right to be considered a separate place of its own. It covers just 6 percent of the earth's total area and is home to just 12 percent of the global population; yet Europe has 40 percent of the world's wealth and accounts for more than half of all global commerce. European countries comprise five of the world's ten richest nations. The continent was the birthplace of "Western values," the combination of individual rights, democratic governments, and free markets that has spread around the world. It is the home of most of the world's Christian denominations and an important locus of Jewish and Muslim belief as well. European art, music, architecture, literature, and legal concepts have been copied everywhere, with local variations. The increasingly common language of the continent, English, has spread from its small island birthplace to become the second most widely spoken language on earth (after Chinese).

Europe is densely populated compared to the other continents, largely urbanized, and heavily industrial. In Roman times, great forests blanketed most of the continent. Population pressure over the centuries cut down most of the trees. Without the "carbon sink" provided by forest cover, Europe faces bigger problems from global warming than most other continents, which helps explain why the Europeans are such forceful advocates of the Kyoto accords. In the twenty-first century, however, Europe faces a different population problem; low birth rates across the continent mean there will soon be too few workers to finance the generous menu of subsidies and benefits that are central to the cherished welfare state. The answer to this problem—although it's a solution that many European nations don't like—will probably be immigration, as tens of millions of working-age people from Africa, the Middle East, and East Asia make their way by hook or crook to wealthy Europe in search of jobs and freedom.

For much of the twentieth century, Europe seemed determined to divide itself, shifting borders and creating new countries so rapidly that mapmakers could never catch up. This habit continued even after the collapse of the Soviet Empire; between 1990 and 1995, the number of European countries grew from thirty-three to forty-three. But amid all those border changes, Europe as a whole has been unifying itself to a revolutionary degree (which is the central point of this book). The borderless single market, the pancontinental government and currency, the huge investment in high-speed transit and communications, and the spreading common culture championed by Generation E are turning the states of Europe into a new kind of "nation" that fulfills Churchill's dream of a "United States of Europe." The impact of this wealthy, ambitious, and politically powerful pan-European nation will be one of the major themes of twenty-first-century history.

But just as Texas and Vermont are different places, the states of the United States of Europe each have their own local culture and flavor, which we will consider briefly here. The following list moves roughly from west to east across the map of Europe. For each of the European states, the roster provides the land area, with a comparison to a U.S. state that is close to the same size; population (drawn in almost every case from a census at the start of the twenty-first century); per capita income, in U.S. dollars, which is a good measure of how rich the country is; the major national language(s); and the name of the country in its national language. These demographic data are drawn largely from the 2004 edition of the CIA's excellent *World Factbook.* The Reid Anti-American Index, or RAA Index, created specifically for this book, measures the general attitude in each country toward the United States at a particular time—in the fourth year of the George W. Bush administration. This is a subjective measure, but it is based on objective data: opinion polls, governmental positions, and popular media depictions of America. The RAA Index ranges from 1 to 100; a high number (as in France) means that the country particularly dislikes America; a low number (as in Poland or Ireland) reflects a populace that still feels respect and admiration for the United States. The Europhile Index, another subjective measurement created by the author of this book, reflects how strongly the people and the government are committed to the European Union; in several cases, the Europhile Index is based on recent referenda to determine whether the nation should join the EU. On a scale of 1 to 100, a high number (as in Luxembourg) represents a country that is strongly committed to the idea of unification; a low number (as in Norway) means a more Euroskeptic population. The Globalization Index, created by the AT Kearney company and *Foreign Policy* magazine, ranks how connected each nation is to the rest of the world—through economic links and personal contacts. That index ranks sixty-two countries; a high ranking means that a country is highly globalized. Ireland's ranking of 1 means that it was judged the most global nation on earth.

Ireland (Eire)

Land area	27,137 square miles (roughly the size of West Virginia)
Population	3.7 million

Per capita income	$25,060
Currency	euro
Languages	English, Irish Gaelic
RAA Index	30
Europhile Index	80
Globalization rank	1 of 62
National Day	March 17, Saint Patrick's Day
EU member since 1973	

Ireland has been one of the major winners in the unification of Europe; its status as an English-speaking stepping stone between American industry and the single EU market has brought wealth never before seen on the green and misty island. The prosperous, highly educated, high-tech Ireland of the twenty-first century is vastly different from the quaint, God-fearing, beer-swilling, rural nation that Americans like to celebrate each year on Saint Patrick's Day (an anniversary that is a much bigger deal in New York and Chicago than it is in Ireland). The Irish are great talkers and wonderful writers; this tiny nation has produced four Nobel Prize winners in literature (George Bernard Shaw, William Butler Yeats, Samuel Beckett, and Seamus Heaney). Ireland today has half the population it had at the start of the great famine in 1840, but in the twenty-first century the tide of outward emigration has turned. In a historic shift, Ireland now is receiving economic immigrants, and the population is growing again. The rapid increase in wealth has caused problems, but these are problems that most of the Irish welcome. When Bertie Ahern, the *taoiseach*, or prime minister, was running for reelection in 2002, he came upon a voter in county Kildare who complained bitterly about heavy traffic jams on the road from Carlow to Kilkenny. Ahern, a world-class politician, came up with a perfect response: "I remember when the only Irishmen who complained about traffic jams were the fellows living in New York," Ahern said. "Now we have the money to buy our own cars and create our own jams. That's the new Ireland, and I like it better." So do his countrymen, who gave Ahern a resounding victory as an endorsement of his pro-growth, pro-Europe policies.

Great Britain

(The United Kingdom of Great Britain and Northern Ireland)

Land area	94,248 square miles (roughly the size of Wyoming)
Population	59.1 million
Per capita income	$24,390
Currency	pound sterling
Languages	English, Welsh, Scottish
RAA Index	60
Europhile Index	50
Globalization rank	12 of 62
National Day	Second Sunday in June, the Queen's official birthday
EU member since 1973	

The United Kingdom is a union of three countries—England, Wales, and Scotland—plus a vest-pocket corner of six Protestant-majority counties in Ireland that refused to go along when the rest of Eire left the British Empire in 1922. Britain entered the twenty-first century as a confident, prosperous postindustrial nation. The country is justly proud of its continuing contributions to global culture (from Harry Potter to David Beckham to *Masterpiece Theatre*) and its scientific stature; Brits invented cloning, Viagra, and the World Wide Web. It is the most military-minded of the European countries—although still a minor partner in its alliance with the United States—and the capital of European finance. It has the world's best newspapers and public broadcaster, and universities that rank among the finest on earth. Still, Britain today is confused and divided about its role in the world: Should it try to be a key player in the new, unified Europe, or should it shun the EU and forge closer ties with the United States? Prime Minister Tony Blair is as uncertain on this central question as the rest of his countrymen. He is strongly committed to the EU, and he is the nation's leading advocate for joining the euro. At the same time, Blair is so determined to be friendly with Washington— even if it means alienating the rest of Europe—that he is routinely described in those lively British newspapers as "Bush's poodle." As the twenty-first century progresses, Britain will have to resolve this national schizophrenia and decide whether it wants to be "at the heart of the New Europe" (Blair's phrase) or the fifty-first American state.

Portugal

Land area	35,672 square miles (roughly the size of Maine)
Population	10.0 million
Per capita income	$11,380
Currency	euro
Language	Portuguese
RAA Index	50
Europhile Index	85
Globalization rank	16 of 62
National Day	June 10, Portugal Day, since 1580
EU member since 1986	

This beautiful small country has been another major beneficiary of EU membership, taking advantage of billions of euros in development grants from Brussels to revive its cities, its transit infrastructure, and its industry. Portugal was the first great colonial power, and the last, waiting until 1999 to surrender its last foreign holding, the Chinese city-state of Macau. As an EU member and a euro nation with relatively low wage rates, Portugal has done well at attracting foreign companies that want a toehold in the eurozone. This has been a necessary boon, because the Portuguese seem likely to lose their status as global leaders in one impor- tant product: cork. The sprawling cork plantations south of the river Tejo have produced the nation's main export for decades. But natural cork is losing out in the wine-bottling business to an artificial competitor—plastic corks, made mainly in the United States. In another area, little Portugal has been a global trendsetter: Lisbon's bold decision to decriminalize all drug use, and to treat drug addiction as an illness rather than a crime, has sparked similar change all over Europe and in parts of North and South America as well.

Spain (España)

Land area	195,000 square miles (roughly the size of Arizona and Utah combined)
Population	39.4 million
Per capita income	$15,120
Currency	euro
Languages	Spanish, Catalan, Galician, Basque
RAA Index	70
Europhile Index	85
Globalization rank	24 of 62
National Day	October 12, Hispanic Day
EU member since 1986	

Spain has prospered mightily since it entered the EU in 1986, partly through a huge influx of foreign investment and partly because the warm, green farm country south of Madrid has become a key source of fresh produce for the whole continent. The huge numbers of starving immigrants who cross the Mediterranean from North Africa—often taking to the high seas in canoes or rubber boats—are more welcome in Spain than they might be elsewhere in Europe because they provide the labor for the agriculture industry. Spain has modernized fast; in a heavily Roman Catholic country, divorce and abortion are legal and common. Women play major roles in government and, to a lesser extent, industry. Landmarks like the spectacular Guggenheim Museum in Bilbao and the amazing Gaudi cathedral in Barcelona have made Spain a global leader in contemporary architecture. The Spanish feel a close alliance to their former colonies in Latin America, and this used to make for warm feelings between the Spanish people and the United States as well. But the national fury over the war in Iraq—polls showed that 95 percent opposed Spain's involvement—and the horrifying burst of terrorism in Madrid on March 11, 2004, have contributed to an increasing anti-Americanism, or at least anti-Bushism.

France

Land area	210,026 square miles (roughly the size of Iowa, Kansas, and Nebraska combined)
Population	60.8 million
Per capita income	$23,560
Currency	euro
Language	French
RAA Index	85
Europhile Index	90
Globalization rank	15 of 62
National Day	July 14, Bastille Day
EU member from the start	

The French seem to have a national inferiority complex when it comes to the United States, Japan, and some of their European neighbors. But it's hard to understand why. La Belle France itself is a marvelous place to live, with splendid beach resorts along the Mediterranean, great ski meccas in the majestic Alps, and some of the most cosmopolitan cities in the world. Like other nations, France became concerned about environmental problems in the 1970s; unlike most others, it invested huge sums and changed its way of life to deal with these issues. France has developed the most advanced transit infrastructure on earth—with sleek TGV trains racing everywhere—to get people out of their cars. France has shut down so many fossil-fueled power plants that the country now gets more than three-quarters of its electricity from nuclear power. The French have deep contradictions when it comes to the United States; devout fans of American pop culture, from McDonald's to Beyoncé, they are nevertheless among the most virulent critics of American politics and foreign policy. The French welfare state gives people plenty of time to savor the pleasant side of life, and they love their luxuries. To see hundreds of thousands of Frenchmen with their Beaujolais, baguettes, and big tubs of Brie enjoying hillside picnics while waiting for the riders of the Tour de France to flash by on a bright summer's day is to see a people who know how to be happy. During the Iraq war, when angry Americans organized boycotts of French products, *Le Monde* columnist Marc Roche remarked that this boycott was typical of Americans, who don't know how to appreciate the finer things. "If Americans are stupid enough to give up wonderful wines and delicious cheese, that's their problem," Roche said. "In France, we know that such delights make life worth living."

Belgium
(België or Belgique)

Land area	11,783 square miles (roughly the size of Maryland)
Population	10.2 million
Per capita income	$24,300
Currency	euro
Languages	Dutch, French, German
RAA Index	75
Europhile Index	95
Globalization rank	not ranked
National Day	July 21, Independence Day, since 1821
EU member from the start	

For two millennia, Belgium was Europe's battleground, which is why this small country marks the dividing line between Europe's Latin and Germanic languages. Thus it is a delightful turnabout for the Belgians to find themselves the capital of the New Europe, the pancontinental union specifically created to end warfare on the continent. Belgium has strongly embraced the European Union from its earliest days, and that's a key reason why Brussels has become the seat of government for both the EU and NATO. The Belgians insist that the popular food known to Americans as French fries was actually invented in Belgium, and the ubiquitous *friteries* on every urban street suggest this is true. Despite language and cultural differences between the Dutch speakers (Flemings) of the north and the French-speakers (Walloons) in the south, Belgium has minimal domestic strife. No matter what their background, after all, they are all Belgians. And today, they are all Europeans.

The Netherlands (Nederland)

Land area	16,023 square miles (roughly the size of New Hampshire and Vermont combined)
Population	16.1 million
Per capita income	$27,200
Currency	euro
Language	Dutch
RAA Index	70
Europhile Index	85
Globalization rank	4 of 62
National Day	April 30, Queen Mother Juliana's birthday
EU member from the start	

Contrary to common usage, "Holland" is not interchangeable with "the Netherlands." Rather, North Holland and South Holland are constituent states of the country. The Holland region, on the North Sea coast, is actually below sea level. Pumps and dikes turned it into habitable terrain, giving rise to the Dutch aphorism "God made the earth, but the Dutch made Holland." The nation's traffic jams are more likely to be caused by swarms of bicycles than by cars; in a flat country crisscrossed by bike paths, two-wheeled human-powered transit remains the most popular way to get around. The huge "Europoort" at Rotterdam is the world's busiest cargo port, shipping out not only Dutch agriculture and manufactures but also the products of the whole of northern Europe. As a result, the Dutch have profited considerably from the single pan-continental market. No wonder they are such strong supporters of the European Union.

Luxembourg

Land area	998 square miles (a little smaller than Rhode Island)
Population	454,000
Per capita income	$48,900
Currency	euro
Languages	Letzeburgesh, French, German
RAA Index	50
Europhile Index	99
Globalization rank	not ranked
National day	June 23, Grand Duchess Charlotte's birthday
EU member from the start	

The only grand duchy in the world, Luxembourg has used its linguistic skills and its tax laws to make itself a global banking center, with a higher ratio of banks to people (one bank company for every 2,500 residents) than any other nation. That explains the astronomical per capita income figure of almost $50,000, the highest of any nation. Luxembourg has also benefited from its status as headquarters for several European Union operations, which offer well-paid white-collar jobs in large numbers. No wonder the residents of the Grand Duchy like to paint its national motto on the walls: "We want to remain what we are."

Norway (Norge)

Land area	125,182 square miles (roughly the size of Florida and Georgia combined)
Population	4.52 million
Per capita income	$35,840
Currency	kroner
Languages	Norwegian, Sami
RAA Index	40
Europhile Index	20
Globalization rank	17 of 62
National Day	May 17, Constitution Day

Not an EU member

Norway has rightly been called "the lucky country of Europe," and the Norwegians indeed have multiple blessings to count as they enter the twenty-first century. Already a wealthy nation because of its globe-spanning fishing fleets, Norway hit the stratosphere of economic success in the 1970s, when large oil reserves were found off the Norwegian coast in the North Sea. The country doesn't use much oil itself, because the rivers running down from its glacier beds provide most of the nation's electricity through hydropower. Thus virtually all of Norway's oil production can be exported. That helps explain why Norway ranks second only to Luxembourg among the European nations in per capita wealth. The Norwegians are doing so well on their own that they show minimal interest in joining the EU. But they do share their riches, partly through a typically generous Scandinavian welfare state, and partly by giving away a higher proportion of their GDP to poor regions than any other nation except their neighbors Denmark and Sweden. A sizable chunk of Norway lies north of the Arctic Circle, a forbidding part of the world where the sun never rises during the four-month winter. In Tromsö, the biggest northern city, there's a huge municipal party each year on January 21, when the sun sneaks above the horizon for about fifteen minutes right at noon—a pale harbinger of long, bright summer days to come.

Denmark
(Danmark)

Land area	16,638 square miles (roughly the size of New Hampshire and Vermont combined)
Population	5.4 million
Per capita income	$29,450
Currency	kroner
Languages	Danish, Norwegian
RAA Index	45
Europhile Index	55
Globalization rank	10 of 62
National Day	June 5, Constitution Day

EU member since 1973

Sweden (Sverige)

Land area	173,732 square miles (a little bigger than California)
Population	9.0 million
Per capita income	$25,080
Currency	kroner
Language	Swedish
RAA Index	65
Europhile Index	55
Globalization rank	11 of 62
National Day	June 6 (Flag Day)

EU member since 1995

The two Nordic neighbors Denmark and Sweden have a good deal in common. Both are industrious, highly educated states that have prospered by building well-designed and well-built manufactured goods for shipment to the world's other wealthy countries. Both have used their wealth to finance unusually generous—indeed, luxurious—versions of the welfare state, and both give away significant portions of their money to the world's poorer nations. Sweden and Denmark have both been in the forefront of women's advancement, in industry as well as government. And yet these two Scandinavian countries do not consider themselves to be cultural twins. They find fundamental differences when it comes to national psyche and worldview. The national self-portraits depict Denmark as a fun-loving nation, the home of the world's oldest amusement park (Copenhagen's charming Tivoli Gardens), while Swedes consider themselves more cautious and serious, with enormous taxes on alcohol to discourage such frivolities as drinking. These attitudes are reflected in a shared joke: A Dane and a Swede get together for dinner. Immediately, the Dane pops open a beer and says, "Drink up!" The Swede replies, "Not so fast! I haven't had time to read the list of contents on the label yet."

Finland (Suomi)

Land area	130,558 square miles (a little bigger than New Mexico)
Population	5.2 million
Per capita income	$26,200
Currency	euro
Languages	Finnish, Sami, Swedish
RAA Index	40
Europhile Index	80
Globalization rank	5 of 62
National Day	December 6, Independence Day
EU member since 1995	

Stuck in the snow on a cold, isolated peninsula, speaking a language different from almost any other (except their Estonian neighbors), the Finns decided long ago that they would have to think harder and work harder than more happily situated nations to succeed. During the cold war, Finland fared fairly well in its niche role as the commercial and financial middleman between Moscow and the rest of the world. The demise of the Soviet Union and the economic collapse of Russia meant the end of that useful arrangement, but the resourceful Finns found themselves a new niche: wireless communications. With the entire Finnish nation acting as boosters—the nation has the highest rate of mobile phone use in the world—Finland's Nokia used technical, design, and marketing skills to become the world's leading supplier of cellular phones and equipment. A Nokia cell phone is the most popular thing to come out of Finland since the sauna, and Nokia's success has had spin-off benefits for the entire economy. The Finns have a national sense of community that sometimes makes the whole nation feel like one big family. The prime minister, who lives in a small, simple official residence on the shore of Helsinki Bay, routinely walks down to the waterfront on summer evenings to chat with kayakers who happen to be paddling by.

Germany (Deutschland)

Land area	137, 857 square miles (a little smaller than Montana)
Population	83.3 million
Per capita income	$26,600
Currency	euro
Language	German
RAA Index	40
Europhile Index	80
Globalization rank	18 of 62
National Day	October 3, the day when East and West were unified in 1990

EU member from the start

Germany—or, more precisely, the fear of Germany—was a driving force behind the initial steps toward the unification of Europe following World War II. Ever since, as the biggest, and richest, member nation,

Germany has played a sort of sugar daddy role for the smaller EU members. For years, whenever the union needed a cash infusion, the Germans would dutifully ante up, as if they were paying voluntary reparations for the horrors of World War II. But then, in 1989, Chancellor Helmut Kohl reached out and embraced the former East Germany as the Soviet empire ended: "We are all Germans, after all," Kohl said. The booming (West) German economy was suddenly burdened with the enormous costs of rebuilding the East. With that new responsibility, Berlin became increasingly reluctant to ship money to the rest of the EU. Despite the cost involved, though, the Germans are enthusiastic EU participants. Perhaps they see the union—as do many others—as an effective way to make sure that Germany never again goes to war against its neighbors.

Switzerland (Schweiz, Suisse, Svizzera)

Land area	15,941 square miles (roughly the size of Maryland and Delaware combined)
Population	7.3 million
Per capita income	$31,700
Currency	franc
Languages	German, French, Italian
RAA Index	50
Europhile Index	40
Globalization rank	3 of 62
National Day	August 1, the day the Swiss Confederation was founded in 1291

Not an EU member

The central paradox of neat, efficient Switzerland is that a profoundly pacifist country has mandatory national military service that sees virtually the entire population affiliated with a local militia. The extensive civil defense network is the price Switzerland (willingly) pays for its centuries-old status as a neutral in world affairs. The Swiss take enormous pride in

their stature as a historic noncombatant, although critics have been asking for half a century whether anybody should be proud to have been
neutral toward the Nazis. Swiss pride was tarnished badly in the 1990s,
when investigators showed that those famous Swiss banks profited
hugely from doing business with Hitler and his regime while most of
Europe was fighting the Reich. Switzerland almost always ranks among
the top five nations in the world in per capita income. The Swiss have
made themselves rich with their finance and manufacturing industries,
but they share the wealth generously with poorer nations.

Austria
(Oesterreich)

Land area	32,377 square miles (roughly the size of Maine)
Population	8.2 million
Per capita income	$27,700
Currency	euro
Language	German
RAA Index	65
Europhile Index	85
Globalization rank	9 of 62
National day	October 26, the day the Allied occupation ended in 1955

EU member since 1995

You have to like a country that spends more of its national budget on
opera (the Vienna Opera, in particular) than on its military. And the
Austrians have a lot of money to spend; their meticulous manufacturing
skills, coupled with cheap hydropower, make for a profitable export trade.
A hundred years ago, Vienna was arguably the most important city on
earth in both art and science. The intervening century was a difficult
one, with the Austrians losing badly in both world wars; the luckiest
moment came in 1945, when Churchill saw to it that Austria stayed on

the free-market side of the Iron Curtain. That gave the Austrians the elbow room they needed to rebuild their lovely country and its thriving industries.

Italy (Italia)

Land area	116,324 square miles (twice as big as Florida)
Population	57.7 million
Per capita income	$25,000
Currency	euro
Languages	Italian, German
RAA Index	65
Europhile Index	85
Globalization rank	25 of 62
National day	June 7, the day the post-Mussolini republic was born in 1946

EU member from the start

All Italian cities have named their boulevards after the heroes of Italian unification—Via Cavour, Via Garibaldi, and so on—but even today the unified Italy looks and feels like two different nations: the northern industrial belt at the top of the peninsula is a modern, prosperous industrial power, while the rural south (the "Mezzogiorno") seems far behind. With its wonderful food and fascinating history—Roman, Renaissance, Roman Catholic—Italy has the biggest tourist industry in Europe. Along with Spain and Britain, Italy supported the United States in the Iraq war, contributing a small but symbolic troop presence—even though most of the population opposed that war. Italians are also responsible, in a sense, for one of the great American success stories of recent years: In the delightful espresso bars of Milan, where the baristas in their bright red vests expertly whip up each *machiatto* and caffe latte, a coffee bean salesman from Seattle named Howard Schultz got the idea that he turned into a new kind of retail outlet—a place he called Starbucks.

Poland (Polska)

Land area	120,725 square miles (roughly the size of New Mexico)
Population	39 million
Per capita income	$9,500
Currency	zloty (committed to adopt euro)
Language	Polish
RAA Index	20
Europhile Index	80
Globalization rank	31 of 62
National day	May 3, Constitution Day, since 1794
EU member as of 2004	

Poland suffered through much of the twentieth century at the hands of powerful and cruel neighbors. First the Nazi blitzkrieg roared in (1939). Victory over Germany served only to deliver the Poles into the equally harsh control of Stalin's Soviet Union (1945). The Poles fought back against both conquerors; in the 1980s, when the Berlin Wall still stood, a Polish pope and a group of determined shipyard workers showed that resistance to Moscow's control was not unthinkable. When the Soviet Union and its empire collapsed, Poland retained its leadership role, demonstrating how a Communist economy could shift to the free market without massive unemployment. Nearly everybody in Poland has a friend or relative living in the United States, which makes the nation one of America's strongest European friends. The United States is hoping that this new member of the European Union will provide a pro-American voice and vote in EU deliberations. It is not certain that Washington's hope will be fulfilled.

Czech Republic
(Ceska Republika)

Land area	30,450 square miles (roughly the size of South Carolina)
Population	10.3 million
Per capita income	$15,300
Currency	Czech koruna (committed to adopt euro)
Language	Czech
RAA Index	50
Europhile Index	82
Globalization rank	14 of 62
National day	October 18, the day Czechoslovakia was founded, 1918

EU member as of 2004

Slovakia
(Slovensko)

Land area	18,291 square miles (roughly the size of New Hampshire and Vermont combined)
Population	5.4 million
Per capita income	$12,200
Currency	Slovak koruna (committed to adopt euro)
Language	Slovak
RAA Index	50
Europhile Index	85
Globalization rank	21 of 62
National day	September 1, the day Czechoslovakia was divided, 1992

EU member as of 2004

The nation of Czechoslovakia, created at the end of World War I, was always something of a shotgun marriage, with the two partners separating in World War II and then forcibly reunited by the Soviets after the war. The so-called Velvet Divorce in 1993 highlighted the fundamental differences. The Czechs in the west have built a fairly successful industrial economy with significant foreign investment; the Slovaks in the mountainous east have struggled, depending largely on agriculture. Both nations' populations strongly supported European Union membership, and both hope for the kind of economic miracles that lifted Ireland and Portugal when those once-poor nations joined the EU.

Hungary
(Magyarorszag)

Land area	35,919 square miles (roughly the size of Indiana)
Population	10.1 million
Per capita income	$13,300
Currency	forint (committed to adopt euro)
Language	Hungarian
RAA Index	40
Europhile Index	80
Globalization rank	26 of 62
National day	August 20, the Feast of Saint Stephen
EU member as of 2004	

Hungary was always one of the toughest satellites for the Soviets to control; from the time of the 1956 revolt through the development of so-called goulash communism, Budapest found ways to permit some political and market freedom while still under the thumb of Moscow. The Hungarians basically opened their border with Austria before the Berlin Wall fell, and the "Home of the Magyars" was one of the first former Soviet-bloc nations to embrace democracy. Comfortable with capitalism, Hungary should flourish in the open market of the united Europe.

Slovenia (Slovenija)

Land area	7,719 square miles (roughly the size of New Jersey)
Population	1.9 million
Per capita income	$18,000
Currency	tolar (committed to adopt euro)
Languages	Slovenian, Serbo-Croatian
RAA Index	50
Europhile Index	80
Globalization rank	19 of 62
National day	June 25, Independence Day, since 1991

EU member as of 2004

Slovenia actually had to fight for independence when it split from Yugoslavia in 1991, but the "war" lasted only ten days because the Slovenes were so determined to break away. With a manufacturing economy that made it the richest of the Yugoslav republics, Slovenia always felt closer to its prosperous neighbors, Austria and Italy, than to the government in Belgrade. So far, it is the only piece of the former Yugoslavia to qualify for EU membership. This is not to suggest that Slovenia is anything like a Western industrial state; its dusty, aging cities and sleepy countryside will need considerable economic aid from Brussels over the next decade.

Greece (Hellas)

Land area	50,962 square miles (roughly the size of Alabama)
Population	10.6 million
Per capita income	$19,000
Currency	euro
Language	Greek
RAA Index	30
Europhile Index	85

Globalization rank	28 of 62
National day	March 25, the day of independence from the Ottomans, 1821
EU member since 1981	

The Greeks, of course, gave democracy—both the word and the concept—to Europe and the world. But the Greeks themselves had to throw out a military junta and restore democratic rule before they qualified to join the European Union in 1981. EU membership has been a huge boon, providing development money to built a transit infrastructure and a Western-style banking industry. The Greeks, in turn, developed enough self-confidence to host the Summer Olympics in 2004 and to start demanding that their European neighbors send back the great art treasures of the Periclean Age that now grace museums far from Athens. The Greeks themselves, meanwhile, are finally taking steps to protect their ancient monuments from the ravages of air pollution and from tourists who want to touch, or carve on, everything they see. A cruise around the Greek isles, which float like shimmering emeralds atop Homer's wine-dark sea, remains one of the most beautiful ocean voyages on the planet.

Cyprus

Land area	2,277 square miles (roughly the size of Delaware)
Population	767,000
Per capita income	$15,000, in Greek Cyprus; $7,000, in Turkish Cyprus
Currencies	Cypriot pound, Turkish lira (committed to adopt euro)
Languages	Greek, Turkish, English
RAA Index	30
Europhile Index	90
Globalization rank	not ranked
National day	Greek Cyprus: October 1 (independence from Britain, 1960);Turkish Cyprus: November 15
EU member as of 2004	

Malta

Land area	122 square miles (about twice the size of the District of Columbia)
Population	397,000
Per capita income	$17,000
Currency	lira (committed to adopt euro)
Languages	Maltese, English
RAA Index	40
Europhile Index	90
Globalization rank	not ranked
National day	September 21 (independence from Britain, 1964)
EU member as of 2004	

These two small island nations were admitted to the EU largely because of the support of their former colonial ruler, Great Britain. Both depend on tourism, with Malta drawing Italian vacationers and Cyprus getting visitors from Turkey (in the Turkish sector, in the north) and Greece (in Greek Cyprus, to the south). Both are desperate for development funds from Brussels, but it is not clear how much the European Union will want to invest in its two smallest member states. The Greek majority on Cyprus angered Brussels in 2004 by refusing to approve a referendum calling for union with the Turkish sector. So Cyprus, while united with the rest of Europe, will remain divided at home.

The Baltic States

ESTONIA (EESTI)

Land area	17,413 square miles (roughly the size of New Hampshire and Vermont combined)
Population	1.4 million
Per capita income	$10,900
Currency	kroon (committed to adopt euro)

Languages   Estonian, Finnish, Russian

RAA Index   20

Europhile Index   75

Globalization rank   not ranked

National days   February 24 (independence from Russia, 1918);

                           August 20 (independence from USSR, 1991)

EU member as of 2004

LATVIA (LATVIJA)

Land area   24, 942 square miles (roughly the size of

                               West Virginia)

Population   2.4 million

Per capita income $8,300

Currency   lat (committed to adopt euro)

Languages   Latvian, Lithuanian

RAA Index   20

Europhile Index   75

Globalization rank   not ranked

National days   February 24 (independence from Russia, 1918);

                           August 21 (independence from USSR, 1991)

EU member as of 2004

LITHUANIA
(LIETUVA)

Land area   25,174 square miles (roughly the size of

                               West Virginia)

Population   3.6 million

Per capita income $8,300

Currency   litas (committed to adopt euro)

Languages   Lithuanian, Polish

RAA Index   20

Europhile Index   75

Globalization rank   not ranked

National days   February 16 (independence from Russia, 1918);
                                 March 11 (independence from USSR, 1991)
EU member as of 2004

Like defenseless badgers living beside the den of a giant bear, the three small Baltic States spent most of the twentieth century under the stern control of the Russian bear that looms over them to the east. All three countries recognize two Independence Days, one marking their (short-lived) freedom from Soviet Russia in 1918, and the other marking the break from the collapsing Soviet Union in 1990–91.

Accordingly, the newly independent Baltic trio are desperate to build stronger ties toward the west; hence their rush to join NATO and the European Union the minute they were invited to do so. In cultural and economic terms as well, the three small countries are racing to western-ize. They have glitzy all-night casinos and busy stock markets and grow-ing tourist industries.

The Former Yugoslav Republics

To the statesmen who redrew the map of Europe at the end of World War I, the idea of a single Slavic state on the Balkan Peninsula evidently seemed like a good idea. In fact, the resulting nation of Yugoslavia was so badly divided on ethnic, religious, and linguistic lines that it added an adjective to the language: the word *balkanized* is now in the dictionaries, meaning "divided into small, quarrelsome, ineffectual groups." After World War I, the anti-Nazi partisan Josip Broz Tito held the various republics together through sheer force of character and a clever foreign policy that made him the West's favorite Communist. Yugoslavia actually survived for a decade beyond Tito's death in 1980, but then fell apart in a series of lethal civil wars. Of the six former Yugoslav republics, the rich-est, Slovenia (see above) has become a market economy and joined the European Union. The remaining units of the former nation have divided into four separate countries: Bosnia-Herzegovina, Croatia, Macedonia, and Serbia and Montenegro. All four say they hope to join the European

Union eventually. In the first decade of the twenty-first century, only Croatia seems a likely candidate.

The Enclaves of Europe

Smaller even than Malta and Cyprus, five postage-stamp principalities in Western Europe have been permitted to operate as quasi-independent states (mainly because that status was convenient for their larger neighbors). Vatican City (.2 square miles, population 900) is the seat of the world's biggest Christian denomination and thus enjoys enough clout with the Italian government to govern itself. Andorra (175 square miles, population 5,000)—high in the Pyrenees between France and Spain—and Liechtenstein (62 square miles, population 31,000)—in the Alps between Switzerland and Austria were useful trading zones and thus never taken over by the larger countries. San Marino (24 square miles, population 25,000) in northern Italy and Monaco (.6 square miles, population 27,000) have been allowed to remain nominally independent because the local rulers cut smart bargains with the kings of the larger countries many centuries ago. All these enclaves are prosperous. They make money from tourism, but they also do a brisk business issuing coins and stamps—far more than their own populations could use, but sought after by collectors all over the world.

Inside the Belgeway

The Governing Structure
of the European Union

If a camel is a horse designed by a committee, as the old joke goes, then the ridiculously complicated structure of European Union councils, commissions, courts, committees, and Parliament scattered around various European cities makes up a huge camel of a government—an awkward, ugly beast that somehow manages to perform its necessary functions in a difficult environment. Nobody would have deliberately designed a government as complex and as redundant as the EU. Rather, the union's unwieldy architecture simply evolved, the product of decades of treaties and agreements involving hundreds of compromises along the way. As Robert Schuman predicted in his May 9, 1950, declaration, the New Europe was created not according to some grand overall plan but rather piece by piece, as necessity and experience suggested. The Schuman prescription holds true of its government as well. Over fifty years, a whole series of committees designed a large, ungainly camel.

And it has proven hard to change. With a budget in excess of $150 billion and some 30,000 Eurocrats (or *fonctionnaires,* to use the preferred Brussels terminology) on the EU payroll, there is enormous resistance to any effort to streamline the operation or eliminate any of its overlapping positions. In 2004, after Valéry Giscard d'Estaing's Constitutional Convention spent more than a year trying to modernize the governmental apparatus to serve a union of twenty-five nations, the resulting document left intact much of the existing system. Under the new constitution, the EU will merge its two distinct foreign minister positions (the "high representative" and the "commissioner for external relations") into a single "foreign affairs minister." That simplification represents a clear gain for common sense. But simplicity did not prevail in other areas. The constitution did not eliminate the confusion caused by the fact that the EU has two different people called "president"—one being the president of the European Council, and the other serving as president of the European Commission. (Just to complicate matters further, the presiding officer of the European Parliament is also called the president, and a revolving presidency used to rotate from one country to another. But this last "presidency," at least, has been eliminated by the constitution.) And then there are the councils. There's a Council of Ministers, which is vaguely subordinate to an institution called the European Council. This should not be confused with a different entity known as the European Commission, which is the EU's executive branch. And neither of these august bodies should be confused with the Council of Europe, which is a completely separate organization with members from forty-five European nations— all the EU states, plus twenty more—that drafts pancontinental conventions and treaties.

For all the overlap and the complicated nomenclature, however, the basic structure of the European Union is relatively easy for an American to understand. The continent's federal government is divided, roughly, into legislative, executive, and judicial branches, just like the federal government that America's founding fathers designed in 1789. But you can't carry this comparison too far. For one thing, the individual states of the European Union are sovereign countries; each one is a member in its own right of the United Nations. That means that the governments in London and Lisbon have more independent authority within the overall union than, say, the governments in Sacramento and Springfield have in the American polity. For another, the branches of the EU government have to answer to a fourth branch of government—a sort of Board of

Directors supervising the whole operation—that does not exist in the American system.

This **Board of Directors**, with ultimate authority over most issues within the EU, is made up of the prime ministers and presidents of the member countries. They all get together in a European Summit four times per year. Theoretically, these important figures—the highest elected official from each member nation—are not supposed to mess around with minor issues. Their job (on paper, at least) is to set the broad direction of the union and resolve disputes that could not be managed by the EU's executive branch, or Parliament. In fact, the summits have often turned into extended arguments about fairly mundane issues, like which country gets to serve as headquarters for each new EU board or commission, or how the last few million euros of the EU's huge program of agricultural subsidies should be divided. Many of these disputes turn into extended arguments between the "nationalists"—those prime ministers who want to keep most governing authority with the various national governments—and the "federalists," who want to expand the collective authority of the EU government. One of the reasons the EU has never settled on a common tax code—although this was one of the great passions of Jean Monnet and his fellow founding fathers—is because debates about Europe-wide tax rules tend to turn into a ferocious argument between the federalists and the nationalists. The virtue of this supervisory board of directors is that it puts elected officials at the top of the organization chart. It means that Brussels can't do anything important unless the democratically chosen leaders of Europe agree.

When the twenty-five heads of state are meeting, the collective body is known as the European Council. In many cases, though, the prime ministers delegate authority over particular issues to their cabinet ministers. When the member states discussed a Europe-wide effort to track down members of Al Qaeda, for example, after the 9/11 attacks, the project was approved by the various ministers of justice. Similarly, the national agriculture ministers get together to discuss food issues, and the health ministers discuss projects on disease control. When the various ministers from the member states are meeting this way, the group is called the Council of Ministers. This acts as a sort of sub-board of directors under the European Council. Until the Giscard constitution, the chairmanship, or "presidency," of this supervisory board used to rotate from country to country every six months. When Spain had the presidency, then, the Spanish premier chaired the European Council and the Spanish justice minister or finance minister chaired the appropriate Council of Ministers. That six-month rotation worked reasonably well when there were nine member nations—each country got to serve as "president" every four and a half years—and it still worked, more or less, in the fifteen-member EU. But the expansion to twenty-five members in 2004 made the six-month "presidency" fairly ridiculous. After Ireland served its presidency in the first half of 2004, it would have had to wait until 2017 to get another chance. So the new constitution eliminated the rotating presidency.

Instead of one prime minister serving as a "president" of the European Council for a six-month term, the new system creates an important new job—arguably the most powerful government position in all of Europe. Once the twenty-five-nation EU is in place, the twenty-five heads of state are to elect a president of the European Council—in effect the president of Europe—for a two-and-a-half-year term. This is the person who will finally answer Henry Kissinger's sarcastic question from the 1970s: "If I want to pick up the phone and talk to Europe, whom do I call?" Even before the Giscard constitution was ratified, the campaigning was under way for this spot. The early favorite, according to just about every major European newspaper, was Tony Blair. The British prime minister was one of the most admired politicians on the continent (at least, he was until he became an outspoken advocate of the enormously unpopular war in Iraq), and a man who could command respect as well from the Americans. Blair offered only the vaguest response to suggestions he run for "president of Europe." In any case, he was still busy at 10 Downing Street when the EU's new system was going into effect, so he presumably could not be the first president of Europe. Under the new constitution, the various ministers for the Councils of Agriculture, Finance, Justice, and so on will continue to meet, with the chairman of each Council of Ministers chosen for a one-year term, and the job rotating among the twenty-five countries.

For a while, Giscard d'Estaing's Constitutional Convention considered an even more dramatic approach to choosing this new "president of Europe." Instead of having the twenty-five heads of government pick the president of the European Council, there was a movement within the convention to have a pan-European popular election to pick Europe's chief executive. The idea here was to deal with an old EU problem known as the "democratic deficit"—the fact that the people of Europe have had a minimal role in choosing the leaders of the continental union. Everybody in Europe gets to vote for a representative in the European Parliament, but the executive branch jobs have always been filled by appointment. The theory was that a continent-wide election might get the people of Europe excited about their leaders in Brussels; it might give them a sense of ownership. Eventually, the constitution writers put aside this fairly daring idea because the smaller nations feared they would always come up the losers in a Europe-wide election. The concern was that the Germans, the Poles, the British, and the French would agree on a joint candidate from one of their countries, and they would have enough voting power to see to it that no candidate from the smaller countries ever won. And so the constitution settled for the less dramatic, and less democratic, approach of having the twenty-five prime ministers elect Europe's chief executive. In theory, that should give an Estonian or a Slovenian as much chance as a German or a Brit to be the voice of Europe.

The **executive branch** of the European Union—the entity that does most of the work, and employs most of the *fonctionnaires*—is the European Commission. This is essentially the cabinet of the European government—the ministers of health, finance, agriculture, and so on who implement the policies of the prime ministers and the European Parliament. Some of the people we've met earlier in this book, such as Mario Monti, the antitrust czar who humbled Jack Welch, and Pascal Lamy, the trade commissioner who forced the U.S. Congress to change its tax laws, are members of the European Commission. These cabinet ministers also represent the EU on international organizations; for example, the EU's commissioner for trade naturally becomes, as the spokesman for the world's biggest trading bloc, a key figure in the World Trade Organization. Before the EU grew to twenty-five members, the rule was that every member country got to name at least one member of the European Commission; thus even tiny Luxembourg, with a population smaller than some rural Irish counties, got to fill one of the cabinet seats. The post-2004 EU, though, could not come up with twenty-five different jobs that required full-scale commissioners. Accordingly, the new Constitution dictates that there will be only fifteen cabinet jobs, and the twenty-five member countries will have to use lobbying and leverage to land one of the slots. Most likely, Luxembourg will be out of luck.

The draft of the new constitution doesn't make it clear what the various cabinet posts will be, but presumably they will roughly match the positions on the commission that sat through 2005. Thus the European cabinet will likely include commissioners responsible for energy; the environment; competition and antitrust; agriculture and fishing; science and research; foreign aid; trade; health and consumer protection; education and culture; budget; regional policy; enlargement of the EU; and a few other jobs. As mentioned, the new EU cabinet will have only one foreign minister, who will represent the united Europe at summit meetings, the United Nations, and so forth. As befits a continent that has little interest in military force, the former European Commission had no job equivalent to secretary of defense, and the new cabinet probably won't, either. In the EU, military matters are left to the national defense ministers, and to NATO.

The European Commission is headed by a president, who oversees the day-to-day operations of the Eurocrats in Brussels. Through 2005, this high-profile job was held by Romano Prodi, an energetic, likable Italian economist-turned-politician who is a passionate disciple of the concept that the EU must stand as a "counterweight" to American power in the world. Until the new constitution, Prodi's job as president of the European Commission made him the most prominent spokesman for the New Europe. But once the prime ministers pick somebody to fill the new position of president of the European Council, that person will presumably become the EU's leading voice in the world. There will still be a president of the commission, but this is likely to become more of a managerial task.

As the outfit that runs most aspects of the EU government and enforces the union's myriad laws and regulations, the European Commission also spends most of the EU's budget. This leads to a totally predictable standoff every few years between the European Commission (that is, the cabinet) and the European Council (that is, the assembly of prime ministers) over how much money the EU should receive in tax payments from the member states. Because the EU is funded by a dedicated sales tax in each country, it is the bigger, richer member nations—particularly Germany, France, and Britain—that provide most of the funds. Inevitably, the biggest donors want the biggest say in determining how big the budget should be and what it should be used for. Every time the budget is discussed, the cabinet suggests cutting the EU's multi-billion-euro program of cash subsidies for European farmers; every time, France and the other big recipients of the agricultural subsidies bitterly resist this change. The addition in 2004 of ten new member states, most of them much poorer than the wealthy industrial nations of Western Europe, created considerable additional budget pressure as the new members sought development help from the old. The tempting models for all the new members are Ireland and Portugal, once-poor countries that have blossomed with new wealth and industrial development thanks largely to the EU's assistance.

With tens of billions of euros sloshing around in the commission's jurisdiction, the temptation to pocket some of the lucre has on occasion proven irresistible. The problem is so real that the EU maintains a full-time Court of Auditors to review spending. In 1998, the auditors found a broad pattern of fraud and kickbacks, with members of the commission passing out EU money willy-nilly to friends and family members. One cabinet member from France decided to put her dentist on the EU pay-roll, although the doctor remained home in Paris treating patients and did no discernible work for the European Commission. The corruption was so blatant, and so widespread, that all twenty members of the EU's cabinet were finally forced to resign. The new commission headed by Romano Prodi replaced the old group, and appears to have maintained a clean record on the money front for its five years in office.

The **legislative branch** of the European Union is the European Parliament, an assembly of members elected to five-year terms by the voters of each of the member states. In typical EU fashion, there was a furious argument in the 1970s about where the Parliament should meet. Most member nations wanted to put it in Brussels, along with the bulk of the executive branch. But France and Germany joined together to lobby for Strasbourg, the border city that was moved back and forth a half-dozen times from one country to the other, depending on which side won the last war; accordingly, Strasbourg is seen as a symbol of Europe's transition from war to peace. In typical EU fashion, this argument was settled by saying yes to both sides. So the parliament now meets half the time at a big, modern building in Strasbourg and half the time in an even bigger modern building in Brussels. In fact, the Parliament building in Brussels, with twenty-six huge flags flapping in the wind outside the imposing central portico, is so grandiose that the Brussels press has dubbed it *la caprice des dieux*, "the folly of the gods."

There are 732 seats in the European Parliament, roughly one for each 600,000 people, which creates a constituency for each member about the same size as a congressional district in the United States. This means Germany, France, Britain, and Poland have the most seats in the Parliament (about eighty seats for each of those large countries), and the tiny states like Malta and Luxembourg get four or five seats apiece. Voting in the Parliament, though, tends not to follow national lines. Rather, the MEPs (MEP is the abbreviation for Member of the European Parliament) have formed various party groupings along policy lines. The biggest "party" in the Parliament is a combine of Christian Democrats and Conservatives, a political alignment that is known in Europe as "center-right," but is actually far more liberal on most issues than left-wing Democrats would be in the United States. There's also a large grouping called the Party of European Socialists (PES), which is generally described as "center-left" but is not at all centrist by U.S. political definitions. The third largest party is a self-described "Reform" camp, which consists largely of people who are fed up with the traditional politics of both the Left and the Right. As you might expect in Europe, there is a large contingent of self-described Greens, who tend to be liberal on social welfare issues and particularly concerned about environmental protection. The Green bloc in the Parliament has been less powerful than it might be because its members are constantly fighting among themselves and dividing into smaller parties—the Nordic Greens, the Southern Greens, the Free Alliance Greens, and so on. There is a party called the Hunters and Fishermen, which seems to exist mainly to oppose whatever the various Green parties want to do. There are also some outright Euroskeptic parties, made up of conservative politicians who ran for the European Parliament in their home countries primarily to advertise their opposition to the whole notion of a united Europe.

The Parliament is the most democratic branch of Europe's government; the only way to get in is to be elected by the people of your home district. But the voters don't seem overly enthusiastic about the opportunity to choose their MEPs. When the first elections were held in 1979, there was an overall voter turnout of 63 percent, which would be a fantastic participation rate in the United States but was actually below average for European elections. The turnout rate has fallen gradually, though, and by the 2004 election for MEPs, voter participation fell close to 50 percent, a dismal figure indeed by European standards. (Voter participation in congressional elections in the United States, in contrast, runs about 40 percent in a nonpresidential election year.) Many of the people who run for European Parliament seats are established politicians already—indeed, a large number are members of their national parliament as well as Europe's. Such double-dippers are generally paid both for their service in the national parliament and for their work in Europe. Perhaps the all-time champion on this score was a triple-dipper: the Reverend Ian Paisley, the fiery head of the most conservative Protestant party in Northern Ireland. Paisley, a man who automatically wins any election he enters in his loyal Protestant constituency, served simultaneously as a member of the British Parliament in London, as a member of Northern Ireland's local assembly in Belfast, and as a member of the European Parliament in Brussels (or, sometimes, Strasbourg). It was obviously impossible for Paisley to give full time and energy to any of these three jobs in four different cities, but he told me, with no evident shame, that he accepted full pay for each one, earning a total income of about $300,000 per year from these parliamentary posts.

Members of the European Parliament can get away with that kind of thing because the parliament, frankly, doesn't do much. There are some policy areas—environmental law and public health law, for example— where the member nations have ceded some of their legislative authority to Brussels; authority in these fields is generally split between the Eurocrats at the European Commission, the EU's cabinet, and the parliament. The parliament has some control over the budget, and it must vote on appointments to the commission. But the big issues that most legislatures deal with, things like crime and taxes and national security, are not the jurisdiction of the European Parliament. Generally, the parliament in Brussels gets the most attention from the nonlegislative resolutions and proclamations it churns out on a regular basis. Since the politicians who serve in this parliament know their constituents, many of these official pronouncements focus on America-bashing of one sort or other: The European Parliament has repeatedly denounced the use of the death penalty in various American states. It has officially complained about the economic impact of America's balance of payments deficit. It passed a strong condemnation of the war in Iraq, reflecting the consensus view of people all over the continent.

The **judicial branch** of the European Union centers on an institution based in Luxembourg called the Court of Justice of the European Communities. This is one of the EU's oldest institutions; it was created in 1951 along with Jean Monnet's original European Coal and Steel Community. In some 5,000 decisions over the past forty years, this court has been concerned with two main issues: First, it wants to establish that the law of the EU is the supreme law within the union; where there is a conflict, the Court of Justice upholds the EU law and orders national governments to follow it. The court declared this point firmly in a 1963 decision (back when the EU was still known as the "European Community"): "The Community constitutes a new legal order of international law, in favor of which the states within certain areas have limited their sovereign rights." A year later, the same court held firmly that national courts in the member states must follow the law created by the supranational European court. A good example of how this works was the case of poor Steve Thoburn, the Metric Martyr in Sunderland, England whom we met in chapter 2 of this book. The EU issued a directive requiring that produce be sold in kilograms rather than pounds. The Court of Justice upheld this regulation as a legitimate act of the EU government, and that meant the British courts had to enforce the rule as well. This fundamental principle, that EU law is superior to the laws of the twenty-five member nations, has now been enshrined in Title I of the new EU Constitition: "The law of the Union shall prevail over the law of the member states."

With that rule established, the court is often called upon to rule on the question of whether a particular law from, say, Spain or Italy is in conflict with EU rules. In answering that question, the court generally holds that a national law is all right if it happens to be stricter than the EU directive on the specific point. In the famous case called *In re Disposable Beer Cans,* the European court said that Denmark had the right to set tougher recycling laws for beer cans than the EU had done. But if the national law is weaker, the court will require a member country to follow the EU rule. In a bankruptcy case from Italy, the Court of Justice ruled that the Italian government had to provide benefits for people left unemployed when their company went bust; EU regulations required this kind of assistance, even though Italian law did not.

The second main concern of the Court of Justice is determining whether actions by the EU commissioners and the Eurocrats are legal under the EU's treaties and statutes. Companies that lose an antitrust case against Mario Monti's Directorate for Competition can take Signor Monti to court and argue that his ruling is a violation of EU antitrust law; generally, Monti prevails in these cases, but a few times the court has told Monti that his decision was illegal and must be reconsidered. With the expansion of the EU and the increasing jurisdiction of the Eurocrats over every aspect of European life, the number of cases challenging EU actions has snowballed in recent years. Accordingly, the union has created a lower court, the Court of First Impression, to hear many of these cases and thus reduce the backlog of the Court of Justice. The two courts also consider disputes among member countries that don't agree on some aspect of EU law; for example, can France use its health regulations to ban the import of British beef? (The court ruled that France could not legally do that; predictably, the French maintained their import ban for years anyway, until Tony Blair and Jacques Chirac finally settled the issue in a face-to-face summit meeting.)

In 2004 Europe saw a daring new use of the Court of Justice when the European Commission—that is, the EU's own cabinet—went to court to charge that Germany and France were both in violation of the union's Stability and Growth Pact, the treaty that requires all the euro-using nations to hold their budget deficit below 3 percent of GDP. Both countries, beset by stagnant economies, were in fact running deficits in violation of that rule—but Paris and Berlin were both outraged that Romano Prodi and his commission would actually try to enforce it. Although the court has the legal power to compel both countries to cut government spending, or raise taxes, so as to reduce the deficit, nobody expects a judicial order along those lines any time soon. Rather, the suit was more likely just a way to send a message—telling France and Germany to get to work on their budget problems, and telling all the other member countries that the EU intends to hold them to the letter of the stability and growth agreement.

As we saw in chapter 6 of this book, there is a separate European court in Strasbourg, the Court of Human Rights, which deals primarily with cases involving the European Bill of Rights. This court, too, acts as a sort of pancontinental Supreme Court, with national courts and governments required to follow its rulings. When the Court of Human Rights ruled that homosexuals have a fundamental right to serve in the military, a half-dozen European countries had to change their laws to reflect this decree from Strasbourg. The Court of Human Rights is not specifically an EU institution—for one thing, its jurisdiction covers more than a dozen European countries that are not yet members of the EU—but in practice it is a part of the overall EU governing apparatus.

The **European Central Bank** is based in Frankfurt—a natural choice, since the former German central bank, the Frankfurt-based Bundesbank, was the institutional model for the ECB. The bank does the same thing for all the euro countries that the Federal Reserve does for the United States. The central bank is responsible for monetary policy in all the euro countries, which is to say it sets the basic interest rate. It also oversees currency exchange among the euro countries and the EU members that have not yet joined the euro. Following the principles of its model, the Bundesbank, the ECB has followed a policy aimed primarily at keeping inflation extremely low; to do so, it has maintained some of the highest interest rates in the industrialized world. The bank has been extremely successful at achieving this anti-inflation goal, but it has been criticized sharply for setting the wrong goal. The critics say the bank's policy was responsible for Europe's slow recovery from the recession of the early twenty-first century. And the high interest rates were one of the key reasons for the explosive strength of the new currency on global exchange markets. The strong euro, in turn, made things difficult for European exporters.

As if it weren't difficult enough to design a government for a new kind of supranational state unlike any other political entity on the planet, the EU has to do all its governing in a cacophony of different languages. Since the Treaty of Rome in 1957, the EU has been committed to the principle of "ever closer union." But within that union, the Europeans also want to preserve their cultural and regional diversity. A key element of diversity is the multipart harmony of different languages heard around the continent. That determination is enshrined in Regulation No. 1 of the European Union, which says that the official language of each member country will be accepted as a working language at all EU gatherings. Since the current twenty-five members have twenty different official languages, it's a costly commitment. The EU spends well over €1 million per day to turn one man's *meat* into another's *viande* (or *carne* or *kjott* or *liha* or *fleisch*). Thick reports from the various EU committees and commissions and study panels—many of them hundreds of pages long—have to be printed twenty different times, one for each language. There may be very few readers for the Maltese version of the annual publication *Operating Budget of the European Union*, but the document is printed nonetheless. The EU union employs some 4,000 full-time interpreters and translators, not to mention the translating titan called EC-Systran, a software program that can pump out 2,000 pages of translation per hour. Human readers of this book may be pleased to know that Systran's stuff usually needs to be proofread by a person before it's usable.

The EU's complex linguistic stew leads to some long days at the office for Marco Benedetti, an Italian who grew up in France, works in Belgium, and smokes tiny Dutch cigars. He's the head of interpretation—that is, oral translation—for the European Union. That means he has to provide simultaneous interpreters in various combinations of the twenty official languages for 200 or more meetings every week. But Signor Benedetti told me that his real headaches come when he looks into the future.

"Under Regulation No. 1, we will accommodate any member's official language. This was a challenge with eleven languages, but beginning in May 2004, with our ten new members, the job became vastly more difficult. Just to think about it, we need people who can interpret from Hungarian to Dutch. From Latvian to Portuguese. From Estonian to—but there are fewer than one million Estonian speakers in the whole world! And I need about fifty Estonian interpreters!

"As you know," he went on, sounding rather wistful, "the United Nations has only six official languages. No other international organization would pay the price we do for interpretation and translation. But we're happy to pay it, to preserve cultural diversity." Now Signor Benedetti was getting emotional "Europe is an orchestra," he said. "But the violins are still violins. We must guarantee that each violin, each instrument, has its own voice."

One place where every violin has a voice is the European Parliament. When any MEP stands up to speak, every word is translated into the other nineteen official languages, generally with less than one second's delay. The only exceptions to this rule come up on scattered occasions when some member starts speaking in a regional European language like Gaelic or Catalan or Basque, which the interpreters don't translate. The presiding officer generally lets these out-of-bounds orators have their say, even though nobody else in the room may understand a word of it. On the other hand, the EU is also determined to preserve regional languages, dialects, and even Europe's defunct languages. The new constitution decrees an official motto for the European Union—and this motto is to be considered official in several dozen national, regional, and classical languages:

* Unity in diversity — English
* Unité dans la diversité — French
* Unidad en la diversidad — Spanish
* Grupa za drugacije — Croatian
* Jednotnost v rů znorodosti — Czech
* Forenet i mangfoldighed — Danish
* Eenheid in verscheidenheid — Dutch
* Ühtsus erinevuses — Estonian
* Erilaisina yhdessä — Finnish
* Einheit in Vielfalt — German
* Διαφορετικοί αλλά ευωμένοι — Greek
* Sokféleképpen - egyutt — Hungarian
* Unità nella diversità — Italian
* Vienotība dažādībā — Latvian
* Jednosc w róznosci — Polish
* Unidade na diversidade — Portuguese
* Unitate în diversitate — Romanian
* Förenade i mångfalden — Swedish
* Undod mewn amrywiaeth — Welsh
* Unueco en la diverseco — Esperanto
* In varietate concordia — Latin

Notes

Chapter Two: The Invention of Peace and the Pursuit of Prosperity

1. Soames, now a Conservative member of Parliament, told this charming story in June 2002 at Blenheim Palace, the fantastic mansion outside Oxford where Churchill was born.

2. Just as they did in the United States, farm subsidies proved addictive, and politically impossible to curtail. Today, in a twenty-five-nation European Union, the Common Agricultural Policy, or CAP, consumes about 40 percent of the $100-billion-plus EU budget. The subsidies are so generous they make even Washington's multibillion-dollar ag programs look skimpy. The U.S. government pays some $40 billion per year in agriculture subsidies (about $8,200 annually for each person employed in agriculture); the EU pays $120 billion, about 15 percent more subsidy per farmer. Every living U.S. cow gets about $120 per year in federal ag subsidies; a European cow gets $600 per year in subsidies from the EU.

Chapter Five: L'Europe Qui Gagne;
or, I Can't Believe It's Not American Butter

1. This list represented ownership records in mid-2004. Because multinationals are buying and selling subsidiaries all the time, the affiliations will change.

Chapter Six: The European Social Model

1. In most big cities in the United States, the combined city, county, and state sales tax runs from 8 to 12 percent. California, during its fiscal crisis at the beginning of the century, set "temporary" rates that pushed the combined sales tax rate in Los Angeles to 15.5 percent.

Chapter Seven: Showdown at Capability Gap

1. These figures were compiled by the OECD, which provides totals for individual countries, for the European Union itself, and for all EU countries combined.

Chapter Eight: Generation E and the Ties That Bind the New Europe

1. INRI stands for the Latin title *Iesus Nazarenus Rex Iudaeorum,* or "Jesus of Nazareth, King of the Jews."
2. Saint Francis of Assisi.

Thanks

"You know, I've had some experience with conflict resolution," John Hume said to me one morning in his lilting Derry brogue as we were driving past the huge office buildings of the *Quartier Européen* in Brussels, the capital city of the European Union. It was a fair statement. A teacher-turned-politician in the British province of Northern Ireland, John Hume spent most of his adult life working to end the lethal sectarian warfare that divided his homeland. He was cursed, threatened, jailed, beaten, and firebombed. But he never gave up—and he won the Nobel Peace Prize for his work on the Good Friday Agreement, which promised peace for Ulster. As the man said, he has had some experience with conflict resolution. But John told me that spring morning that "the European Union is the best example of conflict resolution in the world. Europe made a conscious decision to leave war and differences behind, and then found a way to do it. It's been a phenomenal success." John Hume was so impressed with the European achievement that he ran for and won a seat in the European Parliament, largely so that he could further his own study of conflict resolution and bring the lessons home to Northern Ireland.

We pulled up at the massive meeting hall, two city blocks long, with the name "European Parliament" across the front in eleven languages, and John Hume, M.E.P., got ready to go to work. As he was getting out of the car, though, he glanced at my reporter's notebook and said, "You know, this New Europe is probably more important than most of the stuff that gets in the newspaper. You ought to write something about it."

It is largely because of help, advice, and encouragement from Europeans like John Hume that I have been able to write something about the United States of Europe and its emergence as a "counterweight" to American power in the twenty-first century. A broad network of journalists, scholars, politicians, business people, and just plain friends all over the continent provided generous guidance and assistance for this book. Some of these people, it must be said, helped me even though they disagreed with me on various points. Accordingly, anything that's wrong in these pages is strictly my fault, and can't be blamed on those whom I now want to thank.

Along with John Hume, I'm particularly grateful to my friend Donald Graham. Don has risen to the lofty post of CEO of a $3 billion corporation, but he still has the reporter's instinct for a good story—an instinct he developed as a cub on the *Washington Post* city desk about thirty years ago. I realized this one typically rainy day in London when Don was visiting and happened to ask, just casually, what I had planned for the coming weekend. In tones laced with sarcasm, I replied that I would have the high honor and privilege that weekend of attending a European Union summit, and if the thing turned out to be like all the other EU summits, it would amount to a bunch of gasbag prime ministers droning on and on about the new superpower they were building on the European continent. Don replied, in his gentle way, that my cynicism might be blinding me to something important. "If these guys really can unite Europe, after all the warfare and conflict they've been through, that's a fantastic achievement," he said. "I think you've got a significant piece of history playing out right in front of you." It was excellent advice, diplomatically delivered. That weekend, I left my sarcasm behind when I set off to the ancient castle town of Cardiff, Wales, for the summit meeting. With my eyes open, I saw that those long-winded European politicians had something important to say, something that most Americans had simply ignored. I spent the next four years digging into the "significant piece of history" that is playing out right now across the European continent.

Accordingly, I am grateful to Don Graham—and to my other bosses at the *Washington Post,* including Jackson Diehl and Phil Bennett—for steering me in the direction of this European revolution, and giving me the time and space to cover it. Other editors who encouraged me to look closely at the New Europe included Bill Allen and Bob Poole of *National Geographic Magazine* and Bob Edwards, Ellen McDonnell, and Loren Jenkins at National Public Radio's estimable *Morning Edition.* I'm grateful to many colleagues, including Adam Boulton, William Drozdiak, Peter Finn, Martin Fletcher, Jonathan Freedland, William Glauber, Simon Jenkins, Ian Black, Thomas Kielinger, Marjorie Miller, Marc Roche, and Michael White, for helping me in Brussels and elsewhere. A great reporter, Keith Richburg, did great work on the emergence of Generation E. Stuart Franklin drove me all over Europe in a big black BMW and used his photographer's eye to show me how the continent is changing. I feel a particular debt to several producers and presenters at the BBC, including Nick Guthrie, Gavin Esler, Nicky Campbell, Jeremy Vine, Sue MacGregor, and James Naughtie, who gave me the chance to try out several of the ideas in this book before the British public, a demanding and generally Euroskeptic audience.

Several distinguished scholars, in the United States and in Europe, were generous with their help. The brilliant Norman Davies played a key role, both through the model of his marvelously readable text *Europe: A History*—a 1,365-page volume that rode the wave of European unification to become a best-seller across the continent—and through sage advice passed along over pints of bitter in the pubs of Oxford. Professors Wolfgang Danspeckgruber, Laurence Freedman, Nan Kirk de Graaf, Amy Gutmann, Chip Hauss, Mark Mazower, Andrew Moravcsik, Richard Portes, Peter Kenen, and Donald Smith all helped me with different aspects of the New Europe, its new money, and its new political clout. In

Copenhagen, the ethnologist Mette Kirk instructed me in the characteristics that tend to bind all Europeans, and in their differences.

I had extensive assistance from the political leadership. Tony Blair, Gordon Brown, Peter Hain, and the Baroness Scotland in Britain, Bertie Ahern in Ireland, Paavo Lipponen in Finland, and Valéry Giscard d'Estaing in France, among many others, all found time amid impossible schedules to talk to me about the European project. In Brussels, I owe thanks to Romano Prodi, Pascal Lamy, Mario Monti, and Chris Patten, all members of the European Commission. Emma Udwin of the commission staff provided steady help and guidance. Many elected members of the European Parliament assisted me, but of course I owe particular thanks to John Hume, the man who showed me the EU from the inside and urged me to "write something about it." In the corporate community, I must thank Sir John Browne of British Petroleum, Ernesto Illy of Illycaffe, Toomas Luman of EE Grupp Estonia, Dietrich Mateschitz of Red Bull, Jorma Ollila of Nokia, and Sir Ian Prosser of Six Continents, all leaders of great enterprises who were willing to help an American understand how business works in a united Europe. Steve Thoburn, the Metric Martyr, ran a smaller enterprise but was equally helpful; sadly, Steve died just a few months before this book was published. Some members of the General Electric board helped me; you know who you are, and I thank you. Jack Welch didn't talk to me, but he did the next best thing by providing a typically frank, no-nonsense description of his clash with the EU in his autobiography *Jack—Straight from the Gut*.

I benefited enormously from the reporting talent of the British journalist Adi Bloom, who did prodigious research for this project and who was never reluctant to tell the author when he was all wet. Teresa Horwich in London, Johanna Lemola in Helsinki, Bruno Soares in Lisbon, Tom Mudd in Dublin, Gretchen Hoff in Paris, and Rob Thomason in Washington, D.C., also provided excellent research help.

The British Library, the City of Westminster (Greater London) Libraries, the Denver Public Library, and the university libraries at Oxford,

Goteborg, Trinity College Dublin, the London School of Economics, and the University of Colorado were generous to a stray researcher who wandered in asking for help. I'm particularly grateful to Karin A. Trainer, the librarian of Princeton University, for providing me regular access to Princeton's vast collections on contemporary Europe in the Firestone and Stokes Libraries.

I'd double the length of this book if I tried to mention all the friends who helped me along the pathways of Europe, but I would particularly like to thank Thomas Benghauser, Guy Bracq, Hans Robert Eisenhauer, Charles Grant, Joan and John Hindle, David Hogarth, Veiko Kesksalu, Jan and Tony King, Hana and Jeremy Kinsman, Signe and Doug Lansky, Bill Mules, Penny Pilzer, William Shawcross, Perti Salolainen, Herve de Treglode, and Dan Waters.

I owe enormous thanks to my agent, Gail Ross, who saw what this book could be even before the author did. Not for the first time, the great editor Ann Godoff figured out how to make a book of mine work, with invaluable help from Meredith Blum and Sophie Fells.

Last but foremost, on two continents for two years, Margaret M. McMahon, McMahon Thomas Homer Reid, Penelope Reid, and Willa Reid put up with this manuscript and its author in cheery fashion, a task far more formidable than writing any book.

London   Denver
2002   2004

Index